SELF-DIRECTEDNESS:

Cause and Effects Throughout the Life Course

SELF-DIRECTEDNESS:
Cause and Effects Throughout the Life Course

Edited by

Judith Rodin
Yale University

Carmi Schooler
National Institute of Mental Health

K. Warner Schaie
The Pennsylvania State University

LAWRENCE ERLBAUM ASSOCIATES, PUBLISHERS
1990 Hillsdale, New Jersey   Hove and London

Lawrence Erlbaum Associates, Inc., Publishers
365 Broadway
Hillsdale, New Jersey 07642

Library of Congress Cataloging-in-Publication Data

Self-directedness : cause and effects throughout the life course /
edited by Judith Rodin, Carmi Schooler, K. Warner Schaie
    p.   cm.
  ISBN 0-8058-0562-1
  1. Control (Psychology) 2. Developmental psychology. I. Rodin, Judith.
II. Schooler, Carmi. III. Schaie, K. Warner (Klaus Warner).
  BF611.S4 1990
  155—dc20   89-37927
                                                                 CIP

Printed in the United States of America
10 9 8 7 6 5 4 3 2 1

Contents

Foreword: The Life Course and the Crisis in Social Science

Matilda White Riley
National Institute on Aging

This book, the third in a series on the life course sponsored by Pennsylvania State University, has strategic symbolic significance in today's world of research, professional practice, and public policy, for the set of books to date symbolizes the gradual reemergence of power of the social sciences. In recent decades, this power has often been lost. Within the secular swings of intellectual dominance of some disciplines over others, the "hard" sciences have been in the ascendant, while the social and psychological sciences have been approaching the nadir. Nowhere has this disciplinary crisis been more apparent than in studies of the life course; yet it is precisely in these studies that signs of resolution of the crisis seem particularly auspicious.

Even today, aging research still often appears as it has too often appeared in the recent past—as primarily the province of medical researchers, legislators, lobbyists, and vested pharmaceutical interests. In this world aging is stereotyped as "afflicted with Alzheimer's disease," "imprisoned in a nursing home," or dependent on *medicine* as the only means of preventing either disease or institutionalization. Yet, we social and behavioral scientists, as contributors to this volume and to the conference from which it sprang, know that aging research involves not only a biomedical concern with disease; perhaps more importantly, it also involves social, psychological, and economic concerns with human lives in families, in social institutions of all kinds, and in society as a whole. This social scientific focus takes full cognizance of the potency of the biomedical perspective; but it broadens the view by recognizing the complementary potency of the psychosocial perspective in probing the mysteries of the life course. Thus, the volume reflects and stimulates the incipient resurgence of the social and behavioral sciences.

A word about the history of the volume, and a glimpse into the future, suggests its intimate relationship to this resurgence. An exciting blueprint for this set of books grew out of a series of planning meetings held several years ago at the Social Science Research Council (SSRC). Those meetings were built on a decade of work done by the Council's Committee on Life-Course Perspectives, and funded in large part by the National Institute on Aging (NIA)—hence my own dual commitment to the enterprise. Yet unfortunately, characteristic of the travails of the social sciences, neither the SSRC nor the NIA were able to provide sustenance for implementation of the carefully wrought blueprint. Fortunately, however, and characteristic of the vigor and ingenuity of the social science community, Warner Schaie and the Gerontology Center at Pennsylvania State University did find means for maintaining the momentum, and did find colleagues—in this instance, Judith Rodin and Carmi Schooler—as collaborators in conference planning and manuscript editing.

Focusing on "self-directedness and efficacy" over the life course, the conference posed questions that reflected the original blueprint. These were formerly set out as follows:

"What are the causes of changes in self-directedness and efficacy over the life course? These changes can be intrinsic and developmental, or caused by changes in the environment, such as shifts in roles, work status, or relationships.

"How do changes in self-directedness and efficacy throughout the life course affect the individual, the family system, social groups, and society at large?

"How do various disciplines—anthropology, sociology, psychology, epidemiology—approach the study of self-directedness and efficacy throughout the life course, considering common themes and differences? An effort is made to develop a multidisciplinary perspective unique to the study of self-directedness and efficacy."

The responses to these questions are reported in this volume. They go far beyond the original blueprint, both to extend and to specify it. Much progress has been made since our early SSRC planning meetings. We could not then have envisaged:

How, since then, the concept that once went under the rubric of "sense of control" has developed—and ramified in several directions.

How an entire body of research has demonstrated the power of "control" in differentiating between those individuals who lead long, healthy, effective, and fulfilling lives; and those others who succumb early in life to ill health, loneliness, and withdrawal from affairs.

How clues are being uncovered that may explain the mechanisms through which a sense of control exerts its power.

How developmental, cultural, and social–structural antecedents of control are being identified; and the consequences for health and cognitive functioning are being specified.

The scientific progress manifested in the chapters of this book thus bring to reality the broad vision of the SSRC Planning Committee. This vision was to "view life-course development as interdependent with social structure and social change." The aim was to understand the interplay between human aging and changes in society, and to achieve such understanding through a multidisciplinary approach. Three sets of interrelated variables identified by that Committee are put to use in these chapters. They demand restatement here:

1. Processes of *aging* (or development)—that is, aspects of the ways in which people grow old biologically, psychologically, and socially;

2. Age-related *social structures* and social changes—that include (a) *roles* (e.g., work roles, political roles) with their associated expectations, facilities, and rewards or punishments; (b) *values* that are built into these structures (i.e., standards of what is true, good, beautiful); and (c) *other people* who interact and are interrelated within these structures;

3. *Linkages*—that is, mechanisms that link aging processes with changing social structures. Such mechanisms may be (a) psychological (e.g., coping, self-esteem, sense of personal control); (b) biological (e.g., changes in neural, sensori-motor, endocrine, immunological, and other physiological systems that can impact directly on the aging process); and (c) social (e.g., supportive or hostile relationships, opportunities, or constraints affecting productive performance.

It is clear from the chapters in this volume that the nature of the interdependence among these three sets of variables can be illuminated by intensive focus on specific aspects of the life course, such as self-directedness and sense of control.

What is also clear from these experiences is the strongly integrated effort required to initiate and sustain the production of a cumulative body of significant social science findings. In this instance, the program of life-course analysis required a tripartite arrangement that involved the SSRC and its Committees, which were to foster intellectual vision and integration; the NIA, which was to stimulate research and provide facilities and funds; and academic centers, like the Pennsylvania State University, which were to translate the larger vision into concrete research activities. The program began when all three components were strong, in an era of high confidence in the social and behavioral sciences. Then, in the meantime, there was an erosion of confidence, a period of mounting obstacles, even insults to those sciences regarded as "soft." Nevertheless, neither the original vision nor the potential for its realization has been lost. The SSRC is currently in process of reorganizing, and will be headed by an outstanding leader in research on the life course—a concept that is now widely recognized as seminal. The NIA, although staggering under threats of Congressional budget cuts, has become *the* major source of funding for basic social and behavioral research. And splendid university centers, like the sponsor of this book, are demonstrating the renascent power of the social sciences.

We are still haunted by threats to our disciplines, and challenged by the need to overcome these threats. The crisis of the social sciences is not entirely at an end. But we can look on this book as a harbinger of a brighter future.

Control By Any Other Name: Definitions, Concepts, and Processes

Judith Rodin
Yale University

The purpose of this introductory chapter is to review the various definitions of *control* and to outline the implications of the use of one definition or another for our views about how control has its effects. I take largely an ahistorical and acultural approach for two reasons. First, this reflects the general state of the field with only a few exceptions. Second, the rest of this volume has been designed to remedy this situation, by taking as an explicit focus the role of sociocultural and historical factors, and by considering the individual across the life span in a variety of domains in which control is thought to be operative.

I begin by describing several perspectives on defining and operationalizing control. Theorists have defined *control* in various ways, some focusing on achieving behavioral outcomes, others on making choices, and still others on cognitive processes. This has led investigators to operationalize control in a variety of ways. Even the construct has been called many different things including, besides control, self-directedness, choice, decision freedom, agency, mastery, autonomy, self-efficacy, and self-determination. Next I discuss the domains of individual thought and action where control-relevant processes are important. I conclude by pointing to the importance of considering these issues from a life-course perspective, to set the stage for the following chapters.

DESIRE FOR CONTROL

It has been argued that the desire to make decisions and affect outcomes, that is to exercise control, is a basic feature of human behavior (White, 1959). Many theorists in fact view behavior itself as arising from people's need to be causal agents in their environment (deCharms, 1968). For example, DeCharms (1968) asserted that "man's primary motivational propensity is to be effective in producing changes in his environment. Man strives to be a causal agent. His nature commits him to this path and his very life depends on it" (p. 269). Others (e.g., Kelley, 1967, 1971) believe that attributional or explanatory processes occur because the individual is motivated to attain cognitive control. This view proposes that cognitive processes are a means of encouraging and maintaining feelings of control. The tendency for individuals to overestimate their degree of personal control over events that are objectively random (e.g., Langer, 1975; Wortman, 1975) is consistent with the assumption that they are motivated to believe that they are able to control their environment.

SELF-EFFICACY

The importance of perceived self-efficacy in human agency is under-scored by the work of Bandura and his associates (Bandura, 1977; Bandura, Adams, Hardy, & Howells, 1980). Bandura has argued that, among the different mechanisms of personal agency, none is more pervasive than people's beliefs in their capabilities to exercise control over their own motivations and behaviors and over environmental demands. Self-efficacy depends on the individual's belief that he or she can cause an intended event to occur and can organize and carry out the courses of behavior necessary to deal with various situations.

Perceived self-efficacy has directive influence on people's choice of activities and settings. Through expectations of eventual success, it can also affect coping efforts. Expectations of self-efficacy determine how much effort people will expend and how long they will persist in the confrontation of obstacles and aversive experiences. The stronger the perceived efficacy, the more active the efforts. According to Bandura (1986), those who persist in subjectively threatening activities that are in fact relatively safe, will gain corrective experiences that reinforce their sense of efficacy, thereby eventually eliminating their defensive behavior. Those who cease their coping efforts prematurely will retain their self-debilitating expectations and fears. Expectations of personal efficacy are based on four principal sources of information: direct performance accomplishments, vicarious experience, verbal persuasion, and physio-logical states. The most effective of the four is direct mastery experience. Successes help develop a greater sense of efficacy, whereas failures undermine it. In addition, redoubling one's efforts in the face of occasional failures can strengthen self-motivated persistence if experience comes to show that even the very difficult obstacles can be mastered by sustained effort. The effects of failure on personal efficacy consequently depend on the timing and total pattern of experiences in which the failures occur.

INTERNAL–EXTERNAL LOCUS OF CONTROL

Bandura's view of self-efficacy is quite different from the viewpoint proposed by Rotter (1966). Rotter's conceptual scheme, focusing on internal versus external locus of control orientation, is mainly concerned with causal beliefs about action-outcome contingencies rather than with personal efficacy. Perceived self-efficacy and beliefs about the locus of causality must be distinguished because convictions that outcomes are determined by one's action are different from, although they affect, self-efficacy and behavior. These concepts also differ in how they are measured. Rotter used a general scale to measure views about the locus of causality. This scale and others that followed it usually are comprised of multiple factors involving different domains or types of control. In the standard self-efficacy assessment procedure, individuals are presented with graduated self-efficacy scales representing specific tasks varying in difficulty, complexity, or some other dimension depending on the domain of functioning being explored. Subjects designate the tasks that they judge they can do and their degree of certainty regarding the judgment. In contrast to global dispositional assessments of control such as Rotter's internal versus external locus of control orientation, self-efficacy is measured within task and situation specificity, for example, a measure of cold pressor tolerance self-efficacy used by Litt (1988) asked subjects to indicate how much time they believed they could keep their hand in ice water and to rate their confidence in that judgment.

OUTCOME EXPECTANCY

Outcome expectancies are judgments regarding the potential controllability of an outcome in general, regardless of whether a particular individual is able to influence the outcome. Theoretical difficulties in self-efficacy theory have emerged around the conceptual distinctions made between self-efficacy expectations and outcome expectancy. According to Bandura (1977), efficacy expectations are assumed to be unrelated to outcome expectancies. Although the distinction may seem conceptually clear and logical, operationalization difficulties have occurred with different experimental manipulations (e.g., Davis & Yates, 1982; Manning & Wright, 1983), and several investigators have complained of ambiguity between the two constructs (Eastman & Marzillier, 1984; Kazdin, 1978a).

Self-efficacy theory has also been criticized (Scheier & Carver, 1987) for its inability to account for the fact that some outcome expectancies derive from sources outside of those involving personal self-efficacy. Bandura's theory, for example, provides no conceptual niche for such influences on the anticipated outcomes as a benign or hostile environment, religious faith or lack thereof, or beliefs in the effectiveness or ineffectiveness of a placebo. To remedy this situation Scheier and Carver (1987) proposed that efficacy expectancy determines what action is chosen but outcome expectancy determines whether to engage in the outcome-relevant behavior. Maddux, Norton, and Stoltenburg (1986) manipulated self-efficacy and outcome expectancy and found that both were non-redundant, independent predictors of behavioral intentions. In another study, Schorr and Rodin (1984) found that the motivation for control over an outcome was independent of feelings of self-efficacy.

PERCEIVED CONTROL

The constructs of self-efficacy, outcome expectancy, and locus of control orientation all relate strongly to other notions dealing with *perceived* control. Baron and Rodin (1978) defined perceived control as the expectation of having the power to participate in making decisions in order to obtain desirable consequences and a sense of personal competence in a given situation. By comparison, objective control is the actual ability to regulate or influence intended outcomes through selective responding. Although a substantial portion of the empirical work that has been done in the area of control has examined the results of manipulations of actual outcome contingencies on behavior or cognition, in fact actual control may not be nearly as important as a person's perception of the situation's controllability.

Generally, not enough information is available in the environment to assess accurately whether or not there is contingency. Thus, we necessarily are forced to rely on our perception of control. There is even corroborating physiological evidence that suggests that it is the perception of control rather than actual behavioral control that may be more important in reducing physical indicators of distress (Blankenstein, 1984). Langer's (1975) studies support the hypothesis that often people overestimate the amount of control they have in situations that are primarily chance determined. The illusion of control is in a sense the inverse of Seligman's notion of learned helplessness (Langer, 1983). Although learned help-lessness is the erroneous belief that one has no control to affect the outcome of a given event when contingency does in fact exist between response and outcome, the illusion of control involves the erroneous belief that one can produce a positive outcome when such a contingency does not exist. It is the perception of independence between response and outcome, even when response outcome co-variation does exist, which is responsible for the deleterious effects of learned helplessness, accord-ing to the theory (Seligman, 1975). Reciprocally, the perception of contin-gency between response and outcome may immunize against deleterious effects, even when such a contingency does not exist. There is evidence to suggest, for example, that more accurate and realistic perceptions of personal control are seen primarily in depressed individuals (Abramson & Alloy, 1981) and that an illusion of control may be characteristic of much adaptive human functioning (Taylor & Brown, 1988).

It has been suggested that the illusion of control may actually serve to promote mental and physical health (Cantor & Hunt, 1987; Taylor & Brown, 1988). Taylor and Brown emphasized that, in and of itself, the ability to assign meaning to a particular event has been associated with improved adjustment. Because the sense of control appears to be a pre-requisite for effective action taking and decision making, even illusory control may be beneficial. Notions of cognitive control also figure in the conceptual distinctions of Rothbaum, Weisz, and Snyder (1982), who have emphasized the importance of what they call *secondary control*, which is cognitive control, in contradistinction to primary, behavioral control.

In summary, it appears that perceived control is often the more avail-able and the more effective aspect of control-relevant processes on impor-tant outcomes. Nonetheless, we should not conclude that explicit aware-ness of the availability of control is a necessary condition for control to exist as a psychologically relevant event. It may be that control is per-ceived or cognized at a tacit level of awareness (Turvey, 1977), that is, to paraphrase Polyani (1958), we may know more of control than we can say. It is assumed, however, that although control is sometimes not repre-sented at the level of explicit verbal awareness, it can still be operative as a psychologically relevant process (see Erdelyi's, 1974, and Shiffren & Schneider's, 1977, analyses of the conditions under which selective re-sponding may occur without awareness).

DECISION CONTROL

Other theorists have been more interested in what has been called *decision control* or choice (Steiner, 1970). Decision control is a person's belief that he or she rather than other people or circumstances selects both the goals sought and the means to obtain them (Steiner, 1970). The notion of decision control is linked conceptually to the model of control advanced by Deci and Ryan (1985), who posit that decision control and feelings of self-determination are central to intrinsic motivation to achieve. They argued that events have varied functional significance, which influences self-determination. Informational events, the most important ones, are those that are experienced as providing effectance-relevant feedback in the context of choice or autonomy. Unlike self-efficacy theory, which emphasizes perceived effectance alone, self-determination theory specifies that effectance feedback is most influential when decision control, (that is, choice) is present. The defining characteristic of intrinsic motivation, they argued, is the experience of self-determination. Ryan (1982) extended this theory by suggesting that not only environmental events, but a variety of intrapsychic events, can influence the sense of self-determination. For example, various forms of self-control or intrapersonal feedback influence perceived competence.

MULTIPLE TYPES OF CONTROL

Several forms of control may be operative at a single time. For example, in the behavior-change area, high levels of both efficacy and outcome expectancy are associated with intent to change behavior, but with respect to the maintenance of the behavior change, the results point to the greater importance of perceived efficacy (Godding & Glasgow, 1985; Maddux & Rogers, 1983; Strecher, Becker, Kirscht, Eraker, & Graham-Tomasi, 1985).

Different types of control might also arise sequentially. Consider how control might be operative in the health context. Different aspects of the disease process may be controllable at different times and the types of control that are most effective undoubtedly shift on the basis of a variety of situational and temporal factors. For example, Cantor and Hunt (1987) emphasized that early in the course of coping with a threatening disease, the illusion of control may serve to cushion the individual. This cognitive cushioning produces the necessary security to enable the person to prepare for appropriate action in the face of uncertainty concerning the etiology, treatment, and outcome of the disease. This recognition that at earlier points in the disease process illusory control may be more relevant than actual control, speaks to the necessity of adopting a flexible and dynamic perspective concerning what may be the most adaptive type of control at different phases in the disease process. Similarly, apparent discrepancies in the literature regarding individuals' reaction to loss of control may be better understood when viewed within this temporal framework (Derogatis, Abeloff, & Meliasavatos, 1979; Levy, 1984; Wortman & Brehm, 1975).

As suggested by Wortman and Brehm one might expect that a patient's initial response to the loss of control, which is an inherent part of most disease processes, would be psychological reactance—including hostile and aggressive feelings toward involved medical personnel or the disease process itself. After this initial period of reactance, however, patients may attempt cognitively to restructure and reframe their understanding of the disease process and its role in their lives (thereby exercising cognitive control of the situation). This cognitive redefinition may sometimes superficially resemble learned helplessness in that it may involve a relative absence of behavioral responding, but is probably not accompanied by the motivational and emotional deficits thought to result from learned helplessness.

Finally, the necessity for most chronically ill individuals to make decisions regarding which medical facility to utilize for care, the choice of personal physician, and the decisions regarding various sorts of medical treatments allows the individual a form of vicarious control—the belief that even if he or she cannot control the course of disease, there are powerful others (i.e., physicians) or agents (i.e., certain medical treatments) that can. Taylor (1983) reported that in her study one third of the respondents with breast cancer believed that the cancer could be controlled by the doctor or through continued treatments even though they did not believe that they had personal control of their cancer. Interestingly, both the belief in personal control and the belief that the physician or treatment could control the cancer were strongly associated with overall positive adjustment, and both these beliefs in combination (perceived control and vicarious control) resulted in even better adjustment (Taylor, 1983). This finding provides support for the idea that it may be possible and efficacious for an individual to utilize different types of control in combination. Particularly evident from Taylor's results is that the specific attribution for the cause of the disease and the specific aspects of the disease the patients thought they could control apparently mattered less than the function these attributions served (Taylor, 1983). In addition, the multiple attributions made by many patients suggests that the disconfirmation of the effectiveness of any single explanation or element would not result in profound psychological disturbance as long as some range of options was still available to the individual (Taylor, 1983).

One should recognize that the type of control a given individual utilizes at a given point in the disease process will probably also be affected by individual differences and personality characteristics. Rodin, Timko, and Harris (1986) pointed out that individuals vary in their desire for personal control. Similarly, an individual's degree of optimism may also affect an individual's response to the disconfirmation of control and the type of control individuals prefer and the manner in which they attempt to exert control (Scheier & Carver, 1987; Wortman & Dintzer, 1978). Those individuals who are more optimistic would be expected to view themselves as able to personally control at least some aspects of their disease in contrast to more pessimistic individuals.

PROCESSES IN WHICH CONTROL HAS IMPORTANT EFFECTS

There are numerous pyschological and behavioral processes that are strongly influenced by control. These include, among others, cognition, motivation, emotion, and choice. These are reviewed more fully by Bandura (1990), and are simply highlighted here, based on his review.

Cognitive Processes. One's sense of control may have a variety of cognitive effects. First, people typically have a view of their plans and goals, which is framed by their appraisals of their own capabilities. People set higher goals for themselves and are more firmly committed to them when they have a greater sense of self-directedness (Bandura & Wood, 1988; Locke, Frederick, Lee, & Bobko, 1984; Taylor, Locke, Lee, & Gist, 1984).

Most people also have derived a series of strategies for predicting events in probabilistic environments. In order to discern predictive rules, people must effectively process complex and ambiguous information. In figuring out predictive rules, they must rely on their prior knowledge and experience to develop hypotheses about probabilistic factors, which serve as mechanisms for interpreting events and guiding behavior. People who believe strongly in their problem-solving capabilities are more efficient in their analytic thinking in complex decision-making situations (Bandura & Wood, 1988; Wood & Bandura, 1988). Those who are plagued by self-doubts are erratic in their analytic thinking. Quality of analytic thinking, in turn, affects performance accomplishments.

It is hardly surprising that people who are high in perceived control, construct scenarios in which they visualize and experience themselves enjoying future successes. Mental enactment and rehearsal of these scenarios appear actually to serve as guides for performance. On the other hand, people who judge themselves as inefficacious are more likely to visualize failure scenarios that undermine performance by dwelling on how things will go wrong (Bandura, 1990). Numerous studies have shown that cognitive reiteration of scenarios in which individuals visualize

themselves executing activities skillfully enhances subsequent performance (Bandura, 1986; Corbin, 1972; Feltz & Landers, 1983; Kazdin,
1978b).

Markus, Cross, and Wurf (1988) suggested that people actually construct mental images of their several possible selves, which serve as the
guidance system for competence. When possible selves are well-articulated, they help to organize behavior and motivate people to pursue
selected goals. To best serve this function, self-systems must contain
articulate plans and well-defined strategies for realizing desired futures.
Ill-defined possible selves are not adequate guides for behavior.

Motivation.   It is clear that perceived control influences people's per-
severance and endurance, especially in the face of obstacles. Difficulties
are viewed as challenges by people high in perceived self-efficacy,
whereas those who doubt their own capabilities tend to give up. Although
not always so, in general greater accomplishment is associated with strong
persistence (Bandura & Cervone, 1983; Cervone & Peake, 1986; Jacobs,
Prentice-Dunn, & Rogers, 1984; Weinberg, Gould, & Jackson, 1979).

Emotion.   Feelings are also greatly influenced by perceived control.
Worrisome thoughts are undoubtedly effectively arousing but feeling
that one can control the extent to which they escalate or persevere
strongly influences the extent of the affective component (Kent, 1987;
Kent & Gibbons, 1987). Bandura (1990) has shown that the incidence
of frightful cognitions is unrelated to anxiety level when variations in
perceived thought control efficacy are controlled for. As Bandura (1990)
noted:

> analysis of the aversiveness of obsessional ruminations provides support for
> efficacious thought control as a key factor in the regulation of cognitively-
> generated arousal (Salkovskis & Harrison, 1984). It is not the sheer fre-
> quency of intrusive cognitions but rather the perceived inefficacy to turn
> them off that is the major source of distress. (p. 319)

There is yet another way that perceived control is emotionally calming.
When people believe they can exercise control over potential threats,
they're not perturbed by them because they do not dwell on everything
that might go wrong and all the ways that they might fail. If, on the
other hand, people believe they cannot handle potential threats, they
experience considerable stress and dysphoric emotions. They worry
about coping poorly and see threat of possible failure looming large.
They dwell on their own inefficacy, thus distressing themselves and constraining and impairing their level of functioning (Bandura, 1990;

Lazarus & Folkman, 1984; Meichenbaum, 1977; Sarason, 1975). Studies suggest that perceived coping efficacy operates as a cognitive mediator of anxiety (Bandura, Reese, & Adams, 1982; Bandura, Taylor, Williams, Mefford, & Barchas, 1985).

Choice.   Judgments of personal control not only influence how people operate in various activities but also determine which activities and environments they choose to expose themselves to. Bandura (1990) argued that people pick environments they judge themselves capable of handling. This sets in motion a process by which the selection of more challenging environments in turn cultivates further competencies (Bandura, 1986; Snyder, 1986). Perceived control has great power to affect the course of our lives by influencing the types of choices we make. Nowhere is this shown more clearly than in the impact of perceived control on educational and career choices (Deci & Ryan, 1987; Lent & Hackett, 1987).

THE ORIGINS OF PERCEIVED CONTROL

Infancy.   There is evidence that even young infants show a clear delight in exercising causal agency. Although their realm of influence is relatively small at first, they are able to control the sensory stimulation from objects they can manipulate and the attentive behavior of those around them. For example, hitting a crib mobile produces predictable movements and sounds.

Infants begin to acquire a sense of personal agency when they perceive environmental events as being personally controlled. But first they must learn through repeated experiences of response-outcome contingency that their own actions cause events to occur. Bandura (1990) argued that because manipulating physical objects produces rapid and readily observable effects, the infant's sense of personal control may be initially more affected by his or her exercise of influence over the physical environment than over the social environment (Gunnar, 1980). Control may be more difficult to discern in social interactions where actions have variable social effects and some of them occur independently of what the infants are doing (Bandura, 1990). As cognition develops, and schematic processing increases, children come to be able to learn even from those of their actions that provide more delayed responses. Thus, not too far along in childhood, the sense of control over the social environment begins to play an important role in the development of the sense of personal agency as well.

During the course of development, children and parents operate as reciprocal interactants. Children become more competent when their parents are more responsive, and these increasing infant capabilities elicit still greater parental responsiveness (Bradley, Caldwell, & Elardo, 1979). Initial efficacy experiences are centered in the family but the growing contacts soon extend to a broader and more diverse group of people. Experiences with peers begin to contribute importantly to children's development and self-knowledge of their capabilities.

With development, the sense of control depends on accurate judgments of environmental contingencies. Sometimes the child has to judge whether someone will respond to his or her own act, but sometimes the child must learn to judge the environment's responsiveness to individual action in general. Responsiveness, for example, implies a causal theory about the way the environment operates. The self is often a weak causal contender when act-outcome contingencies are judged, especially when it is the environment's general responsiveness to individual action that is being judged (Bandura, 1990). Weisz and his coworkers (Weisz, Yeates, Robertson & Beckham, 1982) noted that judgments of contingency were crucial in developing children's sense of control. Until accurate perceptions of contingency are developmentally possible, it is more difficult for children to develop a full sense of their own efficacy.

Life Course Trajectory. Across the life span, every significant developmental transition provides new challenges for perceived and actual control. Young adulthood must prepare the way for learning about adult commitments and responsibilities, while still being in many ways a child. Issues of control and self-determination loom large in adolescence and a sense of one's own efficacy can make the transition to adulthood more successful. Yet uncertain physiological changes, induced by puberty, transition to new school environments and friendship groups, and increasing desire for intimacy and bonding, threaten the adolescent's sense of control and predictability (Hamburg, 1980). Learning by social comparison may diminish competencies unless the adolescent has sufficient assurance in his or her own capabilities.

Through middle adulthood and into old age, new demands and issues impact on one's sense of control. The work of Gurin and Brim (1984) shows that perceived control and judgment of outcome expectancies have different temporal features and individual stabilities. Their data show dramatically that historical trends influence both a sense of personal efficacy and views about environmental components of control, but there is greater stability of personal than environmental components of control. Historical events, actual shifts in responsiveness of authorities, and adult experiences with many arenas of action influence individuals' evaluations

of the external world more than their evaluations of their own competence.

Why are the personal components of control more steadfast? Gurin
and Brim (1984) argued that the need for perceived control produces
forces for stability. Change in personal aspects of the sense of control
may occur in adulthood, but probably in response to success experiences
and to gains instead of losses throughout the middle years. Threatening
experiences and losses may not have much power to change people
because there are many ways of protecting the self from threat. People
avoid such experiences if they can. They hold on to illusions about their
control. They try to manipulate relationships and the social environment
to see themselves as effective. Life events that lower feelings of control
would have to be quite compelling in order to change perceptions of
control. I have argued that these compelling events often do occur with
the onset of old age, however (Rodin, 1986a, 1986b).

Some older people experience a decline in objective control because
many environmental events that accompany old age result in limits on
the range of outcomes that actually are attainable. These environmental
factors include the losses of roles, norms, and appropriate reference
groups that are often created by major life events, such as retirement
and bereavement. Weisz (1983) emphasized the association between old
age and loss of actual contingency for a number of important outcomes.
For example, retirement entails a loss of contingency in the world of
work and one's health status depends less on voluntary behaviors and
more on biological forces. Indeed, the biological changes that occur in
late adulthood may induce restrictions in control (Rodin 1986a, 1986b).

Although actual control might diminish, the evidence at present does
not provide a clear picture that *perceived* control decreases as a function
of age per se (Rodin, Timko, & Harris, 1986). For example, as people
age, new roles may provide direct substitutes for former roles. Therefore
one's overall level of self-efficacy may remain stable, although the domains in which one feels competent are likely to change and become less
numerous.

LIMITATIONS TO BENEFITS OF CONTROL-RELEVANT PROCESSES

Despite the demonstrated importance of perceived and actual control, it
is not universally beneficial to feel increased control. There are some
conditions in which perceived control is more likely to induce stress than
to have a beneficial impact, for example when decision making is difficult,
the circumstances ambiguous and the possible outcomes unpleasant (cf.

Averill, 1973). There is also evidence that individuals' preferences for control vary widely. In laboratory studies, there is always a minority of subjects who opt for uncontrollable rather than controllable aversive events when they are given a choice (e.g., Averill & Rosenn, 1972). Field experiments in health-care settings have shown that some individuals benefit more than others from being highly informed about and/or involved in their own medical treatment (Berg & LoGerfo, 1979; Cromwell, Butterfield, Brayfield, & Curry, 1977; Mills & Krantz, 1979). I suspect that variability in optimal or preferred levels of control increases with age, in line with increasing variability in perceptions of control (cf. Lachman, 1986).

Engaging in futile attempts to control events that are actually uncontrollable is likely to have psychological and physiological costs (Janoff-Bulman & Brickman, 1980; Schulz & Hanusa, 1980; Wortman & Brehm, 1975). Excessive feelings of responsibility may be aversive (Averill, 1973; Rodin, Rennert, & Solomon, 1980; Thompson, 1981), and personal control often places heavy demands on people in the form of a high investment of time, effort, resources, and the risk of the consequences of failure. Lack of sufficient information to support effective control over an outcome has also been proposed to decrease the desirability of control (Rodin et al., 1980).

The possible physiological costs of control also merit attention. Specifically, there is evidence that in some individuals, excessive efforts to assert control can have negative effects on many of the physiological systems that show benefits with increased control. The work of Glass (1977), for example, considers Type A individuals who are so hard driving that they exert continued effort to exercise control even in the face of maladaptive outcomes or uncontrollable situations. Glass postulated that this repeated and frustrated desire for control may be related to increased catecholamine output, which in turn contributes to atherosclerosis. It seems quite clear therefore that more thinking is needed to explicate fully the conditions under which perceived and exercised control are beneficial and when they are not, and for whom. The remaining chapters begin to unravel this complex issue.

In studying control from sociohistorical, individual, and life-span perspectives, many challenges emerge. Each chapter is informed by a database unique to the author's discipline with its own terminology and focus. The discussants were asked to comment and broaden the perspectives so that conceptual integrations were pointed to, where possible, and issues for new research raised. What follows, then, explores a range of topics, drawing from a variety of disciplines, to enrich our understanding of the multiple determinants and consequences of control and self-directedness.

REFERENCES

Abramson, L. Y., & Alloy, L. B. (1981). Depression, nondepression, and cognitive illusions: A reply to Schwartz. *Journal of Experimental Psychology, 110,* 436–447.

Averill, J. (1973). Personal control of aversive stimulation and its relationship to stress. *Psychological Bulletin, 80* (4), 286–303.

Averill, J. R., & Rosenn, M. (1972). Vigilant and non-vigilant coping strategies and pathophysiological stress reactions during the anticipation of electric shock. *Journal of Personality and Social Psychology, 23,* 128–141.

Bandura, A. (1977). Self-efficacy: Toward a unifying theory of behavioral change. *Psychological Review, 84,* 191–125.

Bandura, A. (1986). Self-efficacy mechanisms in physiological activation and health promoting behavior. In J. Madden IV, S. Matthysse, & J. Barchas (Eds.), *Adaptation, learning and affect.* New York: Raven Press.

Bandura, A. (1990). Reflections on nonability determinants of competence. In J. Kolligian, Jr. & R. J. Sternberg (Eds.), *Competence considered: Perceptions of competence and incompetence across the lifespan* (pp. 315–362). New Haven, CT: Yale University Press.

Bandura, A., Adams, N. E., Hardy, A. B., & Howells, G. N. (1980). Tests of the generality of self-efficacy theory. *Cognitive Therapy and Research, 4,* 39–66.

Bandura, A., & Cervone, D. (1983). Self-evaluative and self-efficacy mechanisms governing the motivational effects of goal systems. *Journal of Personality and Social Psychology, 45,* 1017–1028.

Bandura, A., Reese, L., & Adams, N. E. (1982). Microanalysis of action and fear arousal as a function of differential levels of perceived self-efficacy. *Journal of Personality and Social Psychology, 43,* 5–21.

Bandura, A., Taylor, C. B., Williams, S. L., Mefford, I. N., & Barchas, J. D. (1985). Catecholamine secretion as a function of perceived coping self-efficacy. *Journal of Consulting and Clinical Psychology, 53,* 406–414.

Bandura, A., & Wood, R. E. (1988). *Effect of perceived controllability and performance standards on self-regulation of complex decision-making.* Manuscript submitted for review.

Baron, R., & Rodin, J. (1978). Perceived control and crowding stress. In A. Baum, J. E. Singer, & S. Valine (Eds.), *Advances in environmental psychology* (pp. 145–190). Hillsdale, NJ: Lawrence Erlbaum Associates.

Berg, A. O., & LoGerfo, J. P. (1979). Potential effect of self-care algorithms on the number of physician visits. *New England Journal of Medicine, 300,* 535–537.

Blankentstein, K. R. (1984). Psychophysiology and perceived locus of control: Critical review, theoretical speculation and research directions. In H. M. Lefcourt (Ed.), *Research with the locus of control construct* (Vol. 3, pp. 73–95). Orlando, FL: Academic Press.

Bradley, R. H., Caldwell, B. M., & Elardo, R. (1979). Home environment and cognitive development in the first two years: A cross-lagged panel analysis. *Developmental Psychology, 15,* 246–250.

Cantor, N., & Hunt, T. M. (1987, June). *Positive and negative frames for health relevant information.* Paper prepared for MacArthur Health and Behavior Network Conference on The Effects of Pharmacology, Technology, and other Modern Interventions on Women's Health, Key Biscayne, FL.

Cervone, D., & Peake, P.K. (1986). Anchoring, efficacy, and action: The influence of judgmental heuristics on self-efficacy judgments and behavior. *Journal of Personality and Social Psychology, 50,* 492–501.

deCharms, R. (1968). *Personal causation.* New York: Academic Press.

Corbin, C. (1972). Mental practice. In W. Morgan (Ed.), *Ergogenic aids and muscular performance* (pp. 93–118). New York: Academic Press.

Cromwell, R. L., Butterfield, D. C., Brayfield, F. M., & Curry, J. J. (1977). *Acute myocardial infarction: Reaction and recovery.* St. Louis: Mosby.

Davis, F. W., & Yates, B. T. (1982). Self-efficacy expectancies versus outcome expectancies as determinants of performance deficits and depressive affect. *Cognitive Therapy and Research, 6,* 23–25.

Deci, E. L., & Ryan, R. M. (1985). *Intrinsic motivation and self-determination in human behavior.* New York: Plenum Press.

Deci, E. L., & Ryan, R. M. (1987). The dynamics of self-determination in personality and development. In R. Schwarzer (Ed.), *Self-related cognitions in anxiety and motivation* (pp. 171–194). Hillsdale, NJ: Lawrence Erlbaum Associates.

Derogatis, L. R., Abeloff, M., & Milesaratos, N. (1979). Psychological coping mechanisms and survival time in metastatic breast cancer. *Journal of the American Medical Association, 242,* 1504–1508.

Eastman, C., & Marzillier, J. S. (1984). Theoretical and methodological difficulties in Bandura's self-efficacy theory. *Cognitive Therapy and Research, 8,* 213–229.

Erdelyi, M. H. (1974). A new look at the new look: Perceptual defense and vigilance. *Psychological Review, 81,* 1–25.

Feltz, D. L., & Landers, D. M. (1983). Effects of mental practice on motor skill learning and performance: A meta-analysis. *Journal of Sport Psychology, 5,* 25–57.

Glass, D. C. (1977). *Behavior patterns, stress and coronary disease.* Hillsdale, NJ: Lawrence Erlbaum Associates.

Godding, P. R., & Glasgow, R. E. (1985). Self-efficacy and outcome expectations as predictors of controlled smoking status. *Cognitive Therapy and Research, 9,* 583–590.

Gunnar, M. R. (1980). Contingent stimulation: A review of its role in early development. In S. Levine & H. Ursin (Eds.), *Coping and health* (pp. 101–119). New York: Plenum Press.

Gurin, P., & Brim, O. G., Jr. (1984). Change in self in adulthood: The example of sense of control. In P. B. Baltes & O. G. Brim, Jr. (Eds.), *Life-span development and behavior* (Vol. 6, pp. 281-334). New York: Academic Press.

Hamburg, B. A. (1980). Early adolescence as a life stress. In S. Levine & H. Ursin (Eds.), *Coping and health.* New York: Plenum Press.

Jacobs, B., Prentice-Dunn, S., & Rogers, R. W. (1984). Understanding persistence: An interface of control theory and self-efficacy theory. *Basic and Applied Social Psychology, 5,* 333–343.

Janoff-Bulman, R., & Brickman, P. (1980). Expectations of what people learn from failure. In N. T. Feather (Ed.), *Expectancy, incentive and action.* Hillsdale, NJ: Lawrence Erlbaum Associates.

Kazdin, A. E. (1978a). Conceptual and assessment issues raised by self-efficacy theory. *Advances in Behavior Research and Therapy, 1,* 177–185.

Kazdin, A. E. (1978b). Covert modeling—Therapeutic application of imagined rehearsal. In J. L. Singer & K. S. Pope (Eds.), *The power of human imagination: New methods in psychotherapy. Emotions, personality, and psychotherapy* (pp. 225–278). New York: Plenum.

Kelley, H. H. (1967). Attribution theory in social psychology. In D. Levine (Ed.), *Nebraska Symposium on Motivation* (Vol. 15, pp. 154–215). Lincoln, NE: University of Nebraska Press.

Kelley, H. H. (1971). *Attribution in social interaction.* In E. E. Jones, D. Kanouse, H. H. Kelley, R. E. Nisbett, S. Valins, & B. Weiner (pp. 1–26). Morristown, NJ: General Learning Press.

Kent, G. (1987). Self-efficacious control over reported physiological, cognitive, and behavioural symptoms of dental anxiety. *Behaviour Research and Therapy, 25,* 341–347.

Kent, G., & Gibbons, R. (1987). Self-efficacy and the control of anxious cognitions. *Journal of Behavior Therapy and Experimental Psychiatry, 18,* 33–40.

Lachman, M. E. (1986). Personal control in later life: Stability, change, and cognitive correlates. In M. M. Baltes & P. B. Baltes (Eds.), *Aging and the psychology of control* (pp. 207–236). Hillsdale, NJ: Lawrence Erlbaum Associates.

Langer, E. (1975). The illusion of control. *Journal of Personality and Social Psychology, 32*, 311–328.

Langer, E. (1983). *The psychology of control.* Beverly Hills, CA: Sage.

Lazarus, R. S., & Folkman, S. (1984). Coping and adaptation. In W. D. Gentry (Ed.), *The handbook of behavioral medicine* (pp. 282–325). New York: Guilford.

Lent, R. W., & Hackett, G. (1987). Career self-efficacy: Empirical status and future directions. *Journal of Vocational Behavior, 30*, 347–382.

Levy, S. (1984). The process and outcome of "adjustment" in the cancer patient: A reply to Taylor. *American Psychologist, 39*, 19–27.

Litt, M. (1988). Self efficacy and perceived control: cognitive mediators of pain tolerance. *Journal of Personality and Social Psychology, 54*, 149–160.

Locke, E. A., Frederick, E., Lee, C., & Bobko, P. (1984). Effect of self-efficacy, goals, and task strategies on task performance. *Journal of Applied Psychology, 69*, 241–251.

Maddux, J. E., Norton, L. W., & Stoltenburg, C. D. (1986). Self efficacy expectancies, outcome expectancies and outcome value: Relative effects on behavioral intentions. *Journal of Personality and Social Psychology, 5*, 783–789.

Maddux, J. E., & Rogers, R. W. (1983). Protection motivation and self-efficacy: A revised theory of fear appeals and attitude change. *Journal of Experimental Social Psychology, 19*, 469–479.

Manning, M. M., & Wright, T. L. (1983). Self-efficacy expectancies, outcome expectancies, and the persistence of pain control in childbirth. *Journal of Personality and Social Psychology, 45*, 421–431.

Markus, H., Cross, S., & Wurf, E. (1988). The role of the self-system in competence. In J. Kolligan, Jr. & R. J. Sternberg (Eds.) *Competence considered: Perceptions of competence across the life span.* New Haven, CT: Yale University Press.

Meichenbaum, D. H. (1977). *Cognitive-behavior modification: An integrative approach.* New York: Plenum Press.

Mills, R. T., & Krantz, D. S. (1979). Information, choice and reactions to stress: A held experiment in a blood bank with laboratory analogue. *Journal of Personality and Social Psychology, 37*, 226–228.

Polyani, M. (1958). *Personal knowledge: Toward a postcritical philosophy.* Chicago: University of Chicago Press.

Rodin, J. (1986a). Health, control, and aging. In M. M. Baltes & P. B. Baltes (Eds.), *Aging and the psychology of control* (pp. 139–165). Hillsdale, NJ: Lawrence Erlbaum Associates.

Rodin, J. (1986b). Personal control through the life course. In R. Abeles (Ed.), *Implications of the life span perspective for social psychology* (pp. 103–120). Hillsdale, NJ: Lawrence Erlbaum Associates.

Rodin, J., Rennert, K., & Solomon, S. K. (1980). Intrinsic motivation for control: Fact or fiction. In A. Baum & J. E. Singer (Eds.), *Advances in environmental psychology* (Vol. 2, pp. 131–148). Hillsdale, NJ: Lawrence Erlbaum Associates.

Rodin, J., Timko, C., & Harris, S. (1986). The construct of control: Biological and psychological correlates. *Annual Review of Gerontology & Geriatrics, 5*, 3–55.

Rothbaum, F., Weisz, J. R., & Snyder, S. S. (1982). Changing the world and changing the self: A two-process model of perceived control. *Journal of Personality and Social Psychology, 42*, 5–37.

Rotter, J. B. (1966). Generalized expectancies for internal versus external control of reinforcement. *Psychological Monographs, 80* (1, Whole No. 609).

Ryan, R. M. (1982). Control and information in the intrapersonal sphere: An extension of cognitive evaluation theory. *Journal of Personality and Social Psychology, 43*, 450–461.

Salkovskis, P. M., & Harrison, J. (1984). Abnormal and normal obsessions—A replication. *Behavior Research and Therapy, 22*, 549–552.

Sarason, I. G. (1975). Anxiety and self-preoccupation. In I. G. Sarason & C. D. Spielberger (Eds.), *Stress and anxiety* (Vol. 2, pp. 27–43). New York: Wiley.

Scheier, M. F., & Carver, C. S. (1987). Dispositional optimism and physical well-being: The influence of generalized outcome expectancies on health. *Journal of Personality, 55*, 169–210.

Schorr, D., & Rodin, J. (1984). Motivation to control one's environment in individuals with obsessive-compulsive, depressive and normal personality traits. *Journal of Personality and Social Psychology, 46*, 1148–1161.

Schulz, R., & Hanusa, B. H. (1980). Experimental social gerontology: A social psychological perspective. *Journal of Social Issues, 36*, 30–46.

Seligman, M. E. P. (1975), *Helplessness: On depression development and death.* San Francisco: Freeman.

Shiffrin, R. M., & Schneider, W. (1977). Controlled and automatic human information processing: II, Perceptual learning, automatic attending and a general theory. *Psychological Review, 84*, 127–190.

Snyder, M. (1986) *Public appearances, private realities: The psychology of self-monitoring.* New York: Freeman.

Steiner, I. (1970). Attributed freedom. In L. Berkowitz (Ed.) *Advances in experimental social psychology* (Vol. 5, pp. 187–249). New York: Academic Press.

Strecher, V. J., Becker, M. H., Kirscht, J. P., Eraker, S. A., & Graham-Tomasi, R. P. (1985). Psychosocial aspects of changes in cigarette-smoking behavior. *Patient Education and Counseling, 7*, 249–262.

Taylor, M. S., Locke, E. A., Lee, C., & Gist, M. E. (1984). Type A behavior and faculty research productivity: What are the mechanisms? *Organizational Behavior and Human Performance, 34*, 402–418.

Taylor, S., & Brown, J. (1988). Illusion and well-being: A social psychological perspective on mental health. *Psychological Bulletin, 103*, 193–210.

Taylor, S. E. (1983). Adjustment to threatening events: A theory of cognitive adaptation. *American Psychologist, 38*, 1161–1173.

Thompson, S. (1981). Will it hurt less if I can control it? A complex answer to a simple question. *Psychological Bulletin, 90*, 89–101.

Turvey, M. T. (1977). Preliminaries to a theory of action with reference to vision. In R. Shaw & J. Bransford (Eds.), *Perceiving, acting and knowing: Toward an ecological psychology* (pp. 211–267). Hillsdale, NJ: Lawrence Erlbaum Associates.

Weinberg, R. S., Gould, D., & Jackson, A. (1979). Expectations and performance: An empirical test of Bandura's self-efficacy theory. *Journal of Sport Psychology, 1*, 320–331.

Weisz, J. R. (1983). Can I control it? The pursuit of veridical answers across the life span. *Life-span Development and Behavior, 5*, 233–300.

Weisz, J. R., Yeates, K. O., Robertson, D., & Beckham, J. C. (1982). Perceived contingency of skill and chance events: A developmental analysis: *Developmental Psychology, 18*, 898–905.

White, R. W. (1959). Motivation reconsidered: The concept of competence. *Psychological Review, 66*, 297–333.

Wood, R. E., & Bandura, A. (1988). *Impact of conceptions of ability on self-regulatory mechanisms and complex decision-making.* Manuscript submitted for review.

Wortman, C., & Brehm, J. (1975). Responses to uncontrollable outcomes: An integration of reactance theory and the learned helplessness model. In L. Berkowitz (Ed.), *Advances in experimental and social psychology* (Vol. 8, pp. 278–336). New York: Academic Press.

Wortman, C. B., & Dintzer, L. (1978). Is an attributional analysis of the learned helplessness phenomenon viable? A critique of the Abramson-Seligman-Teasdale reformulation. *Journal of Abnormal Psychology, 87*, 75–90.

Individualism and the Historical and Social-Structural Determinants of People's Concerns Over Self-Directedness and Efficacy

Carmi Schooler
National Institute of Mental Health

The social and cultural backgrounds of most of the people likely to read this volume would probably lead them to assume that the desire to be an autonomous and effectual individual is a human universal. They might, therefore, readily conclude that the topic of this chapter—the historical and social–structural determinants of concern over self-direction and efficacy–is a nonquestion. The evidence, however, suggests that this is far from the case. Being an independent and efficacious individual has been the goal of only a small portion of mankind (Inkeles & Smith, 1974; Macfarlane, 1978, 1986; Redfield, 1956). In fact, societies with such individualistic values are so relatively rare that Meyer has formulated a theoretical approach aimed at specifying the nature of the institutional supports that Western societies provide for such an individualistic view of the self (Meyer, 1986, 1988).

As we see later, I have reservations about some of the specifics of Meyer's view. Nevertheless, I think it is clear that the varied cultural, social–structural, and institutional processes brought about by different historical circumstances lead to differences in the emphases placed on the importance of self-direction and efficacy for the individual. Furthermore, such differences in emphasis may exist not only between cultures, but may also exist within societies, particularly those that are not homogenous socially or culturally.

Although the questions of the determinants of concern over self-direction and efficacy are interesting in themselves, the importance of these questions goes beyond the merely academic. It is quite plausible that some of the psychological and medical consequences of believing oneself to be self-directed and effectual found among Americans do not occur in other societies. It is an open empirical question whether feelings of self-directedness would have the same effects where self-direction and individualism are not valued, for example among Japanese, Javanese, or Iranians, as they do among Americans. Nor do we even know for certain whether these effects are the same among Americans from different social statuses or ethnic groups.

Because valuing self-directedness and efficacy is apparently relatively rare, identification of the historical and social–structural circumstances in which such concern develops becomes of real importance. In examining the historical and social-structural determinants of concern over self-directedness and efficacy, my primary focus is on factors influencing the growth of individualism. The reason for this focus is my belief that high levels of individualism form the major basis for concern over self-directedness and efficacy. This belief is closely linked to my definition of individualism (Schooler, in press). I envision individualism as representing (Schooler, in press) one pole of an individual versus group-oriented dimension and define the individualistic pole as follows:

1. The individual, in contrast to some larger social grouping, is the unit of central importance both in the selection of means and the evaluation of ends. The individual is conceived of as "essentially" existing independently of society. In a group-oriented culture such an ontological distinction between the individual and his or her group is not readily conceivable (Hamaguchi, 1985).

2. Evaluation of ends takes place in terms of consequences for the individual. Individuals are reinforced as a result of the perceived positive effect of their acts on themselves. In group-oriented societies individuals are more likely to be reinforced in terms of the outcomes for the group(s) with which they are identified.

3. A high reinforcement value is placed on the individual's subjective experience, particularly on the phenomenological experience of choice, including the freedom to choose one's beliefs unhindered by official constraints. The sense of autonomy, self-direction, and freedom of thought, rather than interdependence and behavioral and ideological conformity, are valued.

4. Relevant societal institutions provide legitimization for such a set of individual aspirations for personal satisfaction and autonomy. The status "individual" is seen as inherently including legal-moral-religious rights in contrast to more group-centered cultures where such rights are more likely to adhere to various social entities.

5. Because individuals are viewed as autonomous, self-directed entities, they can legitimately be seen as responsible for their own actions. The individ-

ual is hence the moral unit. Culpability can only be assigned to individuals rather than to other social units.

Using such a definition of individualism requires a clarification of individualism's relationship to several concepts with which it is closely connected—self-direction, autonomy, egalitarianism, and open society. From the perspective of the individual, self-direction and autonomy are the same, *autonomy* being defined as "self-directing freedom" (Webster's Ninth New Collegiate Dictionary, 1985), or being "controlled from within" (Webster's New International Dictionary, 2nd Ed., 1961). Individualism, as I have described it, presupposes such self-direction because individuals are seen as responsible for the selection of both their goals and their means of attaining them. In addition, according to this view of individualism a central goal of the individualistically oriented is the phenomenological experience of choice and self-directedness.

The occurrence of individualism implies the valuation of self-direction or autonomy. However, it is possible that self-directedness may be valued in societies where individualism, in the full sense that the term is used in this chapter, is not a fully accepted social norm. This may occur because individualism, as it has been defined here, involves a tendency to evaluate outcomes in terms of their effects on the individual rather than some group. It is possible to imagine forms of self-directedness in which individuals who value their autonomy choose actions on the basis of whether these actions promote some group's well-being rather than their own. Thus, the occurrence of individualism is a sufficient, but not necessary, predictor of a self-directed orientation. All individualists should value self-direction, but all those people who value self-direction are not necessarily individualistic. Nevertheless, socioenvironmental conditions that increase the value placed on self-directedness probably act to increase the importance of the individual in evaluating outcomes. Although very strong countervailing norms of group identification may hinder such an increase of individualism, it is improbable that such norms can completely stop the development of individualistic values under socioeconomic conditions leading to a high valuation of self-directedness. Nevertheless, it is unlikely that either tendency (i.e., individualistic or group-based evaluation of outcomes) ever becomes the sole determinant of behavior. In most circumstances, most people's choice of actions probably represents some balance of the two.

There is also a relationship between the cultural espousement of individualism and egalitarianism. As we see later, cultures that stress the importance of the role of the individual are likely to give that role primacy above other roles that can be used to formally stratify individuals. Thus, individualistic societies tend to be relatively open societies and not rigidly hierarchical. The cultural emphasis on equality, however, can take at least two forms: one is an emphasis on equality of opportunity, the other an emphasis on equality of reward. The former emphasis is congruent with societies with major disparities in socioeconomic status, but whose norms imply that all individuals have equally inalienable rights to "the pursuit of happiness." The latter emphasis is congruent with societies characterized by relatively flat social hierarchies in which individuals "give according to their abilities and receive according to their needs," and in which the goals of the individual may be subordinated to the societal goal of maintaining equality in wealth and status.

All in all, in terms of the question of the determinants of concern over self-directedness and efficacy, my definition of individualism implies that persons in individualistic societies would seem likely to wish themselves to be self-directed and to highly value the phenomenological experience of freedom of choice. They would also seem likely to place a high value on being personally effective rather than having their well-being depend on others or on fate. Personal efficacy would be valued not only because individuals value their independence, but also because they see themselves as primarily responsible for what happens to them, while believing that they have a relatively weak moral claim on the help of others.

I see the development of individualism as arising from a combination of many levels of phenomena ranging from the cultural to biological. My present focus is on how historical/cultural, social–structural/institutional and economic/production factors interact in the relatively unusual development of individualistic belief and consequent concern over self-directedness and efficacy. I discuss these interactions in three apparently disparate circumstances in which individualism has historically arisen— hunting–gathering societies, England between 1300 and 1840, and 16th-century Japan. My discussion of the first two examples is based on the data and theories of others; my discussion of the last example, on my own marshalling of the evidence (Schooler, in press).

These examples are chosen in the belief that their discussion elucidates the causal interconnections among a society's historically determined cultural institutions, social structure, modes of production, and the development of individualistic thought. I also try to link the conclusions drawn from these historical examples to the findings of research conducted in modern industrial societies by Mel Kohn, me, and our coworkers (Kohn & Schooler, 1983). This research, which uses linear structural equations modeling techniques on survey data from representative samples in the United States, Poland, and Japan, shows how social–structurally determined occupational conditions affect psychological functioning, in part through affecting the complexity of the environment. Most relevant to the question of the origins of individualism and concern over self-directedness and efficacy are our findings that job conditions that increase the self-directedness and cognitive complexity of work, not only increase intellectual flexibility, but also raise levels of concern over and feelings of personal autonomy and efficacy.

In describing and comparing these different historical circumstances in which individualism has developed, I do not claim to present anything close to an integrated theory of the interrelationship of historical patterns, social institutions, modes of production, and the growth of individualism. To complicate matters, for the various societies we examine, we have different forms of evidence, often about quite different aspects of their functioning. These differences come about, in part, because the data about the different societies come from a variety of different disciplines (i.e., anthropology, history, sociology, psychology), each of which has its own interests, as well as its own canons of acceptable proof. Thus, for example, the anthropological conclusions about the hunting–gathering societies are based on the similarity of the findings of relevant field work studies conducted by different anthropologists who are generally more concerned about characterizing a culture than in looking for differences among its members. On the other hand, the sociological evidence that is used generally involves statistical analysis of data from representative samples aimed at understanding why people within a given culture differ. This disciplinary diversity raises difficulties that must be taken into account (Schooler, 1989a). Nevertheless, the only way progress can be made in understanding issues such as the development of individualism is by collating and juxtaposing the research findings of the various disciplines that have dealt with the topic.

An additional complication is that, not only are there similarities in such things as individually oriented modes of production among the individualistic societies we examine, there are also profound differences. For example, they differ dramatically in the nature and complexity of their social institutions and social controls. They clearly also differ in the economic consequences of individualism, and may even differ in the nature of its causes. Still, congruences and similarities emerge—hopefully, enough to provide some of the grist from which an integrated, and necessarily complex, theory of individualism can eventually be made. Attempting to develop such a theory should contribute substantially to our understanding of the social and cultural determinants of people's concern over self-directedness and efficacy.

HUNTING–GATHERING SOCIETIES

I suspect that I was not alone, even among reasonably knowledgeable people, in holding the general belief that nonliterate societies are characterized by one or another form of group orientation (e.g., age-grade societies, clans), and that *individualism* as I have defined it only arises in complex literate societies. I was therefore surprised when, in the course of preparing this chapter, I came across clear examples of the development of individualism in two types of essentially nonliterate, hunting and gathering societies—immediate-return societies and subartic hunting societies. An examination of each of these societies brings to light important interrelationships between the modes of production, cultural values, and individualism, while providing us with some examples of how individualism can exist in situations in which social institutions of any kind seem to be few and simple.

Immediate-Return Societies.   One type of setting in which individualism seems to have developed in preliterate societies is described by Woodburn (1982). Defining a type of society found in Africa, Southern India, and Malaysia, he noted:

> greater equality of wealth, of power and of prestige has been achieved in *certain* hunting and gathering societies than in any other human societies. These societies, which have economies based on *immediate* rather than delayed return, are assertively egalitarian. Equality is achieved through direct, individual access to resources; through direct individual access to means of coercion and means of mobility which limit the imposition of control; through procedures which prevent saving and accumulation and impose sharing; through mechanisms which allow goods to circulate without making people dependent on one another. People are systematically disengaged from property and therefore from the potentiality in property for creating dependency. (p. 431)

In describing the economic and social conditions of the immediate return societies, Woodburn did not go into the level of detail about the psychological functioning of their members that would show that these societies fit all of the aspects of our definition of individualism. Nevertheless, the picture he did draw was congruent with that definition. He strongly made the point that the equality that characterizes immediate-return societies is not the neutral absence of inequality or hierarchy; it is an equality that is actively asserted by the culture. Individual autonomy is highly valued. Whatever leaders there are must be modest and egalitarian, while their opinions hold only a bit more weight than the opinions of others.

In providing evidence for his conclusions, Woodburn portrayed the egalitarian immediate-return systems as having the following basic characteristics. "People obtain a direct and immediate return from their labour. They go out hunting or gathering and eat the food obtained the same day or casually over the days that follow. Food is neither elaborately processed nor stored. They use relatively simple, portable, utilitarian, easily acquired, replaceable tools and weapons" (p. 432).

In contrast, in delayed-return systems "people hold rights over valued assets of some sort, which either represent a yield, a return of labour applied over time, or, if not, are held and managed in a way which resembles and has similar social implications to delayed yields on labour" (Woodburn, 1982, p. 432). In hunter–gatherer societies, such assets may include, among other things, technical facilities used in production (e.g., boats, nets, traps), and processed and stored foods; in other types of societies such assets may include land or other forms of ownership of the means of production.

In terms of their social organization, Woodburn saw immediate-return societies as having the following basic characteristics: (a) social groupings are flexible and change frequently; (b) individuals are free to choose whom they associate with in their residence, in the quest for food, in trade and in ritual contexts; (c) people are not dependent on specific other people for access to basic requirements; (d) interpersonal relationships do not involve long-term binding commitments and dependencies.

Drawing on the fieldwork of a number of anthropologists, Woodburn showed that among the societies that fit into this pattern are the Mbuti Pygmies of Zaire; the !Kung Bushmen of Botswana and Namibia; the Pandaram and Paliyan of south India; the Batek Negritos of Malaysia, and the Hadza of Tanzania. In all of these societies nomadism is fundamental. Dwellings are not fixed. People live in frequently moving small camp units of one or two dozen people. Individuals can and do move from one camp to another and from one area to another, either temporarily or permanently. There is no economic penalty for such moves and no question of tightly defined groups monopolizing the resources of their areas and excluding outsiders. These cultures do not see movement as a burdensome necessity, but as something positive that is healthy and desirable in itself. Neither the frequency nor spatial patterning of such moves is the result of ecological factors alone.

As Woodburn noted, arrangements such as these are subversive for the development of authority. Because individuals are not bound to fixed areas, to fixed assets or to fixed resources, they are able to move away rapidly and easily from constraints that others may seek to impose on them. The possibility of such free and easy movement acts as a powerful leveling mechanism.

Another important leveling mechanism that Woodburn described is the access that all males have to effective weapons. Hunting weapons are generally lethal to people as well as to game animals. Because all men, however physically weak, possess the means to kill those they perceive as threats or sources of grievance, inequalities of wealth, power, and prestige that can lead to envy and resentment can be dangerous for their holders.

> What we have here is direct and immediate access to social control, access which is not mediated through formal institutions or through relationships with other people. It is directly analogous to and matched by, the direct and immediate access, again not normally mediated through formal institutions or through relationships with other people, which people have to food and other resources. (Woodburn, 1982, pp. 436–437)

In most of these societies, neither kinship status nor age serve as qualifications for access to particular hunting and gathering skills or equipment. Consequently, adults of either sex can, if they wish, readily obtain enough food to feed themselves adequately and are thus potentially autonomous.

The genuine equality of opportunity that individuals enjoy in their access to resources does not result in equality of yield. The quantities of desirable items that individuals obtain vary greatly depending on skill, persistence, and luck. It is in the face of such inequalities that societal controls on the development of inequality are brought into play. Thus, when large game animals are killed elaborate formal rules are brought to bear that dissociate the hunter from his kill and deny him the privileges of ownership. Also common are forms of gambling and gift giving that result in a relatively random distribution of goods that subverts the accumulation of individual wealth by the hard working or the skilled. Furthermore, these societies are characterized by the absence of leaders or by the presence of leaders who are elaborately constrained from exercising authority or using their influence to acquire wealth or prestige.

The fluidity and spatial mobility of local groupings reinforced by a distinctive set of egalitarian practices that disengage people from property inhibit any intensification of the economy. The difficulties are not due to the absence of technical knowledge. In many instances, individuals are knowledgeable about farming techniques. Farming, however, cannot be carried on without some legitimated means of accumulation and in the absence of grain stores and agricultural tools.

Woodburn noted that the possibility of autonomy together with the limitation of the obligations to specific other people—as opposed to a generalized obligation to share—reduces the sense of commitment that people feel to each other. There are instances in which the seriously ill or elderly are abandoned when camp is moved. On the other hand, these societies are open. Thus, for example, among the Hadza, although lepers are ostracized in surrounding societies, and although the Hadza are aware of the communicable nature of the disease, Hadza lepers are treated exactly like everyone else. "The principle is that Hadza society is open and there is simply no basis for exclusion. Equality is, in a sense generalized by them to all mankind" (Woodburn, 1982, p. 448).

What emerges from the descriptions of these immediate-return societies is a picture of how independence in means of subsistence production, linked to a social system that does not bind the individual tightly to a given geographic or social location, can support an extremely high level of individualism. There evidently also exist some related social institutions, such as organized forms of gambling and gift giving, that have the presumably latent functions of reducing inequality as well as more manifest value systems that directly support the individualistic ethos.

The congruence between individualism and those simple social institutions and modes of production that do exist in the hunter–gatherer societies is clear. What is unclear from these examples is the nature of the direction of causality, both in terms of the origins of these societies and their maintenance. To what extent were the individualistic social organizations, value systems, and modes of production historically responsible for each other's development? To what extent does each at present constrain change in the others? Although we may gain some clarification through the examination of other individualistic societies, the answer to these questions remain unclear. What does seem to be the case is that individualism can develop and continue in societies that do not provide it with elaborate institutional supports—societies that seem to be based on the simplest social contract between individuals that Hobbes (1651/1958) could have imagined. Certainly, the social and physical conditions of life seem to support the high value the individual members of these immediate-return societies place on their autonomy and ability to effectively provide for themselves.

Subarctic Hunting Societies.   In a review article on subarctic hunting societies, Ridington (1988) found that "Native hunter–gatherers of the North American Subarctic have consistently been described as valuing knowledge, power and individual autonomy" (p. 98). (For an extended review providing evidence for this point from a wide range of studies by numerous anthropologists see Christian & Gardner, 1977.) Ridington asked whether there is something special about what it takes to adapt to subarctic life that brings about this association of knowledge, individualism, and power and noted that this subarctic individualism "is very like the individualism Woodburn (1982) describes for what he calls 'immediate return' egalitarian societies" (Ridington, 1988, p. 105). It is noteworthy that these two types of hunter–gatherer societies are also similar in the value placed on movement, the resultant ease with which it is possible to move away from the constraints that others may seek to impose, and the near absence of political organizations and hierarchies of power.

These subarctic societies, however, differ from the immediate-return societies in several ways. First, in the course of the year, periods of isolation alternate with periods of intense socialization. The interdependence of individuals is also greater than in immediate-return societies.

> There is too much to contend with for man to exist without a wife, or for a family to exist without kinsmen. Lone persons are actually pitied and feared, and if isolated . . . lose their humanity. For the native person, isolation *in extremis* is dehumanization in earnest, for people need one another to insure their survival and preserve their nature. (Savishinsky, 1974, p. 44)

The subarctic hunting societies also differ from immediate-return societies in their modes of production and consumption. Thus, they have developed and employ a wide variety of preservation and storage techniques so that food can be saved from seasons when it is available, for use in seasons when it is scarce. They also differ from immediate-return societies in the greater elaborateness and technical complexity of the equipment and clothing they manufacture and use, as well as in the frequency with which individuals cooperate in complex forms of hunting and trapping.

In these societies, people value and "hold in high esteem an individual whom they feel to be malleable, adjustable, and capable of adapting to diverse ecological and social situations" (Savishinsky, 1974, p. 80). A man is respected not only because he has all of the skills necessary for living off of the land, but also because he is alert and innovative enough to meet the challenges of any unusual circumstances that arise. The successful person is thus an individual who can alter materials and develop inventive procedures when necessary. Individuals in these societies clearly value the freedom to live as they choose, to move when and where they please, and to schedule, order, and arrange their lives as they wish. The value they place on freedom "is cognate not only with flexibility, but also with people's stress upon individualism, anti-authoritarianism, and independence. Their dislike of 'bossy' or pushy persons, and their positive evaluation of self-reliance and individual competence, are consistent—though not synonymous—with their emphasis on freedom and flexibility (Savishinsky, 1974, p. 81).

Subarctic hunting people fundamentally depend on their knowledge and technique for their successful adaptation to the environment (Ridington, 1988). The individual's knowledge of animals, the environment, and hunting techniques are the major tools of these hunters. Consequently, what takes place in the individual's cognitive space is seen as very important. This individualism reaches such a level that personal experience is considered the only appropriate validation of knowledge. Thus, "the Chipewyan . . . regard the written word as hearsay. 'Knowledge that has been mediated is regarded with doubt. True knowledge is considered that which derives from experience (Scollon & Scollon, 1979, p. 185)" (Ridington, 1988, p. 104).

The relationship between dealing with complex environments and the development of concern over what one subjectively knows and feels has also been noted in modern societies. The evidence indicates that in modern societies individuals exposed to complex environments "tend to develop a form of subjectivism based on the belief that what takes place within themselves is of primary importance, such a belief deriving both from the feeling that the locus of control is and should be within oneself and from the importance given to mental processes by the emphasis placed on effective cognitive functioning" (Schooler, 1972, p. 300).

On a more general level, exposure to environments demanding intellectually flexible responses has been shown to lead, not only to increased intellectual flexibility, but also to an increased valuation of self-directedness (Kohn & Schooler, 1983; Schooler, 1984, 1987). Thus, it seems plausible that there is a causal connection between the almost incredible degree to which subarctic environments test the individual's flexibility and resourcefulness and the emphasis that these societies place on individualism. Subarctic individualism may well represent a way in which the modes of production within a society affect both its cultural values and the psychological functioning of its members. The environmental demands that must be met to successfully adopt to a hunter–gatherer existence in the subarctic seem to lead to individuals and societies who share a strong concern over self-directedness and efficacy.[1]

---

[1]It is also worth noting that fishing societies have been seen as similar to hunter–gatherer societies both in their individualism and their modes of production. In a discussion of equality and flexibility in maritime adaptation Schoembucher (1988) noted:

> Despite . . . diversity, anthropologists agree that fishing societies have certain factors in common through which they can be distinguished from nonfishermen in general. Unlike an adaptation to a terrestrial environment, an adaptation to a maritime environment is considered to be "one of the most extreme achieved by man" (Acheson, 1981, p. 277). Consequently, exploiting a maritime environment is supposed to have a determinant influence on the psychocultural and sociocultural characteristics of fishermen. . . . Coastal fishermen (or maritime communities) are described as independent, proud, aggressive . . . courageous: qualities that are rarely applied to peasant cultivators. (p. 213)

> An extractive mode of production is considered to be the presupposition for flexibility and equality in hunter and gatherer societies. Despite essential structural differences between hunter–gatherer and fishing societies (the most important of which is that . . . fishing societies are not economically subsistent) we find basically egalitarian and flexible structures in the social organization of the Vadabalija [the South Indian fishing caste Schoembucher is investigating]. (p. 218)

Similar differences in levels of individualism between fishing and peasant societies have also been noted in preindustrial Europe (Lewis, 1958; Schooler, 1976; Slicher Van Bath, 1963).

ENGLAND

The empirical and theoretical basis for the next example of circumstances in which individualism developed is the work of the historian and social anthropologist Alan Macfarlane (1978, 1986). Basing his conclusions on a wide variety of sources, including local records, personal documents, and contemporary descriptions, he made a convincing argument that England, in contradistinction to the peasant societies that characterized most of Europe and Asia, was highly individualistic from the 14th century, if not earlier. Indeed, in its psychological and social characteristics, the historical England that Macfarlane described fits quite closely the definition of individualism I have given. In this England, individuals are viewed as being free to make their own choices in terms of what they believe will make them happy. There are few legal, social, or familial restraints on individuals' freedom of choice of what work they do, where they live, and whether or whom they marry. This liberty in the pursuit of happiness was supported by a wide range of legal and political institutions.

This individualism occurred in an essentially monetary, and not subsistence, socioeconomic context in which the individual, and not the family, was the basic unit of production and consumption. In this society there were high levels of social and geographic mobility. Psychological ties to the extended and even the nuclear family were relatively weak. Marriage was voluntary with individuals being generally free to choose their own spouses. It was seen as being primarily for the psychological and sexual benefit of the individual and not for the good of the family. Similarly, the reasons for having children centered on the individual's personal satisfaction, not on the economic benefit or social status having children might bring. Children were seen as pleasures and pets, not as investments, insurance, or workers in a family-based production system.

Macfarlane viewed this historic individualistically oriented family and production system as causally connected to the development of English industrialization. He drew this conclusion both from the early work of Malthus and from more recent demographic and economic historians. He saw the pivot on which the system leading to economic development turned as being the individually oriented flexible marital regime, which allowed population size to adjust to available economic resources in a way that avoided the negative consequences of overly rapid population growth. According to this view, procreation is strongly encouraged in nonindividualistically oriented systems by cultural and institutional norms influenced by the usefulness of children when the family is the unit of production. Under such circumstances populations tend to grow rapidly even before there is any economic growth, increasing "as soon as mortality loosens its grip. This increase destroys any chance for a rise in the standard of living and economic growth is made difficult because of the diminishing marginal returns on increasing labour input" (Macfarlane, 1986, p. 36).

Thus, as the population increases a negative spiral is produced. Food becomes scarcer. Because of the abundance of labor, wages, if available, become lower and living conditions generally worsen. In this situation, fertility is held back by two major mechanisms. Either there is a perennially high level of mortality, particularly of infants, or more often, a wave-like movement in which the population climbs relatively rapidly and is then savagely cut back by some "crisis," usually the pestilence and famine associated with war. Because increases in the necessities for subsistence are quickly absorbed by population increases, it is extremely difficult to accumulate the long-term investment necessary to capitalize industrial development (Macfarlane, 1986).

England seems to have avoided such a "high-pressure" demographic regime. By the 16th century, and probably even earlier,

it escaped into a 'low pressure' regime, much more like that of present-day 'post demographic' transition societies. That is to say, both fertility and mortality were well below their theoretical maximum and were more or less balanced. Such a homeostatic situation has been observed in some simple hunter–gathering societies [see above discussion of such societies and their individualism] . . . and became widespread in Europe in the nineteenth century. (Macfarlane, 1986, p. 34)

Macfarlane has abstracted the individualistic assumptions underlying the English marriage system, which he noted Malthus was the first to see as undergirding England's low-pressure demographic regime. Many of these characteristics—monogamy, a fairly equal relationship between spouses, permissive remarriage, independent residence after marriage, and a fairly equal contribution to the conjugal fund—would have seemed "extraordinary to those living in China, India, Africa, Eastern Europe and South America at the same time as Malthus" (p. 35).

Even more unusual was the assumption

that there were few positive rules restricting the choice of spouse, and in particular that the individual could marry whomever he or she could catch. . . . All this betrays an even deeper assumption—that there was a choice in the matter of marriage . . . to marry or not to marry at all was a matter for decision by the individual concerned. The almost universal view at the time was that marriage is an automatic "natural" event. . . . A further

cultural assumption which would have startled other parts of the world was
the view that marriage, and particularly the rearing of children, would be
economically and socially costly. (p. 36)

Given these assumptions, marriage came to be seen as a luxury that
could only be afforded by those who could pool sufficient resources to
support their individual households. Under such conditions, incentives
to marry grew greater and disincentives less during times of prosperity,
whereas during times of economic hardship, individuals may choose to
delay or even forego marriage in order to assure that their other wants
are met. Because the preponderance of evidence indicates that before
the middle of this century the major determinant of the birth rate was
age of marriage, those marrying earlier having proportionately more
children. Given this possibility for individual choice, it is noteworthy that
from at least the 16th century until about 1800 a relatively young age of
marriage, and its accompanying increase in birth rate, was associated
with increases in real wages and a decline in real wages associated with
later marriage and a declining birth rate. Thus, the individualistic assumptions underlying the English marriage pattern seem to have provided the mechanisms for the operation of the low-pressure demographic
regime that fostered the accumulation of economic resources that made
industrial development possible.

This demographic linkage is not the only plausible connection between
individualism and English economic development that Macfarlane noted.
He saw England as having been distinguished by a

highly developed and individualistic market society . . . one which would
lead to unusual affluence, distributed widely over the population. It was a
situation of very considerable social mobility, based on wealth rather than
blood, and with few strong and permanent barriers between occupational
groups, town and country, and social strata. The strong sense of individualism was likely to be found embedded in the laws, in the concept of individual
rights and independence and liberty of thought and religion. (Macfarlane,
1978, p. 165)

These individual rights also included rights to private property that
went well beyond those defined either by continental Roman law or by
most nonEuropean legal codes.

The basis of this . . . system was the idea of the impartible, individually
owned, estate which could be bequeathed to specific individuals. . . . This
meant that any individual—man, woman, or child—could have absolute
rights in their "own" property. People could also have complete rights in
themselves. (Macfarlane, 1986, p. 340)

The individual right to own property that cannot be readily or arbitrarily alienated may well have been an important precondition for England's industrialization. Jacobs (1958, 1985) and Braudel (1981) have argued that the absence of such property rights in the patrimonial governmental systems of China and Korea may have represented important stumbling blocks to these countries' economic development.

As we see in more detail when we examine the case of Japan, there are also persuasive historical arguments (Goldstone, 1987) that individual freedom in thought and action encourage economic and technical development. At the very least, the English case provides another example of the congruency between individualistic beliefs and individually oriented modes of production, England being historically characterized by the predominance of a monetary market rather than a family-oriented, peasant, subsistence economy. It is also clear that, in contradistinction to the hunter–gatherers previously discussed, historical English individualism was supported and embodied by a wide range of legal, political, and other social institutions.

What is not clear is why English individualism developed. Macfarlane was uncertain. He tentatively suggested that the roots of the individualism he sees as characterizing 13th-century England lie much further back in an amalgam of Christianity and individualistic Germanic customs. He noted that even in the 17th and 18th century when the differences between England and the rest of Europe were most marked, there was more in common between England and the countries of northwestern Europe that had similar historic backgrounds than there was to divide them. Nevertheless, demographic, ideological, and economic differences existed. One possible reason Macfarlane considered for England's divergence, even from such places as Holland and Northern France and Germany, was the distinctive nature of the English legal system. He argued that although in the 11th century the legal systems of the whole of the northern half of western Europe were almost identical and based almost exclusively on Germanic law, between the 12th and the 16th century much of northern Europe was reconquered by Roman law. By the 16th century, England was an island carrying an old Germanic legal system lying off a land mass dominated by Roman law (Macfarlane, 1986). As we have noted, this English law was much more protective of the individual than was Roman law.

Another difference between England and the continent that Macfarlane noted is that England was sheltered from the effects of the Counter-Reformation.

Protestantism shielded and even encouraged those capitalistic tendencies already present. Ultimately, it protected private judgment and independence of belief. The Inquisition, which destroyed huge trading networks and corroded economic development throughout continental Europe, never took root in England. (Macfarlane, 1986, pp. 340–341)

Thus, even when compared to the individualism of the continental European Renaissance, English individualism was not only more institutionally protected, more deeply embedded and widespread in the society—stretching even into the agricultural sector, but also more long-lasting.

Taken in toto, Macfarlane's explanation of the causal connections between England's individualism, social institutions, economic development, and history suggest a picture in which historical circumstances led to the development of individualistically oriented social institutions, which together with the individualistically oriented value system that they supported, directly and indirectly led to the origination of industrial development. It is unclear whether Macfarlane viewed the direction of causation as ever going from the nature of the modes of production to the level of individualism as I have suggested may be at least partly the case for the subarctic hunters. He did imply that the monetary market economy encouraged individualistic values, but his basic concerns were with the demographic and economic consequences of individualism and its historic background and not with how levels of individualism might be affected by the individual's everyday environment. Macfarlane's work, however, not only elucidates the socioeconomic consequences of individualism, it also provides a striking example of how institutionally embodied societal values can play a strong part in developing and maintaining individuals' desires to be self-directed and efficacious.

JAPAN

Japan provides another example through which to examine the causal interconnections of historical/cultural, social–structural/institutional, and economic/production factors and level of individualism. (For the original, more extended and historically detailed discussion see Schooler, in press.)

If a European had been able to come to Japan during the pre-Meiji Edo era (1603–1867), when Japan was under the rule of the Tokugawa shogunate, he or she would have found a society that, although containing a developed mercantile system, was socially and economically quite different from contemporaneous Europe. In contrast to the expansionist Europeans, during this period, Japan shunned any overseas military, political, or commercial involvements and was relatively closed to foreign intellectual or cultural influences, particularly from the West. Whereas an ideology of equality and individual achievement had developed in several parts of the West and social and economic mobility had come to be seen as a distinct possibility, Japanese society was rigidly stratified into a formal hierarchy of nobles, warriors, farmers, artisans, merchants, and impure untouchables. By the end of the Edo period, Japan was also clearly lagging behind the West technologically. Psychologically, this world was characterized by a hierarchical set of loyalties—to family, to daimyo (lord) and to shogun—that demanded "not mere passive devotion, but active service and performance" (Bellah, 1957, p. 14; see also Caudill, 1973; Caudill & Schooler, 1973; Doi, 1962, 1973; Hamaguchi, 1985; Naoi & Schooler, 1985; Schooler & Naoi, 1987, 1988). This emphasis on diligent group loyalty and de-emphasis on the importance of the "egoistic" goals and feelings of the individual has often come to be seen as inherent in the Japanese people or their culture.

Given the cross-cultural differences readily visible to both Japanese and Westerners at the time of Japan's reopening to foreigners in 1854, a modern observer transported back to 16th-century Japan might be somewhat puzzled by the many psychological, sociological, and economic similarities (portrayed in the next part of this section) of that society to the European Renaissance. The resemblance of 16th-century Japan to Renaissance Europe may not be fortuitous, but the result of a remarkable parallel in historical experience. Like their European visitors, the 16th-century Japanese belonged to a society that had previously (during the Heian Period, 794–1192) been unified under an imperial government (cf. Rome and the Carolingian Empire) that had been developed under the influence of an intellectually dominant classical civilization (China). As in Europe, this imperium broke down into a feudal system (during the Kamakura Period, 1192–1336). When the Europeans arrived in 1543 during the later part of the Muromachi era (1336–1568), Japan was in a period that has been likened to the Renaissance (Grossberg, 1981) and that was marked by opposing tendencies that continued through the Momoyama era (1568–1601). On the one hand, the social controls that regulated the hierarchical social and political systems of the earlier imperial and feudal periods broke down in ways that emphasized the importance of individuals as opposed to that of the social groupings to which they belonged. On the other hand, military, political, and bureaucratic processes were set in motion that could serve as the basis for the development of a repressive central state whose goal was a strongly regulated, ideologically orthodox, and hierarchically defined society. All of these changes took place in an era of great commercial expansion fueled by dramatic increases in agricultural production and by regular and massive injections of gold and silver into the money supply (Atwell, 1986). Renaissance Europe was, of course, marked by a somewhat similar historical background and similar opposing trends toward individualistically oriented open societies and hierarchically structured closed ones.

The trend toward a hierarchically structured closed society was successfully carried through by the Tokugawa Shogunate during the first half century of the Edo period. As a consequence of this success, the Jesuits in Japan were the witnesses and victims of an absolutist counter reformation—different from the one they had in mind—but one that was more complete and long-lasting than any achieved in Europe. This historical pattern seems to have had profound consequences for the levels of technological and economic development and of individualism.

Individualism and Economic Development in 16th-Century Japan

The relatively high level of technology and individualism of 16th-century Japan is revealed in a number of ways when the Japan of this period is compared to Japan of other periods as well as to Renaissance Europe.

Military Capability and Expansionist Orientation. Even at first contact (1543), Japan was militarily so impressive that the Europeans seem never to have given more than a moment's thought to an invasion. Compared both to the Japanese of the later Tokugawa period and their Chinese and Korean contemporaries, 16th-century Japanese were internationally outward looking and expansive. In the beginning of the 16th-century official trade with Ming China was extensive. By the end of the century, the Sendai daimyo had sent one of his retainers on a European mission, one of whose purposes was to open up trade between Japan and Spanish America (Smith, 1981). Two major attempts to invade Korea were also undertaken and plans were made to invade the Philippines, while at home, interest in Western things and thought—including religion—was widespread.

Technological Capability. The 16th-century Japanese were able not only to reproduce European technology, but were also able to further its development and to outproduce the Europeans. This was most strikingly the case in terms of armaments, where the Japanese made important technical innovations, while "in absolute numbers" guns were almost certainly more common in Japan in the late sixteenth century than in any other country in the world" (Perrin, 1979, p. 25).

The technical ability of the Japanese to reproduce Western products was also evident in other spheres. During the 16th century the Japanese both copied and created Renaissance-style pictures. Pipe organs were also built in Japan from 1606 to 1613 (Malm, 1981). This technological capability was also manifested in industries developed before the entry of the Europeans. Japan led the world in the manufacture of paper products. The level of her defensive armor and swords was at least as high as that of contemporary Europe, and there was a major export industry of such armaments (Perrin, 1979). "Her copper and steel were probably better, and were certainly cheaper, than any being produced in Europe at the time. Her copper, indeed, was so cheap that it began to be exported all over the world. . . . In iron and steel, Japan could undersell England . . . the recognized leader among European producers" (Perrin, 1979, p. 9).

The Place of the Individual in the Social and Political Systems. Much of this period was marked by an openness to social mobility, a relative absence of rigid hierarchical distinctions and in places, even an emphasis on equality. One cannot also help being struck by the primacy given to the egoistic concerns for material and social advancement.

This egoism is reflected in political terms, by the characteristic that best describes Japanese behavior during the Muromachi and Momoyama ages—the *absence* of loyalty in formal hierarchical relations between superiors and inferiors (i.e., lords and vassals) and even among members of the same families. The almost legendary 47 ronin, who sacrificed themselves to defend their lord's honor, were an 18th-century, not a 16th-century, phenomenon. It was only during the Edo period that bushido developed into an ethical system and martial cult emphasizing selfless service to one's lord (Collcutt, 1983).

The 16th-century struggle with hierarchical authority and an actual concern for equality and leveling of hierarchical distinctions can be seen in both the form and the activities of the *ikki*—organizations that individual, small-scale landowners originally developed during the turbulence in the middle of the 15th century. "The ikki was . . . in principle egalitarian. Its symbol was the collective oath or compact signed, often in blood, with names written in a circle so that none took precedence over another" (Hall, 1981, p. 11).

During most of this period, the social boundaries between samurai and merchants were relatively open. Compared to the later Tokugawa Bakufu (government)

(t)he Muromachi Bakufu was from its inception, less concerned about erecting rigid class barriers. . . . The name by which . . . early financiers were known—utokunin, "virtuous men"—has a peculiarly Renaissance ring to it and denoted the value that contemporary Japanese society placed on their services. . . . The elite society of Muromachi Kyoto was less rigidly

stratified than that of Edo, due to the relative absence of invidiousness
between samurai and non-samurai. . . . The Muromachi utokunin were not
officially spurned by warrior and polite society. (Grossberg, 1981, p. 58)

Individual cities and towns also had a fair amount of autonomy (Wakita
& Hanley, 1981), the level of which may on occasion have approached
that of the free cities of Renaissance Europe. Finally, there is some
evidence of concern about the legal status of the lower orders. During
the Muromachi period "The Ashikaga (Shogunate) encouraged social
mobility and economic development, as well as cultural egalitarianism of
a sort, and were the first to give commoners (bonjin) specific rights written
into the law" (Grossberg, 1981, p. 59).

*The Place of the Individual in the Aesthetic, Philosophical, and Religious
Spheres.*   The emphasis on the individual in the social and political
systems was paralleled in the aesthetic, philosophical, and religious
spheres where there was an emphasis on individual self-development,
individual aesthetic cultivation and self-expression, and individual salvation—either in the here and now, or in the hereafter.

This relative importance of the individual and absence of class distinctions during the Muromachi and Momoyama periods is visible in the
history of Noh drama. Although its Muromachi "originators held up the
ideal of 'an actor for all audiences,' the samurai class of the Edo period
destroyed the concept of aesthetic democracy and brought the Noh to
what it was in the Meiji period . . . the ceremonial theatre of the elite"
(Raz, 1976, p. 272).

An extremely important focus of Japanese aesthetic concern, the tea
ceremony, remained until the end of the Momoyama period a relatively
open social occasion where samurai freely interacted with merchants
(Varley & Elison, 1981). The ceremony had some highly individualistic
and egalitarian components, especially in its most developed *wabicha*
form. In its rigorously simple physical setting, it actively avoids ostenta-
tion and obvious signs of wealth, and, in fact, stresses the renunciation
of materialism. In social terms, all seems to be done to emphasize the
equality of the participants, the host himself serving the guests with
utensils of "plainness and refined simplicity."

In this context, "the tea ceremony masters of the Momoyama period
sought uniqueness in their utensils that would reflect the owners' person-
alities" (Tokyo National Museum, 1985). The tea ceremony was individualistic in an even more fundamental way—the ultimate concern was with
the psychological state of the individual participants. Despite the care
taken that the social discourse and emotional bonds of the participants

be appropriate, the ultimate measure of the success of the occasion was the subjective state of the individual participants.

Zen has a similar subjective and thus individualistic goal, and the desired state may well be the same if the traditional maxim "Zen and Tea are one" is to be believed. From the present perspective, the important point is that Zen, which was the dominant sect among the samurai and also quite widely spread among the merchant class, is concerned with the subjective state of the individual. Furthermore, although others can help through example or instruction, there are no soul saving sacraments; salvation is an individual affair whose only validation is the individual's enlightenment about the nature of the relationship between what one is and what is.

A Protestant-like concern over the individual's path to salvation was also central to the Jodo and Jodo Shin sects of Buddhism, begun in the 13th century and prevalent in the poorer sectors of society in the 16th. Both of these sects based their reformation of earlier Buddhist practices on the acceptance of the necessity of providing a means to salvation that was accessible to all. In rejecting the temporal and ecclesiastical authorities, they "injected the element of spiritual independence" (Lai, 1983, p. 67). Preachers of these and similar sects were very active in preaching their message to the common people in a manner that has been likened to that of some of the famous Protestant preachers.

All in all, before the full imposition of Tokugawa state control in the 17th-century, 16th-century Japan was remarkably similar to Renaissance Europe. This similarity raises the question of the possible relationships among the historical stages—classical period, feudal period, and renaissance—that seems to characterize both Japan and Western Europe and their oftentimes similar levels of individualism and economic development. Discussion of the possible socioeconomic and psychological consequences of the first two periods is beyond the scope of this chapter.[2]

Evidence for a possible causal connection between relatively open individualistic societies such as that of 16th-century Japan and economic development is suggested when we look for reasons why levels of individualism and technical and economic development did not continue at their 16th-century rates during the Tokugawa period. One source of hindrance to economic development is suggested by the parallelism between Japan and parts of Europe in the movement from relatively open to absolutist social systems. Both the Japanese and the European cases

_____

[2]These issues are discussed in my more extensive examination of this historical pattern (Schooler, in press) where I have suggested why a classical period may be important. Hypotheses put forward in that paper, as well as by Jacobs (1958, 1985), Braudel (1981), and Tominaga (1989), suggest why it may be the very existence of feudalism in Japan that explains why Japan developed as it did during its 15th- and 16th-century renaissance.

suggest that such imposition of a closed society dampens economic and technological development. The combination of economic stagnation with suppression of dissent and free intellectual innovation in 17th-century Japan is remarkably similar to that which seems to have occurred in Hapsburg Spain, as well as in Ch'ing China, and the late Ottoman Empire (Goldstone, 1987).

INDIVIDUALISM, ECONOMIC DEVELOPMENT, AND COMPLEX ENVIRONMENTS

Although the causal connection between ideology and economic and technical development has been one of the most central debates in the history of sociology (Tawney, 1926/1963; Weber, 1904–1905/1958), the Japanese case adds more relevant data to the discussion. The individualistic ideology that developed during the Momoyama and Muromachi periods seems to have been intimately tied to the process of economic development. The critical question is the nature of the causal connection between the two. One possibility is that individualism leads to technical and economic development. Under such a scenario, the individualistic ideologies and viewpoints that seem to develop when feudal controls on the individual break down may be an important cause of technical and economic growth. Such a possibility, of course, underlies Weber's theory about the importance of the Protestant Ethic for the growth of Western capitalism.

Goldstone (1987) also viewed the historical evidence as indicating that individualistic ideology promotes economic development. He attributed the historical economic stagnation of a wide range of countries to the intolerance of innovation resulting from just such a "suppression of alternatives and emphasis on internal cultural orthodoxy" (p. 132). His argument that technical and economic progress is dependent on individuals being open to innovation, pluralism and the taking of risks, also suggests ways in which individualism may be important for technical and economic development. As we have seen, individualism involves an emphasis on the importance of autonomy, self-direction, and behavioral and ideological freedom. Individuals strongly interested in their own success may also be more willing to engage in risky ventures than would those constrained by concerns over the repercussions of their actions to the social groups with which they identify. In addition, such persons may be more free to act without concern for the constraints that such group ties impose, providing for greater flexibility in both the geographical movement and occupational behavior of workers (Macfarlane, 1978,

1986, made the same points in reference to England). Indeed, it was the belief that this was the case that led Inkeles (1983) to see such an individualistic nontraditional orientation of a state's citizens as a necessary precursor to its modernization. It is clear, however, if we remember that in immediate-return hunter–gatherer societies intense individualism actually hampers the accumulation and application of resources necessary for development, that the presence of individualism by itself is not sufficient to guarantee innovation or economic growth.

In any case, Inkeles and his associates (Inkeles, 1983; Inkeles & Smith, 1974) were only able to provide empirical evidence for the reverse hypothesis that the experience of industrialization leads to individualism. Their findings indicate that in a variety of countries, doing factory work, as well as exposure to other aspects of modernization (e.g., formal education, exposure to mass media), consistently leads to autonomous, self-directed, nontraditional values, an openness to innovation and cognitive flexibility. Although Inkeles and his associates described several mechanisms through which such changes may take place (i.e., reward and punishment, modeling, exemplification, and generalization), they never empirically isolate which aspects of the modernization experience have these effects.

If we accept the possibility that technological development can and often does lead to more substantively complex and self-directed work, a possible answer to this question can be found in the work of Kohn and Schooler (1983). We and our associates have found that job conditions offering challenge and opportunity for self-direction result in a self-directed psychological orientation, favorable self-conceptions, flexible orientations, and effective intellectual functioning. Naoi and Schooler (1985) have replicated these findings in the cultural context of present day Japan. More generally, both the Kohn and Schooler and the Naoi and Schooler studies fit together with a large body of research, including that of Schooler and Smith (1978) on Japanese women's role values, from a wide range of disciplines indicating that exposure to complex environments increases both intellectual flexibility and self-directed individualistic orientations. In all of these circumstances exposure to a complex environment increases the value individuals place on being self-directed and effective.

A complete review of the evidence on the effects of environmental complexity and a rough hewn psychological theory of why they occur is presented in Schooler (1984, 1987). Stated briefly in terms of its application to individualism, the theory defines the complexity of an individual's environment by its stimulus characteristics. The more diverse the stimuli, the greater the number of decisions required, the greater the number of considerations to be taken into account and the more ill defined the contingencies, the more complex the environment. To the extent that such environments reward initiative and independent judgment, they should foster a generalized individualistic orientation favoring self-directedness rather than conformity to external authority. On the other hand, values, orientations, and behaviors that are adaptive in complex environments may be maladaptive in simpler ones. The social psychological experiments of Breer and Locke (1965) provide ample evidence of how such successful task performance can affect, not only situationally specific orientations, but also be generalized to abstract beliefs and preferences. (For a full discussion of the issue of generalization from the perspectives of both cognitive and social science see Schooler, 1989b.) Thus, if technical and economic development lead to more complex environments, we have good reason to believe that such environments should lead to an increase in individualism. Such increased complexity would certainly seem likely at the level of economic and technical development involved in the move from rural to urban settings and from agricultural to commercial and manufacturing occupations. If Form (1987), Spenner (1988), and Attwell (1987) are correct, the substantive complexity of work probably does not decrease and may even continue to increase even at later levels of development. But, as we have seen in the case of the immediate return hunter–gatherer societies, individualism and concern for self-directedness and efficacy can also occur where the modes of production and social organization are quite different from those of modern societies.

CULTURE, SOCIAL STRUCTURE, AND INDIVIDUALISM

All in all, the empirical evidence that technical development can lead to individualism and an accompanying concern for being self-directed and efficacious seems strong. Although firm proof that individualism leads to technical and economic development is more difficult to come by, historical patterns such as those just described for England and Japan suggest a complex web of reciprocal causal interconnections among historical/cultural, social–structural/institutional, and economic/production factors and level of individualism and concern for individual autonomy and efficacy. There are, in addition, some tantalizing findings about the nature of the reciprocal effects among these various levels of phenomena that hint that differences in timing differentiate the ways that culture, social structure, and individualism affect each other. (For a fuller discussion of these issues see Schooler & Naoi, 1987.) These findings suggest that a major difference between psychological functioning on the one hand, and social structure and culture on the other, is that psychological functioning may be more readily amenable, and hence quicker, to change. Consequently, superordinate level phenomena (i.e., culture and social structure) may have more rapid effects on subordinate level phenomena (i.e., psychological functioning) than the reverse. This would seem to be particularly the case for those societies that are rich in social institutions supporting particular ways of thinking. Thus, we would expect that the individualism that characterizes English society would be less quick to change in the face of direct pressures on the psychological individualism of its members than would that of immediate-return hunter–gatherers.

The existence of a temporal distinction in the relative speed of the effects of social structure and personality on each other is suggested by the evidence that, although the effects of occupational conditions on psychological functioning are generally contemporaneous, the effect of psychological functioning on occupational conditions is generally lagged (Kohn & Schooler, 1983). These findings imply that, although there is a reciprocal effect between the two, psychological functioning is more quickly affected by occupational conditions than are the occupational conditions by psychological functioning.

Individuals' psychological characteristics can change their occupational conditions in two ways. People either change the way they do their work or they actually change jobs. Both such changes can in the long run affect the structure of society. If enough individuals change the way they carry out a particular occupational role such changes may

> become institutionalized as a changed set of role expectations. Each such role change has ramification through its role set, with resulting modifications in social structure. Similarly, . . . [if many people change jobs] differential availability of personality types for recruitment to particular roles contributes to the shaping of those rules. (Turner, 1988, pp. 8–9)

Not only do the processes of firmly embodying something in a culture also seem to take longer than the processes involved in psychological change, once something is included in the cultural corpus it has a tendency to remain. Consequently, the ensuing cultural conservatism often results in ideologies and customs formed under an earlier set of conditions continuing to affect people's behaviors in later, but quite different conditions. An example of such a cultural lag as it affects individualism is found in the evidence that Americans from ethnic groups with a recent history of serfdom exhibit the nonself-directed orientation and lack of intellectual flexibility characteristic of American men working under conditions limiting the individual's opportunity for self-direction (Schooler, 1976). Although it is impossible to confirm each link in the causal chain, a model emphasizing the lagged effects on an ethnic group's culture of historical conditions restricting the individual's autonomy seems a probable and parsimonious explanation of these ethnic differences.

CONCLUSION

In summary, I have examined the development of individualism and concern over self-direction and efficacy in several very different settings—immediate-return and subarctic hunter–gatherers, 13th- to 19th-century England, 16th-century Japan, and modern industrialized societies. We have seen that in each of these circumstances individualistic values have been congruent with the modes of both production and social organization. The cause of this congruence remains a question. The evidence seems to suggest a reciprocal causal relationship between modes of production and an individualistic psychological orientation. As is the case in both subarctic hunter–gatherers and modern industrial societies, modes of production requiring self-directed responses to complex environmental demands increase individualism and the value placed on self-direction and efficacy. As seems to have been the case in England, individualism, under some circumstances, changes modes of production in ways leading to technical and economic development. Psychological individualism may possibly affect social institutions, modes of production most probably do so. In historical England and Japan, as well as in the modern world, social institutions clearly affect the level of individualism. Individualism, however, can clearly also occur in settings, such as immediate-return hunter–gatherer societies, characterized by an unusual absence of almost any formal social organization but with individualistic modes of production.

The question remains open of how necessary the institutionalization of individualism is to the relationships between it and the socioeconomic process to which it has been linked. Clearly one of the historical differences between England and Japan is the far greater level of institutionalization of individualism in the former than the latter. How important such institutionalization is for the connections between individualism and technical and economic development is unclear. As Macfarlane (1978, 1986) has argued, such institutionalization serves to promote the continuation of individualism in the face of countervailing pressures. Thus, it might not have been as easy for an English monarch, as it was for the Tokugawa Shoguns, to impose a rigidly stratified, nonindividualistically oriented society on his 17th-century subjects. It is also possible that the striking, in comparison to England, absence of any attempt by the wealthy Japanese merchant class to gain political power (Morris, 1981) is due to the lack in Japan of traditions institutionalizing the political activity of citizens. Such institutions have occurred in the West since the time of the Greeks. Nevertheless, it is true that in the overall pattern of Japanese history individualism and technical and economic development are linked in a manner parallel to that of the West. Furthermore, since the question of the nature of the conditions under which different belief systems, such as individualism, become institutionalized remains an open one, explanations of the effects of individualism that make these effects dependent on its degree of institutionalization provide no ultimate answer about why such effects occur.

The evidence that personal levels of individualism are likely to be more quickly affected by a society's modes of production and social institutions than to affect those modes is clearly tentative. What is certain is that the web of causal interconnections is complex. In England, as we have seen, individualistic psychological orientations, together with social institutions supporting such an ideology, seem to have led to dramatic changes in the modes of production—the modern industrial system. Today, as the industrial system spreads to other parts of the world, the psychological changes brought about by the consequences of that system are leading to an increase in individualism resulting in a demographic pattern—the limitation of family size to match the parents' individualistic needs and the shift in the flow of resources from parent to child, instead of from child to parent (Thadani, 1978; Thornton & Fricke, 1987)—that has been seen as one of the underlying causes of the original development of industrialization in England.

These complexities arising in the attempt to understand the causal connections between individualism and the social, economic and cultural conditions in which it is found are daunting. Nevertheless, some understanding of the issue is necessary if we are to come to grips with the basic question asked in this volume—how do feeling self-directed and efficacious affect one's psychological and physical health.

Several things are certain. Although part of their relationship may come about because individualistic orientations affect socioeconomic conditions, it seems clear that different historical and socioeconomic conditions do produce different levels of individualism by affecting both a society's institutions and the characteristics of the demands that everyday life places on its members. Furthermore, although concerns over self-directedness and efficacy may develop in the absence of a fully elaborated individualistic ideology, the growth of individualism is closely linked to the rise in the level of such concerns.

Differences among people and societies in individualism and the value placed on self-directedness and efficacy must be taken into account before any generalizations about the effects of feelings of self-direction and efficacy on people's physical and psychological functioning can be reached. Much of this attempt to unravel the causes and consequences of the development of individualism may seem temporally and geographically remote, and may involve levels of phenomena not usually encountered in psychological or medical investigations. Nevertheless, the causes and consequences of the development of individualism are an integral part of the story of how concerns over self-directedness and efficacy affect our lives in late 20th-century America.

ACKNOWLEDGMENTS

I thank Melvin L. Kohn, Leslie Caplan, and John Meyer for their helpful critiques. As will be clearly obvious to them, I have not accepted all of their points, but they definitely made me think. The research for the Japanese part of this paper was carried out when I was at the University of Osaka on a Fellowship from the Japan Foundation for the Advancement of Science under the sponsorship of Atsushi Naoi. This Japanese research was greatly aided by the fine library and other facilities of the International House of Japan in Tokyo. My thinking on the place of the individual in Japanese history benefitted from discussions with Ken'Ichi Tominaga and Kazimierz Slomczynski, as well as from helpful criticism by William Bartholomew of an earlier attempt I made to treat the subject.

REFERENCES

Acheson, J. M. (1981). Anthropology of fishing. *Annual Review of Anthropology, 10*, 275–317.

Attwell, P. (1987). The deskilling controversy. *Work and Occupations, 14*, 323–346.

Atwell, W. S. (1986). Some observations on the "Seventeenth-Century crisis" in China and Japan. *The Journal of Asian Studies, 45*, 223–244.

Bellah, R. (1957). *Tokugawa religion: The values of pre-industrial Japan.* Glencoe, IL: The Free Press & The Falcon's Wing Press.

Braudel, F. (1981). *Civilization and capitalism, 15th–18th century: Vol. 1. The structure of everyday life: The limits of the possible.* New York: Harper & Row.

Breer, P. E., & Locke, E. A. (1965). *Task experience as a source of attitudes.* Homewood, IL: Dorsey Press.

Caudill, W. A. (1973). The influence of social structure and culture on human behavior in modern Japan. *Journal of Nervous and Mental Disease, 157*, 240–257.

Caudill, W. A., & Schooler, C. (1973). Child behavior and child rearing in Japan and the United States: An interim report. *Journal of Nervous and Mental Disease, 157*, 323–338.

Christian, J., & Gardner, P. M. (1977). *The individual in northern dene thought and communication: A study in sharing and diversity* (National Museum of Man Mercury, Series No. 35). Ottawa: National Museums of Canada.

Collcutt, M. C. (1983). "Bushido." In *Encyclopedia of Japan* (pp. 221–223). Tokyo: Kodansha International.

Doi, L. T. (1962). 'Amae'—a key concept for understanding Japanese personality structure. In R. J. Smith & R. Beardsley (Eds.), *Japanese culture: Its development and characteristics* (pp. 132–139). Chicago: Aldine.

Doi, L. T. (1973). *The anatomy of dependence.* Tokyo: Kodansha International.

Form, W. (1987). On the degradation of job skills. *Annual Review of Sociology, 13,* 29–47.

Goldstone, J. A. (1987). Cultural orthodoxy, risk, and innovation: The divergence of East and West in the early modern world. *Sociological Theory, 5,* 119–135.

Grossberg, K. A. (1981). *Japan's renaissance: The politics of the Muromachi Bakufu.* Boston: Harvard University Press.

Hall, J. W. (1981). Japan's sixteenth-century revolution. In J. W. Hall, K. Nagahara, & K. Yamamura (Eds.), *Japan before Tokugawa* (pp. 7–22). Princeton: Princeton University Press.

Hamaguchi, E. (1985). A contextual model of the Japanese: Toward a methodological innovation in Japan studies. *Journal of Japanese Studies, 11,* 289–321.

Hobbes, T. (1958). *Leviathan: Or, the matter, forme and power of a commonwealth, ecclesiastical and civil.* Oxford: Clarendon. (Original work published 1651)

Inkeles, A. (1983). *Exploring individual modernity.* New York: Columbia University Press.

Inkeles, A., & Smith, D. H. (1974). *Becoming modern: Individual change in six developing countries.* Cambridge, MA: Harvard University Press.

Jacobs, N. (1958). *The origins of modern capitalism and Eastern Asia.* Hong Kong: Hong Kong University Press (Oxford University Press).

Jacobs, N. (1985). *The Korean road to modernization and development.* Urbana, IL: University of Illinois Press.

Kohn, M. L., & Schooler, C. (1983). *Work and personality: An inquiry into the impact of social stratification.* Norwood, NJ: Ablex.

Lai, W. (1983). Jodo sect. In *Encyclopedia of Japan* (Vol. 4, pp. 67–68). Tokyo: Kodansha International.

Lewis, A. R. (1958). *Shipping and commerce in Northern Europe, A.D. 300–1100.* Princeton: Princeton University Press.

Macfarlane, A. (1978). *The origins of English individualism: The family, property and social transition.* Oxford: Basil Blackwell.

Macfarlane, A. (1986). *Marriage and love in England: Modes of reproduction 1300–1840.* Oxford: Basil Blackwell.

Malm, W. P. (1981). Music cultures of Momoyama Japan. In G. Elison & B. L. Smith (Eds.), *Warlords, artists and commoners* (pp. 163–186). Honolulu: The University Press of Hawaii.

Meyer, J. W. (1986). The self and the life course: Institutionalization and its effects. In A. B. Sorenson, F. E. Weinert, & L. R. Sherrod (Eds.), *Human development and the life course* (pp. 199–216). Hillsdale, NJ: Lawrence Erlbaum Associates.

Meyer, J. W. (1988). The social construction of the psychology of childhood: Some contemporary processes. In R. M. Lerner & E. M. Hetherington (Eds.), *Child development in life span perspective* (pp. 47–65). Hillsdale, NJ: Lawrence Erlbaum Associates.

Morris, V. D. (1981). The city of Sakai and urban autonomy. In G. Elison & B. L. Smith (Eds.), *Warlords, artists and commoners* (pp. 23–54). Honolulu: The University Press of Hawaii.

Naoi, A., & Schooler, C. (1985). Occupational conditions and psychological functioning in Japan. *American Sociological Review, 51*, 372–390.

Perrin, N. (1979). *Giving up the gun: Japan's reversion to the sword, 1543–1879*. Boston: David R. Godine.

Raz, J. (1976). The actor and his audience: Zeami's view of the audience of the noh. *Monumenta Nipponica, 31*, 251–274.

Redfield, R. (1956). *Peasant society and culture: An anthropological approach to civilization*. Chicago: University of Chicago Press.

Ridington, R. (1988). Knowledge, power, and the individual in subarctic hunting societies. *American Anthropologist, 90*, 98–110.

Savishinsky, J. S. (1974). *On the trail of the hare*. New York: Gordon & Breach.

Schoembucher, E. (1988). Equality and hierarchy in maritime adaptation: The importance of flexibility in the social organization of a South Indian fishing caste. *Ethnology, 27*, 213–230.

Schooler, C. (1972). Social antecedents of adult psychological functioning. *American Journal of Sociology, 78*, 299–322.

Schooler, C. (1976). Serfdom's legacy: An ethnic continuum. *American Journal of Sociology, 81*, 1265–1286.

Schooler, C. (1984). Psychological effects of complex environments during the life span: A review and theory. *Intelligence, 8*, 259–281.

Schooler, C. (1987). Cognitive effects of complex environments during the life span: A review and theory. In C. Schooler & K. W. Schaie (Eds.), *Cognitive functioning and social structure over the life course* (pp. 24–49). Norwood, NJ: Ablex.

Schooler, C. (1989a). Levels and proof in cross disciplinary research. In D. I. Kertzer, J. Meyer, & K. W. Schaie (Eds.), *Comparative perspectives in age structuring in modern societies*. Hillsdale, NJ: Lawrence Erlbaum Associates.

Schooler, C. (1989b). Social structural effects and experimental situation: Mutual lessons of cognitive and social science. In K. W. Schaie & C. Schooler (Eds.), *Social structure and aging: Psychological processes* (pp. 129–147). Hillsdale, NJ: Lawrence Erlbaum Associates.

Schooler, C. (in press). The individual in Japanese history: Parallels to and divergences from the European experiences. *Sociological Forum*.

Schooler, C., & Naoi, A. (1987). *Social structure, occupational conditions and individualism in Japan*. Paper presented at the 82nd annual meeting of the American Sociological Association, Chicago, IL.

Schooler, C., & Naoi, A. (1988). The psychological effects of traditional and of economically peripheral job settings in Japan. *American Journal of Sociology, 94*, 335–355.

Schooler, C., & Smith, K. (1978). '. . .and a Japanese wife.' Social structural antecedents of women's role values in Japan. *Sex Roles, 4*, 23–41.

Scollon, R., & Scollon, S. B. K. (1979). *Linguistic convergence: An ethnography of speaking at Fort Chipewyan, Alberta*. London: Academic Press.

Slicher Van Bath, B. H. (1963). *The Agrarian history of Western Europe: A.D. 500–1850*. London: Arnold.

Smith, B. (1981). Japanese society and culture in the Momoyama era: A bibliographic essay. In G. Elison & B. L. Smith (Eds.), *Warlords, artists and commoners* (pp. 245–280). Honolulu: The University Press of Hawaii.

Spenner, K. (1988). Occupations, work settings and the course of adult development: Tracing the implications of select historical changes. In P. Baltes, D. Featherman, & R. Lerner (Eds.), *Life span development and behavior* (Vol. 9, pp. 244–285). Hillsdale, NJ: Lawrence Erlbaum Associates.

Tawney, R. H. (1963). *Religion and the rise of capitalism*. Glouster: Smith. (Original work published 1926)

Thadani, V. N. (1978). The logic of sentiment: The family and social change. *Population and Development Review, 4*, 457–499.

Thornton, A., & Fricke, T. E. (1987). Social change and the family: Comparative perspectives from the West, China, and South Asia. *Sociological Forum, 2*, 746–779.

Tokyo National Museum. (1985). *Exhibit history of Japanese pottery.* Tokyo: Author.

Tominaga, K. (1989). Max Weber and the modernization of China and Japan. In M. L. Kohn (Ed.), *Cross-national research in sociology:* ASA Presidential Series (pp. 125–146). Newbury Park, CA: Sage.

Turner, R. H. (1988). Personality in society: Social psychology's contribution to sociology. *Social Psychology Quarterly, 51*, 1–10.

Varley, H. P., & Elison, G. (1981). The culture of tea: From its origins to Sen no Rikyu. In G. Elison & B. L. Smith (Eds.), *Warlords, artists and commoners* (pp. 187–222). Honolulu: The University Press of Hawaii.

Wakita, H., & Hanley, S. B. (1981). Dimensions of development: Cities in fifteenth- and sixteenth-century Japan. In J. W. Hall, K. Nagahara, & K. Yamamura (Eds.), *Japan before Tokugawa* (pp. 295–326). Princeton: Princeton University Press.

Weber, M. (1958). *The protestant ethic and the spirit of capitalism.* New York: Scribners. (Original work published 1904–1905)

Webster's Second New International Dictionary (Unabridged). (1961). Springfield: G&C Merriam.

Webster's Ninth New Collegiate Dictionary. (1985). Springfield: Merriam-Webster.

Woodburn, J. (1982). Egalitarian societies. *Man, 17*, 431–451.

Individualism: Social Experience and Cultural Formulation

John W. Meyer
Stanford University

Schooler's most interesting analysis in Chapter 2 covers two main issues. First, there is the question of the sources of "concern" over, or emphasis on, individual self-directedness and efficacy. The research issue involved has focused on the factors affecting individual scores on psychological measures of self-esteem and related variables. Second, the analysis covers questions of the social effects—indeed societal effects—of such concerns. Does expanded efficacy contribute to social and economic development, as a range of contemporary theories (with roots in Weber, 1930) have suggested?

There is an ambiguity about whose concern with efficacy we are discussing. Consider two different meanings of social individualism: (a) Individuals and their advisors, based on social experience, tend to stress and develop orientations to efficacious self-direction as a useful or necessary quality in life in a given setting. (b) Society, as with our own, tends to develop rules and ideologies supporting individual self-direction as in the general good. This latter kind of collective individualism is a prominent feature of modern societies and nation-states, which place great social value on enhanced and empowered and developed individuals. Almost all modern societies constitutionally emphasize and validate properly socialized individual self-direction as a crucial ingredient of national progress (e.g., Fiala & Lanford, 1987). Since Tocqueville's (1969) analysis, it has been generally assumed that such an emphasis is an important part of American political and cultural life.

TYPES OF SOCIAL SETTINGS

These two different distinctions—whether or not social experience makes individual self-direction a useful or necessary strategy, and whether or not individual self-direction and efficacy are valued as in the collective good—define four types of social settings. First, in classic liberal societies, experience shows the necessity of individual autonomy for the myriad of economic, political, social, and cultural choices allocated to the individual, but economic, political, social, and cultural ideologies also value individual self-direction as contributing to the greater good. Second, in many societies (perhaps Schooler's hunting and gathering ones are good examples), individual self-direction is a necessary individual strategy, but available ideology does not celebrate it as contributing to collective life. Third, one can imagine societies in which individual self-direction is highly valued collectively, but in which much of life experience discourages it: In some accounts, contemporary bureaucratic socialist states are a little like this. Fourth, there are clearly societies—for instance, agrarian peasant ones—in which autonomous individual self-direction is neither strategic nor collectively validated.

The psychological literature on self-direction and efficacy evidences a studied ambiguity toward the issues previously discussed. The researchers desire to show, as a scientific matter, that self-direction as an individual property has various sources and consequences. But they also wish to argue as a collective normative matter that self-direction is a collective good, which we should all value in others as well as ourselves. In thinking of the origins and consequences of individualism, Schooler tends toward his own version of this ambiguity in dealing with the distinction. As is common in the literature, he emphasizes a "concern" with or value on individual self-direction without being quite clear whose concern or value is at issue, and in the name of whose good. Most of his discussion, however, seems to focus on the individual's own concern with, and experience of the advantages of, self-direction and efficacy. In reflecting on the issue, however, we need to consider the alternative perspective.

SOURCES OF SELF-DIRECTION

In discussing the social sources of self-direction and efficacy, Schooler is most clear and forceful. Some kinds of societies, because of economic structure and/or cultural preference, arrange individual life so that self-direction is necessary and rewarded. These societies include, not only our modern differentiated ones, but also very simple hunting and gathering societies—segmented economically right down to the individual level, with life chances dependent on individual choice and initiative.

This argument leads to a clear testable hypothesis. People in hunting and gathering societies, as in the occupational literature to which Schooler has so prominently contributed, might get higher scores on measures of self-direction and efficacy than do more "developed" but group-oriented agrarian peasants. Comparative psychological research is called for. Schooler may be right, but it is possible that high scores on efficacy result less from the individual experience of necessary autonomy than from cultures emphasizing individualism as a collective good. The dramatic effects modern education has on such measures suggest that the self-concept is directly culturally constructed (Inkeles & Smith, 1974). If this is so, hunters and gatherers might show the driven, fatalistic, and pessimistic postures of individuality without much uplifted legitimating theory.

It seems plausible that the main sources of high scores on such psychological measures as those of self-direction and efficacy lie less in private individual experience than in the cultural formulation of values and goods. Modern cultural systems clearly and explicitly instill and value interpretations of the self as competent, autonomous and causal. Child-rearing is explicitly organized to produce these effects, and in good measure so is the educational system. The virtues (for both individual and collectivity) of sovereign individual choice in polity, economy, social relations, and culture are trumpeted in basic modern ideology. Marriages and jobs are to be individual choices, and it is thought to be good (i.e., freedom) that it is so. In liberal ideologies with worldwide hegemony, political authority and economic power are to be allocated by individual choices in appropriate markets, and political and economic development are thought to be natural products. Even central cultural matters— choices among gods, for instance—are to be individual choices (Tocqueville, 1969; see the general review by Jepperson, 1990). The individual lacking self-direction and efficacy is stigmatized as incompetent and unproductive, and programs of therapy are proposed. Every aspect of modern society is ideologically defined as the product of efficacious individuals. Perhaps this cultural or ideological emphasis built into modern society, rather than cumulations of raw experience, accounts for variations in self-conceptions, which are after all rather highly symbolic linguistic constructions.

The question is open. But we have no empirical research showing the modernity of the self-conceptions of hunters and gatherers on the conventional measures. We do have the findings that in modern societies variations in individual work experience affect relevant self-conceptions

(Inkeles & Smith, 1974; Kohn & Schooler, 1983). But these same studies show even larger effects of education on self-conceptions, suggesting that the process may be a cultural or interpretive one.

Further, we have a number of studies showing comparisons among relatively modern national societies. These variations are very large, and appear to reflect variations in political culture more than in immediate individual experience. Hofstede (1980) reviewed some of this literature, and showed great cross-national variations on some relevant indicators even among employees of parallel subunits of the same multinational organization (thus holding in part constant variation in work experience). Americans may get high scores because they think they are Americans, rather than because of any extraordinary individuation in their experience.

We do not get far, in empirically addressing the issue here, by comparing modern societies in which individuation is both experienced and valued with peasant societies in which it is neither experienced nor valued collectively. It is necessary to find out what happens to individual properties when one is true but the other is not. That is why Schooler's proposed examination of the psychological characteristics of people in hunting and gathering societies is interesting. If individual experience and strategy are the governing factors, these people should look surprisingly modern, as Schooler suggests they do—and as the kinds of anthropological observations he summarizes often support. On the other hand, if collective goods and values are the governing variables, hunters and gatherers may well report knowing that their fortunes are their own individual ones without having much of a conception of efficacy or self-direction: perhaps, as the literature on social disorganization in modern mass societies suggests (see the summary in Kornhauser, 1959) individuation in this context generates high scores on measures of alienation, isolation, and anomie. Perhaps these people are likely to see themselves as individuals, but not efficacious ones, with visions of the self as at the mercy, neither of its own direction nor organized social forces, but rather of arbitrary and chaotic natural and supernatural powers.

The other interesting comparative case would involve finding social settings where individualism is a valued cultural recipe but little rooted in individual experience and its strategies. As previously noted, contemporary socialist states might be good cases for inquiry: Do people in these societies report the efficacious self according to cultural recipes or is it devalued as experience might suggest? Data on racial minorities in America—particularly on Blacks—are suggestive. Despite individual experience in settings offering little encouragement for faith in self-direction, researchers uniformly report scores that are much higher than expected on self-concept measures, suggesting the pervasiveness of cultural interpretation as a causal factor. Perhaps a cultural version of Schooler's argument would help explain one of the pervasive problematic results consistently found in an extensive empirical research literature.

EFFECTS OF INDIVIDUALISM

There is a substantial theoretical tradition arguing that individualism, in one or another of its forms, is a crucial source of societal economic and social development. Self-directed and efficacious individuals are thought to generate the economic, political, and social enterprises that bring modernizing social changes; and are also thought to function with more efficiency and commitment in these new structures. Weber (1930) argued that Christian and especially Protestant emphases on the enhancement of individuals were main sources of rapid Western economic development, and many others have followed versions of the same line.

A main issue has always been to decide what kind of individualism is involved. Is it the existence of many persons experienced in isolated and individuated activity? Or is it the presence in many individuals of the social recipes valuing individual autonomous self-direction? Or is it the presence of a legitimating culture treating individual enterprise (say, in economic matters) as something to be valued as in the collective good?

Schooler emphasizes the first line, in his speculations about the advantages hunting and gathering societies might have over peasant societies in adapting to modern development. If hunters and gatherers have much experience in autonomous activity, and if that experience is what is at issue in preparing people for modern society, they should indeed have advantages.

If, alternatively, what matters is the presence of self-conscious psychological efficacy and self-directedness, Schooler's argument turns on the question discussed earlier—do hunting and gathering societies in fact generate the psychologized individualism reflected in the conventional measures? As noted previously, the evidence is not in, but there are good reasons for doubt. Finally, if what matters for social development is the presence of a cultural legitimation of individualism as in the collective good, Schooler's hypothesis would be very unconvincing: Hunters and gatherers have little cultural theory of enhanced individuals as properly reorganizing, mobilizing, and dominating society, and are often notorious for their inability to structure effective collective action on such bases.

The empirical experience with the many confrontations between simple hunting and gathering societies and modern ones (e.g., between native American groups and the European settler colonies) has run sharply against Schooler's speculations. Hunters and gatherers are indeed very individuated, but their social structures and support systems tend quickly to collapse in these confrontations. The persons involved tend to drift into the modern orbit, but by no means in efficacious ways—they tend to be the most peripheral and depressed populations in the modern world. The people involved function as individuals, but not with the orientations and competences suited to effective participation in the collective modern structures.

Whatever individualism is involved, indeed, seems maladaptive. It is often argued that this is precisely because hunters and gatherers lack the normative aspects of the psychology of individualism (that is, the high scores on articulate self-definition) or because they lack the collective values and ideologies locating their individualism in a legitimated wider social order. It is precisely the common experience with the failures of such experiential individualisms that leads modern social theorists to see effective Western individualism as a collective value system—an individualism characterized by high levels of social commitment and conformity.

ENGLAND AND JAPAN

The issue of the cultural versus the experiential character of individualism is implicitly raised by Schooler's interesting and informed discussions of English and Japanese history. Given that individualism is, in the modern system, an engine of social and economic development, is it the collective culture legitimating individualism that does it, or is it more the aggregation of the individualistic virtues of persons? In discussing England, Schooler's summary description of early individualism is convincing. It is much less clear whether (a) the historic force is exercised by culture or economic organization, and (b) the force is exerted through English people or through English political and social history. One can argue that the English were economically innovative and enterprising, or that the English political and cultural system allowed economic individualism (elsewhere considered usury, exploitation, and piracy) to gain an upper hand as collectively valued and authoritative.

In his extraordinary discussion of Japan, Schooler himself notes that Muromachi feudal individualism, unlegitimated in a coherent order as contributing to the collective good, collapsed in a subsequent absolutism. So we do not know how much the earlier individualism contributed to later expansion: As just noted, we also do not know that the zen-infused medieval elites would have gotten high scores on our measures of efficacy and self-direction. Perhaps the high levels of individual activity required of these people generated only attributions of efficacy to cosmic powers for which the person was an agent rather than an actor. In short, nothing in the historical record suggests that medieval Japanese structural fragmentation generated the sorts of self-enhanced individualism we now measure. As a matter of fact, even present-day Japanese people often get much lower scores on the measures of the enhanced self than we imagine are required in the modern order. The whole question of the significance of Japanese culture—and particularly of its medieval roots— for modern development is very much contested and unclear.

Schooler's discussion, here, raises many interesting questions: the nature of the psychology of earlier Japanese individualism, the relation of this system of self-definition to the standard Western (or American) models of psychological virtue, and the impact of both on subsequent social development. These issues are not likely to go away, but may be intensified by the facts of distinctive patterns of development (particularly in Asia, but also in the Middle East) outside the Western orbit. In the future, as a result of this new reality, and of such discussions as Schooler's, there will be much rethinking of Western experience. The older easy attributions of Western success to particular pattern of culture or of selfhood will probably be rethought: The relation between the two will be seen as more arbitrary and less causal. And more distinctions between types of individualism and types of psychologies of self-direction and efficacy will be needed.

CONCLUSIONS

Schooler's discussion broadens the research agenda, and makes it much more comparative and historical. In doing this, interesting new questions are raised—but older answers are also perforce brought into question. It is clearly necessary to more sharply distinguish the culture of collectively valued individualism from the experience of self-dependence, and to discuss the psychological consequences of the latter in the absence of the former. How do hunting and gathering people, or ones caught up in a feudal political system, score on our conventional measures? And how do the different dimensions of individualism—experiential self-dependence, self-consciously articulated stances of efficacy and self-direction, and cultures legitimating individuals as sovereign and collectively valued—affect social changes? We have, operating within our narrow cultural frame, tended to treat experience as central. But our more comparative evidence suggests that the cultural and ideological aspects of individualism may have played a more crucial role than we recognize:

Self-direction and efficacy may be more significant as cultural elements than as experiential realities, both in predicting our individual orientations and in accounting for social change.

ACKNOWLEDGMENT

This discussion is a revised version of my comments at the conference. It has benefited from a number of comments made in the conference discussion. In particular, several distinctions suggested by Professor Ted Forbes were of great use, and are incorporated in the structure of the present revision.

REFERENCES

Fiala, R., & Lanford, A. G. (1987). Educational Ideology and the World Educational Revolution, 1950–1970. *Comparative Education Review, 31,* 315–332.

Hofstede, G. (1980). *Culture's consequences.* Beverly Hills, CA: Sage.

Inkeles, A., & Smith, D. (1974). *Becoming modern.* Cambridge, MA: Harvard University Press.

Jepperson, R. (1990). *Constitutional orders and civic dispositions: How national political organization shapes citizen identities and orientations.* Unpublished doctoral dissertation, Yale University, New Haven, CT.

Kohn, M., & Schooler, C. (1983). *Work and personality.* Norwood, NJ: Ablex.

Kornhauser, W. (1959). *The politics of mass society.* Glencoe, IL: The Free Press.

Tocqueville, A. de. (1969). *Democracy in America.* New York: Doubleday Anchor.

Weber, M. (1930). *The Protestant ethic and the spirit of capitalism.* New York: Scribner.

3

Careers, Career Trajectories, and the Self

David R. Heise
Indiana University

Most social interactions transpire within the framework of standard role relationships like parent–child, employer–employee, minister–worshiper. Everyone has a variety of such roles in different social institutions like family, occupation, and religion, and people often accumulate multiple roles within a social institution as they mature—for example, a woman may be at once a daughter, a sister, an aunt, a wife, and a mother. Acquisition of roles within social institutions occurs in an orderly way with some roles having other roles as prerequisites—for example, one must be a mother before one can be a grandmother—so institutions provide individuals with orderly sequences of status advancement and self-expansion.

Career is a reasonable name for an ordered sequence of roles within an institution. Careers often are viewed—by laypersons at least—as biographical productions of individuals achieving according to personal preferences and peculiar destinies. A career in this view is the record of idiosyncratic accomplishments within a particular life history. Sociologists on the other hand have focused the term mainly on the sharing of ordered experiences as a result of common socialization and of recurrent social reactions to certain kinds of performances (Becker & Strauss, 1956; Glaser & Strauss, 1971; Rains, 1982). In this view, careers are individualistic productions that are shared because they emerge repeatedly under the same conditions. Here, I propose another orientation, that careers are cultural structures that unfold in accordance with institutional rule systems. This orientation still allows that individuals build unique biographies with individualistic flair but suggests that they do so largely by voyaging along standard career trajectories in idiosyncratic combinations. Orderly sharing of experiences still is an aspect of careers but arises because role participants shape similar experiences as they apply culturally given knowledge and sentiments to interpret what is happening to them during status transitions. The new orientation bridges individualism and social structure while also offering precision in studying career paths.

An institutional approach to careers is outlined in the next two sections. First, I discuss careers as sequences of status transitions generated by grammars derived from taxonomies of roles. I then discuss career trajectories—the attainment of varying levels of social valuation and power as a career line unfolds. Two examples are presented—one involving careers in the Catholic Church and the other dealing with kinship.

In the last section I discuss how institutional career structures impact on individuals over the life course. Because different roles confer varying levels of social esteem and power, people with a variety of roles may be richer than those with fewer roles in that people with more roles might be more able to activate interactions that yield desired gratifications. People with a variety of roles also are more likely to experience subjective variety in how they are gratified and in how they gratify others. Thus, a person's life experiences relate to advancement along various career lines within institutions and across institutions, and careers are a relevant topic in studying the development of self, including self-esteem and the sense of self-efficacy.

THE LOGIC OF CAREERS

Anthropologists have studied the logical relations of role identities mainly in terms of typologies constructed through componential analysis (Goodenough, 1956). For example, family roles might be analyzed in terms of gender, generations, and consanguinity (among other things), in which case a "mother" can be interpreted as a female consanguineous relative removed one generation upward (Wallace & Atkins, 1960). Typologies are the intellectual products of analysts who organize semantic systems through the use of externally imposed distinctions that may or may not have reality in the culture to which they are applied (Werner & Fenton, 1970). Thus, a typology that helps anthropologists understand an indigenous culture may not be part of that indigenous culture.

Taxonomies offer a different way of defining the logical organization of constructs. For example, a taxonomy of "living things" might separate "plants" and "animals," with "plants" dividing into "trees," "flowers," and so on and "trees" dividing into "oaks," "maples," and the like. In this case, all of the analytic constructs come from the cultural corpus being analyzed, and relations between constructs are indigenous in that the connections are part of the terms' cultural meanings, part of the way a given group represents knowledge about a topic. Moreover, the relation between constructs is one of inclusion (e.g., "living things" include "plants," which include "trees," which include "oaks"). Consequently a taxonomy is a cultural classification that specifies logical relations: An oak implies a tree, which implies a plant, which implies a living thing.

Anthropologists (Spradley, 1979; Werner & Fenton, 1970; Werner & Schoepfle, 1987) have written in depth about taxonomies, and anthropologists have applied taxonomic methods as a way of organizing folk knowledge about nature. However, taxonomies have not been applied (as far as I am aware) to the study of institutional role identities. This is an important slippage: It is exactly such an approach that leads to the discovery that careers are cultural structures embedded in indigenous knowledge of social institutions.

Taxonomic analysis of role identities requires a different perspective than componential analysis. In componential analysis, one defines a role by asking how a person with that role is different from another person. In taxonomic analysis one asks how the roles of one individual necessarily relate to other roles of the same individual.

Consider this example. In componential analysis, a "mother" necessarily is a different person than a "daughter" because the emphasis is on how one's mother differs from one's daughter, on the generational difference between two women. But in taxonomic analysis, a "mother" always is a "daughter": One cannot possibly be a mother without being a daughter. We actually can say that a mother is a kind of daughter, that mothers are a subset of daughters, that being a mother implies being a daughter.

Having accepted this conceptualization, it is easy to elaborate the taxonomy for conventional female family roles. Here, for example, is one line of the taxonomy. A wife is a kind of daughter; a mother is a kind of wife; a mother-in-law is a kind of mother; a grandmother is a kind of mother-in-law. Daughter is most general among these categories in that daughter embraces all the rest. Grandmother is the most specific category in that grandmothers are a subset of mothers-in-law who are a subset of mothers who are a subset of wives who are a subset of daughters.

Moreover—and this is the key point here—this taxonomic line defines the procreative career for females in our Western institution of family. The cultural taxonomy is not only a system of meanings; it also operates dynamically as a rule system governing status transitions. A woman goes from being a daughter to being a wife to being a mother, then a mother-in-law, and then a grandmother. Individual women may develop their procreative careers idiosyncratically, some terminating as wives, some as mothers, and so on, but each of these variations (and more complex ones I mention later) also is a cultural structure: a pattern that can be generated from the family taxonomy applied as a system for producing status transitions. Some careers are long, some are short, but all obey the same restrictions on movement from status to status.

A taxonomy of role identities provides an institutional grammar (Colby, 1975; Skvoretz, 1984; Skvoretz & Fararo, 1980) for building careers in the same sense that we have a grammar for building sentences from words. A grammar defines how elementary units are to be strung together in order to create a proper and comprehensible serial outcome. In the case of careers, an institutional taxonomy of roles (with some additional understandings) turns into a grammar that defines permissible status transitions and thereby possible careers.

On the one hand, a taxonomy of role identities is a body of knowledge about how people develop and become more and more differentiated (e.g., as members of a family). On the other hand, a taxonomy is a key component of the rule system for generating status transitions: it defines the sequence of status transitions that is necessary in order to attain a particular role. Thus, a taxonomy simultaneously operates as a means of understanding reality and as a means of creating reality. Different cultures may have different taxonomies for the same domain (e.g., different kinship terminologies) and therefore different knowledge about reality, but each knowledge system is correct because each is a rule system generating the reality it describes.[1]

This framework leads neatly to a method for studying careers within social institutions. Obtain the institutional taxonomy of roles with the aid of an expert consultant who has the required knowledge, apply the taxonomy as a grammar for generating conventional status transitions, and examine the career paths which result. Careers thereby can be studied as ideal types, while individuals' actual careers as revealed in life history data (Luborsky, 1987) are empirical manifestations.

I elaborate this approach to careers when I turn to specific examples. First, though, there is another aspect of careers that I want to consider.

---

[1]This chapter is not the place to consider whether taxonomic knowledge is arbitrary—for example, whether biology imposes some limits on kinship terminologies. I also have to bypass the question of what happens when a taxonomic system fails to generate the reality it explains—for example, whether a new American kinship taxonomy ultimately will emerge because some contemporary American women become mothers without being wives.

CAREER TRAJECTORIES

Role taxonomies operating as institutional grammars define which status transitions cannot—or should not—happen. For example, a woman cannot make a transition directly from sister to mother within the family institution; motherhood issuing from the sibling role would violate an incest taboo. However, these grammars do not explain why a person might select a specific career from permissible alternatives or why a person might prefer some roles of a career line while wanting to de-emphasize others. To deal with individual preferences we have to recognize that every institutional role offers a profile of resources, and a career defines a trajectory of gains and losses.

Sociologists generally agree that social valuation and power are two key dimensions of social position. My interpretation of these constructs as social resources derives from Kemper (1972, 1978). Social valuation elicits voluntary patronage from others as others try to exhibit their good will toward one's position. Power elicits involuntary cooperation from others as others act to enhance or to prevent debilitation of their own positions.

I measure the social valuation of a role in terms of averaged ratings on an evaluation scale ranging from "bad, awful" to "good, nice." Relational aspects of power are coded psychologically I presume, and the capacity of a role to enhance or debilitate others' fortunes can be captured by averaging responses to the role on a potency scale ranging from "little, powerless" to "big, powerful."

Graphs of career trajectories allow one to see at a glance how the overall valuation or power of one career line compares with another. The graphs also show how social regard and potency are gained—or lost—at each status transition within a career line.

A career trajectory can be graphed by plotting the evaluation or power of roles in the career line against a time dimension. For some purposes the time dimension in careers might be defined in terms of average age at investiture in each role. However, this introduces a statistical element in the time measure and also may suggest a misleading correspondence between career development and biological aging, so instead, in this chapter, I employ a sociological unit of time derived directly from the logic of careers. Each role is plotted one step beyond the last of its prerequisite roles. This measure of "advancement" is ordinally related to biological time: The unit between one role and the next may represent a period of 1 year or 20 years.

The career trajectory graphs that are presented here show average evaluations or average potency ratings of roles on the vertical axis (actual numerical data are provided in tables in the Appendix). The horizontal axis is the time dimension of advancement. Dotted horizontal lines on the graphs show neutral points in ratings: roles above the dotted lines were rated good, or powerful, and those below the dotted lines were rated bad, or powerless. Roles in a career line are connected by lines, and I use dotted connecting lines to distinguish exceptional kinds of careers (i.e., female Church careers, and kinship careers associated with family splintering or widowhood).

Data for mapping social valuation and perceived potency of roles come from surveys in which respondents rated roles on evaluation and potency scales. Church roles were rated by working-class adolescents attending Catholic schools in the center of Belfast, Northern Ireland. Several hundred students participated in the study, but only a few—about 25 males and females combined—rated any particular role because the project goal was to assemble a dictionary of ratings for more than 1,000 different concepts. Family roles were rated by college students in the U.S. South, and here, too, the original project was designed to acquire measurements on thousands of concepts (Heise & Lewis, 1988b; Smith-Lovin, 1987) so ratings of roles on evaluation and potency are averages based on small samples—about 25 males and 25 females.

Evidence indicates that such ratings represent general cultural phenomena and vary remarkably little by social characteristics of the raters (Heise, 1966), with the same general patterns of ratings even occurring cross-nationally in many Western nations (Heise, 1987a; MacKinnon, 1985). Thus, there is some justification for discussing institutions in terms of evaluation and potency ratings obtained from subpopulations of respondents. On the other hand, it is known (Heise, 1979) that participation in specialized groups affects ratings of selected concepts. Considering this latter point and the small sample sizes, the data on evaluation and power must be treated as suggestive rather than definitive.

CHURCH CAREERS

It is desirable to employ a well-institutionalized set of roles to illustrate the ideas just mentioned about careers and career trajectories so that the rules governing status transitions are well defined and career paths are clear. ("Institutionalization involves the processes by which social processes, obligations, or actualities come to take on a rule-like status in social thought and action," Meyer & Rowan, 1977, p. 341.) As a first example, I examine roles within the Roman Catholic Church. These roles are as institutionalized as any in our culture. Moreover, I have reasonably adequate data on the social valuation and perceived power of these roles from a lay Catholic population.

Figure 3.1 shows a taxonomy of roles in the Catholic Church. The taxonomy is incomplete—especially for female roles (e.g., the diagram includes Abbot but not Abbess)—because I include only the roles for which I have dimensional data. Also, the diagram anomalously suggests that a person could be both a Nun and a Priest, and the taxonomy would have to be elaborated along the lines of the family roles—Fig. 3.4—in order to represent properly the Church's sharp distinction between male and female Catholic careers. However, with these caveats, the taxonomy probably is close to correct because most of the role relations are institutionally defined, and the taxonomy was derived in an interview with a priest. I conducted the interview with the assistance of a portable computer and program ETHNO (Heise & Lewis, 1988a) which elicited the taxonomy by questions like "*a priest* generally is or has been *a deacon* (yes or no)?" The computer program was helpful because it made inferences from prior answers in order to ask the minimum number of such questions. Also, the program composed the initial taxonomic diagrams for this chapter.

The diagram shows which roles are prerequisites for others when reading downward. Thus, for example, being a Catholic is a prerequisite

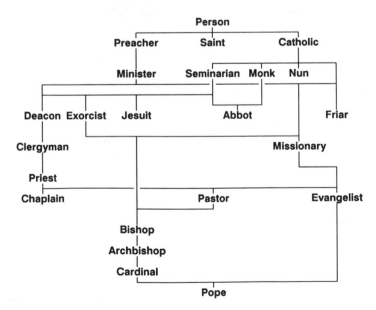

FIG. 3.1 Taxonomy of Church roles.

for being a Catholic seminarian, a monk, a nun, or a friar; being a priest and a missionary both are required to be a Catholic evangelist; and to be a Pope one has to be both an evangelist and a cardinal.

The diagram shows which roles imply others when reading upward, and a role implies all roles which are reachable by tracing upward paths. Thus, being a priest implies being a clergyman, a deacon, a seminarian, a minister, a preacher, and a Catholic.

A career is a sequence of roles ending in a terminal role, and the roles in an ideal career can be defined by starting at the terminal role and tracing upward along every available path in the taxonomic diagram until one reaches the top. The actual career unfolds in the other direction: Starting at the top, roles are acquired until the prerequisites for a target role are fulfilled, and then the target role may be acquired.

A person can have multiple career lines within the same institution. For example, it is possible that a Catholic could become a preacher, a minister, then a friar, which constitutes one career; then later become a seminarian and a deacon to form a second Church career.

Some careers are simple and others are complexly multilayered, and tiers in the diagram help in analyzing this aspect of careers. Thus, for example, the diagram shows that Sainthood is a simple career: One either attains the status or not, and there is no sequence of roles for getting closer. Becoming pope is the longest, most complex career in Catholicism, requiring nine stages of advancement beyond simply being a Catholic.

Now let us consider the trajectories of Church careers on the dimensions of social valuation and power.

Figure 3.2 shows evaluation of Church roles plotted against career advancement. Some specific features of this graph warrant comment. Being a Saint—a career with a single stage that interlocks to nothing else—is the most highly regarded of all Church paths. Exorcist is a stigmatized role—it actually is rated as a bit "bad, awful," probably because of its association with the demonic. (Exorcist used to be a part of the standard priestly career, but Vatican II limited it to Missionaries and to Bishops who invest others in the role.) Minister appears to be a role with low evaluation, but that probably is an artifact of obtaining data from Catholics in Belfast where the term is likely to be understood as meaning "Protestant minister." The same association may be involved in the relatively lower evaluation of deacon.

Aside from these peculiarities, all of the Church roles receive high and almost equal social valuation. Church careers are a way of acquiring social regard and thereby receiving patronization from others who wish to show good will.

Figure 3.3 shows how Church careers vary in terms of perceived

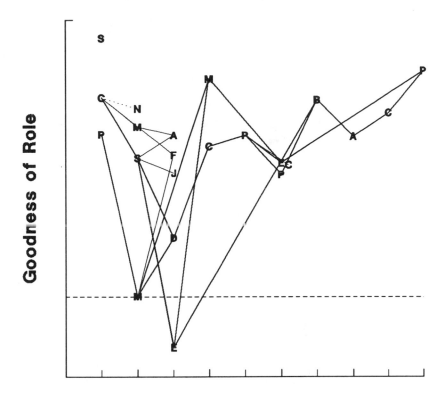

Advancement

FIG. 3.2 Evaluation in religious careers. Stage 1 (top to bottom): Saint, Catholic, preacher; Stage 2: nun, monk, seminarian, minister; Stage 3: abbot, friar, jesuit, deacon, exorcist; Stage 4: missionary, clergyman; Stage 5: priest; Stage 6: evangelist, chaplain, pastor; Stage 7: bishop; Stage 8: archbishop; Stage 9: cardinal; Stage 10: pope.

power. Remembering that minister probably does not fit within this set of Catholic roles and that Exorcist is an almost discontinued role, it becomes evident that embarking on a Church career as a monk (a nun in the case of females), a friar, or a seminarian involves forsaking power, and the level of power attributed to lay Catholics can be regained only by progressing to roles of priest, missionary, or abbot. Sainthood and the high offices of bishop, cardinal, and pope do provide a religious basis for great power, and it is notable that these are select and carefully monitored roles. (The slight loss of power in going from bishop to archbishop, if significant, might relate to the

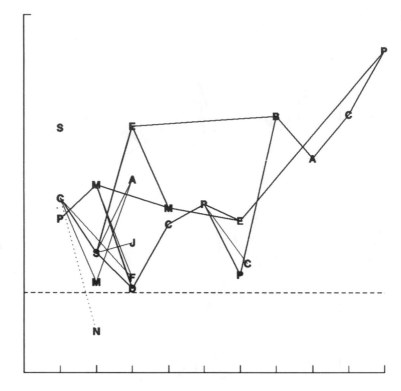

Advancement

FIG. 3.3 Power in religious careers. Stage 1 (top to bottom): Saint, Catholic, preacher; Stage 2: minister, seminarian, monk, nun; Stage 3: exorcist, abbot, jesuit, friar, deacon; Stage 4: missionary, clergyman; Stage 5: priest; Stage 6: evangelist, chaplain, pastor; Stage 7: bishop; Stage 8: archbishop; Stage 9: cardinal; Stage 10: pope.

way role activity changes from pastoral to administrative in the course of this transition.)

Summary

A Church career is defined by any route downward in Fig. 3.1 with termination at any point, and a particular person might develop several different Church careers at once or in succession. The total number of possible careers and career combinations is very large, so the Catholic

Church provides rich opportunities for career development with individual distinction.

Church careers largely are confined to a particular pattern of social resources: high social valuation and low power. Thus, embarking on a Church career entails seeking self-fulfillment through nonthreatening relationships with others who provide one with social support out of admiration. Power in Church careers is available to only a select few and (except for Saint) only to those with very advanced careers.

KINSHIP CAREERS

Kinship is another well-defined institution for which I have data. As before, I begin by offering a taxonomy of roles that can be interpreted as an institutional grammar defining kinship careers. The taxonomy in Fig. 3.4 deals with roles that are central in American families, although others could be added. The taxonomy is based on my own understandings of the kinship terms.

Because nearly all kinship roles are gender specific, the taxonomy divides right at the top into male and female branches, and the branches remain separate except for two roles (cousin and divorcee) which have no gender-specific labels. Because the two branches are completely parallel, I discuss only the male roles.

Son is the most general male kinship role. One of the immediate subtypes, grandson, is a role always acquired simultaneously with son, and that is why son is shaded on the diagram—to show that it instantiates something else, in this case, grandson. Brother branches from son and initiates an avuncular career including brother-in-law and uncle. The branching through nephew initiates a nepotic career that may include cousin. (The abbreviation for cousin is all capitals to signal that the role can be attained by either a nephew or a niece.) Stepson is the entry point for a splintered-family career that may include stepbrother; half-brother is shown as a different splintered-family career line branching from brother.

Alternative careers in an institution ordinarily can develop simultaneously, but kinship careers have a peculiarity in this regard: Becoming a husband eliminates the possibility of becoming a bachelor. I have included unmarried man as a dummy subtype of son in order to deal with this in the institutional grammar; when a man becomes a husband he depletes his status as an unmarried man and thereby eliminates the precondition for being a bachelor.

Getting married instigates two kinship careers at once giving one the

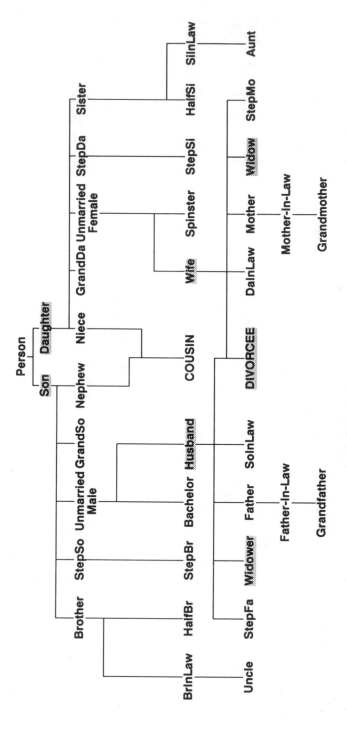

FIG. 3.4 Taxonomy of family roles.

Instantiations: Daughter to Granddaughter; Divorcee to Unmarried Male or Female; Husband to Son-in-law; Son to Grandson; Widow to Unmarried Female; Widower to Unmarried Male; Wife to Daughter-in-law.

role of spouse and also making one an in-law. Thus in the grammar model, husband instantiates son-in-law.

The main reproductive career follows from the husband role and includes father, father-in-law, and grandfather. This reproductive career is the most complex of kinship careers with a total of six stages.

Widower also follows from husband. Here again, a peculiarity of kinship roles has to be addressed in the model. We have to allow that becoming a widower depletes husband but reactivates (instantiates) the status of unmarried man, thereby allowing a repetition of the transition to husband. Divorcee also follows from husband, and operates in the same way as widower.

Finally, becoming a husband itself can lead to another splintered family career, that of being a stepfather.

Now let us turn to the trajectories of kinship careers, employing data from U.S. college students. I use male ratings of evaluation and potency to graph the trajectories of male kinship careers and female ratings to define female kinship trajectories. (The actual numbers are presented in Tables 2 and 3 in the Appendix.)

The evaluation of male kinship roles is shown in Fig. 3.5. The scales of the kinship graphs are different from the scales of the Church graphs. However, all of the kinship evaluation graphs that I present use the same scales and all of the kinship power graphs have the same scales.

Roles within the reproductive and avuncular careers are held in high esteem, and grandfather is the most positively evaluated of all male kinship roles. In-law roles receive somewhat less appreciation, but they are well regarded. Roles in the nepotic career and bachelorhood are approved, but less so. Splintered-family careers (shown by the dotted lines on the diagram) garner little approval, and stepfather and divorcee actually are touched with stigma rather than favor.

Figure 3.6 shows trajectories of perceived power for male kinship careers. Reproductive and avuncular careers provide substantial power except in relations with in-laws. Fatherhood represents the peak of kinship power, but power declines somewhat in later phases of the reproductive career. Bachelorhood provides modest power.

Roles defining the nepotic career and splintered-family careers are largely powerless. The only exception is stepfather, but even this role is far less powerful than the normal role of father.

Figures 3.7 and 3.8 reveal that the same general patterns occur in the trajectories of female kinship careers. (Unfortunately ratings for mother-in-law were not collected.) The gender differences that do exist mainly apply to all careers about equally. Females obtain somewhat more social valuation in their kinship roles than males do. At the same time, female

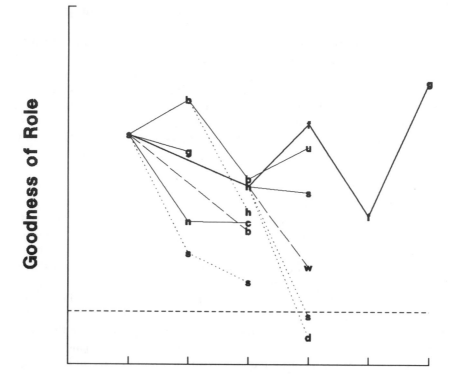

Advancement

FIG. 3.5 Evaluation in male family careers, U.S. Stage 1 (top to bottom): son; Stage 2: brother, grandson, nephew, stepson; Stage 3: brother-in-law, husband, half-brother, cousin, bachelor, stepbrother; Stage 4: father, uncle, son-in-law, widower, stepfather, divorcee; Stage 5: father-in-law; Stage 6: grandfather.

kinship roles generally are less powerful than corresponding male kinship roles.

One specific difference between male and female kinship roles is that the nepotic career is valued more highly for females. Another difference centers around spinster versus bachelor. Spinster is valued less highly than bachelor and is much less powerful.

Summary

The taxonomy of male kinship roles is somewhat simpler than the taxonomy that applies for a male developing careers in the Catholic Church. However, the American kinship system allows for repeated starts through

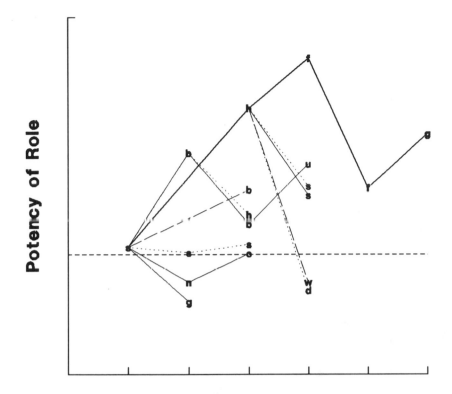

Advancement

FIG. 3.6 Power in male family careers, U.S. Stage 1 (top to bottom): son; Stage 2: brother, stepson, nephew, grandson; Stage 3: husband, bachelor, half-brother, brother-in-law, stepbrother, cousin; Stage 4: father, uncle, son-in-law, stepfather, widower, divorcee; Stage 5: father-in-law; Stage 6: grandfather.

the spouse role, and this adds substantial complexity to the system (e.g., a male could be a husband, father, divorcee, husband, stepfather). In any case, there are a number of different career lines that may terminate at various points and that may be combined in sundry ways, so there is potential for considerable variation in kinship biographies.

Kinship careers are not clustered around a particular profile of social resources the way Church careers are. Rather, different patterns of resources accrue on different career lines and at different stages of a kinship career. Generally speaking, the youthful roles are esteemed and powerless. The reproductive career provides social regard and power. Family splintering yields career lines that are without honor and that are powerless.

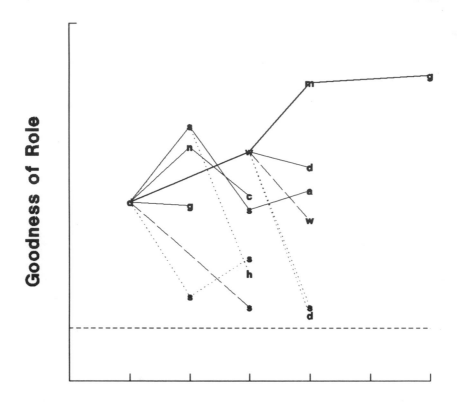

FIG. 3.7 Evaluation in female family careers, U.S. Stage 1 (top to bottom): daughter; Stage 2: sister, niece, granddaughter, stepdaughter; Stage 3: wife, cousin, sister-in-law, stepsister, half-sister, spinster; Stage 4: mother, daughter-in-law, aunt, widow, stepmother, divorcée; Stage 5: grandmother.

CAREERS AND THE INDIVIDUAL

Role Variety

An individual almost always traverses multiple career lines. Nearly everyone has several kinship careers going, an educational career, a lay religious career, often an occupational career. Thus, at any particular time a person owns a variety of roles deriving from careers in several institutions. Given this array of roles, a particular role might be activated in order to accomplish some specific instrumental goal or to fulfill some socioemotional needs. To the extent that the roles invoke socially valued

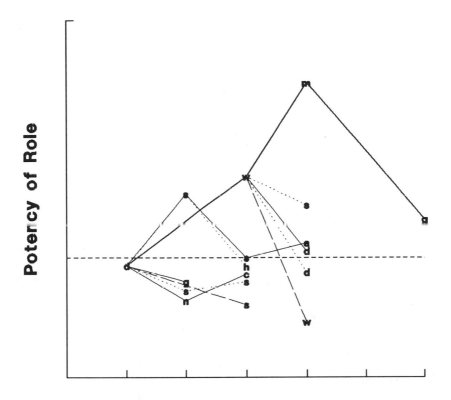

Advancement

FIG. 3.8 Power in female family careers, U.S. Stage 1 (top to bottom): daughter; Stage 2: sister, granddaughter, stepdaughter, niece; Stage 3: wife, sister-in-law, half-sister, cousin, stepsister, spinster; Stage 4: mother, stepmother, aunt, daughter-in-law, divorcée, widow; Stage 5: grandmother.

and powerful statuses, one also can garner others' cooperation in one's own endeavors. Thus, on the whole a person with more identities has more resources in a greater variety of circumstances for attaining a greater range of desires (Sieber, 1974).

People who have more roles can exercise greater selection in the statuses that they get to experience sometimes. They can attain fine tuning of social resources with their preferences at least occasionally. They also can move through a greater diversity of statuses if they so choose and thereby experience a richer life. (We do not usually think of someone wanting low regard or powerlessness, but some of us do crave such states sometimes—call it humility, and the desire does not seem so strange.) A person with a larger self generally has more freedom to experience a range of social statuses and more freedom to match roles to varying personal needs.

So far I have emphasized advantages of owning multiple roles, but I do not want to ignore the other side. Once one owns a role it can be activated not only by oneself but by others as well, and one may have to resign oneself to unwanted low evaluation or low power as others invoke various roles. Moreover, one is obligated to fulfill responsibilities with regard to the statuses of others who are in complementary roles—to offer them esteem or trepidation if their statuses warrant. Devotion to or fear of others siphons one's energies into fulfilling others' goals rather than one's own. Additionally, one may be faced with the dilemma of performing an action that accommodates an activated role but that would be aberrant were the action judged by the standards of some of one's other roles (see Stryker & Statham, 1985, for a review of the role conflict issue).

Obviously, one is more at risk of being buffeted from status to status if one owns many roles rather than a few, that is, if one has multiple institutional affiliations and careers. People with large numbers of roles who do not take charge may find themselves in the service of others, find themselves living a rich life but one without self-direction.

Role Accumulation

Some institutions are organized so that acquisition of new statuses depletes prior statuses. For example, in the military becoming a major requires relinquishing one's captaincy. However, in many institutions, as in the Catholic Church and in kinship, one retains old roles while gaining new roles. For example, becoming a father does not deplete being a husband; becoming a father-in-law does not terminate one's status as father. Although becoming a divorcee does terminate one's status as husband or wife, depletability of the spouse status is a special case within the kinship system. (See Glaser & Strauss, 1971, for an extended discussion of role accumulation and reversibility.) Consequently the number of roles one has increases on the whole as one progresses through careers. Moreover, we have seen in the example cases that career trajectories rarely are flat. Different roles in a career bring more (or less) social valuation and power. Thus, over the life course one's set of available roles tends to get larger and more diverse as well.

A peculiarity of status transitions is that these events always are conducted by others who are chartered to invest people in specific roles (Meyer, 1972). For example, the College of Cardinals makes a man a pope, and superior officers turn a captain into a major. Kinship also works like this. Ministers and justices are chartered to marry couples, thereby investing a set of people in the roles of husband or wife, brother or sister-in-law, father or mother-in-law, and so forth, and marriage charters a couple to reproduce, thereby investing others in the roles of son or daughter, brother or sister, uncle or aunt, grandfather or grandmother, and so on. Deviant identities[2], too, are acquired through the activities of others, as labeling theorists have emphasized (Hawkins & Tiedeman, 1975; Lofland, 1969). In the case of ascribed statuses like kinship, transitions may be totally out of one's hands, as in becoming a grandfather. In the case of achieved statuses, one can assemble a biography that justifies a role transition, but investiture still awaits others' actions.

Thus, one cannot push willfully through a career; one has to wait for others to act, and so career progress and the accumulation of statuses offers little opportunity for immediate manipulation. At any particular time, one has a set of statuses; and more desirable statuses cannot be added, unwanted statuses cannot be voided (voiding of status—as with annulments or pardons—is another status transition in the hands of others). The self as represented in the corpus of one's current roles is a product of past decisions about institutional affiliations and careers, and of other's activities as agents of status transition.

Although one cannot present oneself as someone entirely new, one can promote part of what one already has become (Swann, 1984), managing selections from one's available roles by: (a) frequenting settings where desired roles are invoked and keeping away from settings where disliked roles arise; (b) conducting oneself so as to remind others of one's desired roles and so as not to remind them of one's stigmatized statuses; and (c) maneuvering others into roles that evoke in a complementary way one's own desired roles rather than undesired roles. Those with a greater number of roles have more flexibility in managing their presentation of selves. This may be one reason why they experience less psychological distress than others with fewer roles (Thoits, 1983, 1986), and it perhaps gives them a greater sense of control.

Role Aspirations

Meanwhile, however, culturally defined career lines provide explicit, common knowledge about sequential unfolding of roles, and thereby individuals may develop notions about what roles they expect to acquire

---

[2]People do not always want the statuses to which they are entitled. Sometimes people can avoid an unwanted status by refusing it, but people often are forced to participate in transition ceremonies regardless of their wishes, as in the cases of child initiations in some cultures and of criminal proceedings in our own culture. See Glaser and Strauss (1971) for more on desirability of status transitions.

(Markus & Nurius, 1986). Such conceptions expand psychological fields into the future and can generate an anticipated self that may be more magnificent than the self that actually is operative in current social relations. The future self tenably can be incorporated into one's self-concept as long as the future is being actualized, as long as career development is being planned and managed, as long as one is working for required credentials so that aspirations will be realized as they become logically possible.

Aspirations have a voluntary element—people aspire to roles that provide desired levels of social regard and power. However, social context also is a factor because status transitions ultimately are in the hands of others. There is reason to be optimistic about a future investment when one has few competitors for the role or when investitures are boundless, when chartered authorities are eager to fill the role in order to maintain institutional structure, and when the authorities are receiving information that one is a fitting candidate for the position. On the other hand, an aspiration can be terminated when it becomes clear that vacancies are unforthcoming in the foreseeable future, when authorities neglect the role (e.g., the role of stablemaster in modern cavalry units of the army), or when authorities receive no information about the self or when they receive information disqualifying the self.

Statuses involving stigma or weakness (like divorcee) may damage self-esteem and the sense of self-efficacy just as holding esteemed and powerful roles can enhance self-concepts, and the negative version of aspiration is foreboding that one is being swept toward such statuses. People ordinarily make efforts to avoid events that are likely to precipitate attainment of stigmatized roles, but here, too, much depends on contextual factors—on the efficiency of chartered authorities in processing the given form of stigma, on authorities' eagerness to stigmatize, and on the flow of secret information that qualifies one for a stigmatization.

Careers and Aging

Do youths or middle-aged adults have more control over their lives? A theory of careers offers a complex answer to a question like this.

Youths in embryonic careers with little role accumulation cannot select from a variety of roles in order to fit their needs, and they may be unable to invoke roles with any significant power because powerful positions often are located at the ends of career paths. On the whole, therefore, their social resources perhaps are minimal and their ability to control their own everyday lives may be constrained. In contrast, middle-aged adults with advanced careers in several institutions theoretically should have a multitude of roles from which to choose (e.g., in the family), and they may have attained at least one role with significant power (such as father or mother) as well as having access to less valued and weaker roles (such as those in the nepotic career line). Thus a middle-aged adult often has control in that he or she generally does have a role that can be activated to fit most any mood or to fulfill personal needs.

However, because careers are culturally given structures, youths can project themselves into an imagined future in which they have a complex, prestigious, powerful self. Moreover, because the aspired roles are as yet far from attainable, they are relatively secure against failure and loss. In this sense, youths might enjoy a heady period of invulnerability and psychological control. Meanwhile, middle-aged adults may be in the throes of relinquishing identities as it becomes clear that career lines are being truncated short of aspirations. A middle-aged adult may worry about some gained roles being withdrawn—whether by fate or as punishment for nonconformity. And having so many roles puts the middle-aged adult at risk of being tossed among statuses as others invoke the roles.

In short, youths may not have much control in reality, but psychologically they could feel efficacious; middle-aged folks may exercise significant control over reality, but meanwhile they may feel disappointment about failed aspirations, anxiety about vulnerable statuses, and frustration that they do not have more control in deciding which roles occupy their time. Both youths and middle-aged adults could end up with the same sense of efficacy as a result of career-related processes, but the underlying reasons are different.

A theory of careers suggests that these kinds of social psychological processes are not a consequence of biological aging but of participation and advancement in culturally given social institutions. Indeed, the same variations should be expected when comparing neophytes and old-timers *within* an age level. (See Lachmann, 1988, on New York teenaged graffiti artists for one example of an age-graded institution with several short career lines.) A teenager could be "old" by having advanced too fast through peer-group roles, and a middle aged adult could be "as a youth" by having started over in new institutions or in new career lines. Career advancement occurs in sociological time, measured from one status transition to another, and all of the social psychological phenomena of careers might be found anywhere in the life course.

CONCLUSION

The key idea presented in this chapter is that career lines are predictable sequences of status transitions generated from cultural taxonomies of roles. This conceptualization of careers offers fertile ground for social psychological research on human development. Taxonomic structures provide a determinate framework for cataloging individual differences in role acquisition and accompanying privilege and power, so the formulation allows one to delineate how the self expands and contracts as a function of individual participation and performance in social institutions. Moreover, understanding that role taxonomies act as generative grammars allows one to comprehend how individuals project themselves into the future through aspirations. Meanwhile, the perspective suggests that individual development should vary as a function of differences in institutional participation and as a function of cultural differences in institutions.

My free discussion of relations between career development and psychological aspects of self suggested logical linkages between role processes and development of a sense of efficacy. I conclude by offering a somewhat more determinate set of hypotheses as follows.

1. Once a role is situationally invoked, a person performs in the role until the role is situationally relinquished, and in the process confirms him or herself as the kind of person who participates in the events required by the role (Heise, 1987b).

2. Performing in a role that is esteemed or powerful contributes to a sense of self-efficacy. Indeed, self-efficacy may be largely predictable from the summed evaluation and power of held roles with each role weighted by the time committed to it.

3. Aspiring to esteemed and powerful roles incorporates those roles vicariously into the self as one works to gain the credentials required for those roles. Thus, self-efficacy additionally is a function of future roles (Markus & Nurius, 1986), weighted by the time devoted to preparing for them.

These propositions lead to some expectations that could be tested.

1. Self-efficacy is influenced by institutional affiliations because institutions vary in the social valuation and power of roles they provide. Thus, people affiliating with different institutions should show differences in self-efficacy. Also, considerable variation in the development of self-efficacy is possible within institutions through selection of different career paths. Thus, people should also differ within institutions depending on their career lines.

2. Attained roles and the time committed to them theoretically provide the foundation of efficacious feelings, but aspirations (and forebodings) are another important factor. Consequently, peoples' sense of efficacy should correspond to some degree with the valuation and power of unattained roles in their career paths, and feelings of efficacy should change as career lines open—either through unexpected status attainments of the individual or through institutional changes in roles.

3. Commitment to roles—and the sense of efficacy produced by roles—is influenced by demands of others and by cultural schedules that control the amount of time a person devotes to each held role. Thus, people's sense of efficacy should be influenced by contextual demands for various kinds of role performances apart from individuals' own histories or aspirations. Moreover, institutional changes in scheduling should be found to impact on the sense of efficacy of people in the institution as roles with more (or less) valuation and power are accorded more (or less) time.

The propositions and their extensions surely are debatable (e.g., Thoits, 1983, 1986, presented more complex hypotheses about the psychological impact of multiple identities). However, the propositions listed here are useful if they simply instigate further theorizing and research regarding the fundamental theme in this chapter: that a sense of efficacy has sociocultural determinants, some of which might be analyzed usefully in terms of readily defined maps of institutional careers.

ACKNOWLEDGMENTS

Data collection in the United States was sponsored by the National Institute of Mental Health (Grant # 1-R01-MH29978-01-SSR); data collection in Northern Ireland was sponsored by the Jesuit Council for Theological Reflection, and analysis of the Irish data was sponsored by the National Science Foundation (Grant # SES-8122089). I am grateful to Lynn Smith-Lovin (Cornell University) for her participation in the U.S. data collection and for preparing both the U.S. and the Irish dictionaries of EPA profiles. I give my thanks to Father Dennis Willigan (University of Utah) for collecting the Irish data and to Father Ronald Ashmore (St. Charles Church, Bloomington, IN) for defining careers within the Catholic Church.

Linda Lazowski and Carmi Schooler provided me with extensive and valuable theoretical analyses that allowed me to improve this chapter. They also—along with John Meyer, Sheldon Stryker, and Peggy Thoits—offered concrete suggestions that helped me make the chapter more coherent and readable. Helpful comments also were received from faculty and fellows in the Program on Identity and the Program on Affect at Indiana University when this material was presented to a joint seminar.

REFERENCES

Becker, H. S., & Strauss, A. L. (1956). Careers, personality, and adult socialization. *American Journal of Sociology, 62*, 253–263.
Colby, B. N. (1975). Culture grammars. *Science, 187*, 913–919.

Glaser, B. G., & Strauss, A. L. (1971) *Status passage*. Chicago: Aldine-Atherton.

Goodenough, W. (1956). Componential analysis and the study of meaning. *Language, 32,* 195–216.

Hawkins, R., & Tiedeman, G. (1975). *The creation of deviance: Interpersonal and organizational determinants.* Columbus OH: Charles E. Merrill.

Heise, D. (1966). Social status, attitudes, and word connotations. *Sociological Inquiry, 36,* 227–239.

Heise, D. (1979). *Understanding events: Affect and the construction of social action.* New York: Cambridge University Press.

Heise, D. (1987a). Sociocultural determination of mental aging. In C. Schooler & K. W. Schaie (Eds.), *Cognitive functioning and social structure over the life course* (pp. 247–261). Norwood, NJ: Ablex.

Heise, D. R. (1987b). Affect control theory: Concepts and model. *Journal of Mathematical Sociology, 13,* 1–33.

Heise, D. R., & Lewis, E. M. (1988a). *Programs* INTERACT *and* ATTITUDE. Durham, NC: National Collegiate Software Clearinghouse, Duke University Press.

Heise, D. R., & Lewis, E. M. (1988b). *Program* ETHNO. Durham, NC: National Collegiate Software Clearinghouse, Duke University Press.

Kemper, T. D. (1972). Power, status, and love. In D. Heise (Ed.), *Personality and socialization* (pp. 180–203). Chicago: Rand McNally.

Kemper, T. D. (1978). *A social interactional theory of emotions.* New York: Wiley.

Lachmann, R. (1988). Graffiti as career and ideology. *American Journal of Sociology, 94,* 229–250.

Lofland, J. (1969). *Deviance and identity.* Englewood Cliffs, NJ: Prentice-Hall.

Luborsky, M. R. (1987). Analysis of multiple life history narratives. *Ethos, 15,* 366–381.

MacKinnon, N. J. (1985). *Affective dynamics and role analysis.* (Final report, Social Sciences and Humanities Research Council of Canada Project #410-81-0089). Ontario: Department of Sociology and Anthropology, University of Guelph.

Markus, H., & Nurius, P. (1986). Possible selves. *American Psychologist, 41,* 954–969.

Meyer, J. W. (1972). The effects of the institutionalization of colleges in society. In K. A. Feldman (Ed.), *College and student: Selected readings in the social psychology of higher education* (pp. 109–126). New York: Pergamon.

Meyer, J. W., & Rowan, B. (1977). Institutionalized organizations: Formal structure as myth and ceremony. *American Journal of Sociology, 83,* 340–363.

Rains, P. (1982). Deviant careers. In M. M. Rosenberg, R. A. Stebbins, & A. Turowitz (Eds.), *The sociology of deviance* (pp. 21–41). New York: St. Martin's Press.

Skvoretz, J. (1984). Languages and grammars of action and interaction: Some further results. *Behavioral Science, 29,* 81–97.

Skvoretz, J., & Fararo, T. J. (1980). Languages and grammars of action and interaction: A contribution to the formal theory of action. *Behavioral Science, 25,* 9–22.

Sieber, S. D. (1974). Toward a theory of role accumulation. *American Sociological Review, 39,* 567–578.

Smith-Lovin, L. (1987). Impressions from events. *Journal of Mathematical Sociology, 13,* 35–70.

Spradley, J. P. (1979). *The ethnographic interview.* New York: Holt, Rinehart & Winston.

Stryker, S., & Statham, A. (1985). Symbolic interaction and role theory. In G. Lindzey & E. Aronson (Eds.), *Handbook of social psychology* (Vol. 1, 3rd ed., pp. 311–378). New York: Random House.

Swann, W. B., Jr. (1984). Quest for accuracy in person perception: A matter of pragmatics. *Psychological Review, 91,* 457–477.

Thoits, P. A. (1983). Multiple identities and psychological well-being: A reformulation and test of the social isolation hypothesis. *American Sociological Review, 48,* 174–187.

Thoits, P. A. (1986). Multiple identities: Examining gender and marital status differences in distress. *American Sociological Review, 51,* 259–272.

Wallace, A. F. C., & Atkins, J. (1960). The meaning of kinship terms. *American Anthropologist, 62,* 58–80.

Werner, O., & Fenton, J. (1970). Method and theory in ethnoscience or ethnoepistemology. In R. Naroll & R. Cohen, (Eds.), *A handbook of method in cultural anthropology,* pp. 537–578. Garden City, NY: Natural History Press.

Werner, O., & Schoepfle, G. M. (1987). *Systematic fieldwork: Foundations of ethnography and interviewing.* Beverly Hills CA: Sage.

APPENDIX

TABLE 1
Evaluation and Potency Ratings of Catholic Church Roles Rated by Northern Ireland Adolescent Males and Females
(N: about 25 per word)

	Evaluation	Potency
Abbot	2.0	1.4
Archbishop	2.0	1.7
Bishop	2.5	2.2
Cardinal	2.3	2.2
Catholic	2.5	1.2
Chaplain	1.7	0.4
Clergyman	1.9	0.9
Deacon	0.7	0.1
Evangelist	1.7	0.9
Exorcist	−0.6	2.1
Friar	1.8	0.2
Jesuit	1.6	0.6
Minister	0.0	1.3
Missionary	2.7	1.1
Monk	2.1	0.1
Nun	2.4	−0.5
Pastor	1.5	0.2
Pope	2.8	3.0
Preacher	2.0	0.9
Priest	2.0	1.1
Saint	3.3	2.1
Seminarian	1.7	0.5

TABLE 2
Evaluation and Potency Ratings of Male Kinship Roles
by U.S. College Males (N: about 25 per word)

	Evaluation	Potency
Bachelor	0.8	0.7
Brother-in-law	1.3	0.4
Brother	2.0	1.1
Cousin	0.8	0.0
Divorcee	−0.2	−0.4
Father-in-law	0.9	0.7
Father	1.8	2.1
Grandfather	2.2	1.3
Grandson	1.5	−0.5
Half-brother	0.9	0.4
Husband	1.2	1.6
Nephew	0.9	−0.3
Son	1.7	0.1
Son-in-law	1.1	0.7
Stepbrother	0.3	0.1
Stepfather	−0.0	0.7
Stepson	0.6	0.0
Uncle	1.6	1.0
Widower	0.4	−0.3

TABLE 3
Evaluation and Potency Ratings of Female Kinship Roles
by U.S. College Females (N: about 25 per word)

	Evaluation	Potency
Aunt	1.3	0.2
Cousin	1.3	−0.1
Daughter	1.2	−0.1
Daughter-in-law	1.5	0.1
Divorcee	0.1	−0.2
Granddaughter	1.2	−0.3
Grandmother	2.4	0.4
Half-sister	0.5	−0.1
Mother	2.3	1.9
Niece	1.7	−0.5
Sister	1.9	0.7
Sister-in-law	1.1	−0.0
Spinster	0.2	−0.5
Stepdaughter	0.3	−0.3
Stepmother	0.2	0.6
Stepsister	0.7	−0.2
Widow	1.0	−0.7
Wife	1.7	0.9

Schemas, Sense of Control, and Aging

Ronald P. Abeles
National Institute on Aging

"Cultural taxonomies" are an example of a concept and method for obtaining information about how social structure is represented subjectively. Drawing upon cultural taxonomies as cultural representations of the sequences of roles that constitute careers within social institutions (e.g., family, Catholic Church), Dr. Heise considers three related questions: (a) How people perceive the interrelationships among various social roles and careers that comprise social institutions; (b) how they compare these roles on dimensions of power and prestige; and (c) how such cognitive representations of roles, careers, and social institutions might affect a person's objective and subjective control. My comments as a discussant are both a slight expansion and a redirection of these two sets of questions from the perspective of a "psychological social psychologist."

In particular, my concern is with the individual's sense of control, in line with the conference topic of self-directedness and efficacy (cf. Rodin, chapter 1, this volume). After a brief review of Dr. Heise's contributions to this topic, I introduce my own conceptual model of sense of control that, building on the relevant work of numerous scholars, specifies the main components of control and the processes through which it influences the performance of a particular behavior. Furthermore, recognizing that "aging" through a person's life course involves a long succession of behaviors, I show how the recursive processes in the model emphasize a continuing interplay between self and environment that can influence the nature of sense of control (Abeles & Riley, 1976–1977).

EXPERIENCE AND CULTURAL TAXONOMIES

How does experience with a social institution influence culturally provided taxonomies? This question is prompted by the nature of the respondents, who in Dr. Heise's research provided the information used
in diagraming the cultural taxonomies for two selected institutions: the
Catholic Church and the family. In both instances the respondents were
primarily adolescents or college-age students. (While an expert infor-
mant, a Catholic priest, was used to create the taxonomy of the Catholic
Church, Irish teenagers provided information about the perceived power
and prestige of the various roles within the taxonomy.) This meant that
they were too young to have occupied more than a limited set of roles in
either of these institutions. This experience was limited to just a few roles
and to less prestigious and less powerful roles. This lack of first-hand
exposure might be an advantage, if the goal were to obtain general
cultural taxonomies. The perceptions and evaluations of these young
respondents are "untainted" by personal experience, and they are still in
the midst of being socialized or systematically exposed to cultural belief
systems.

However, it seems highly probable that, as a person moves through
roles in an institution, his or her cognitive map of that institution is
changed. An individual's experience with an institution (as an outsider)
or in it as a role incumbent could change his or her taxonomy in at least
three ways. First, previously unrecognized roles might be added or finer
distinctions between and within role categories might be made. To take
another highly hierarchical institution as an example, experience with the
military quickly reveals meaningful distinctions among different kinds of
generals that go unrecognized amongst civilians. Second, the perceived
relationships between roles or the path between roles might be changed.
As a graduate student, a person might believe that there is only a single
route to obtaining tenure and a professorship. But, experience teaches
that alternative paths exist. Finally, roles might be revaluated in terms of
their prestige and power. From the outside, the general's aide de camp
might appear to hold a low prestige and powerless position. However,
experience with aides de camp could lead to the realization that they
control access to generals and thereby have power, influence, and perhaps even prestige.

In summary, a person's cognitive map that is provided by the surrounding culture is not likely to be immutable, but is likely to change
over time and with experience, as in the case when one moves from being
a novice to an expert in a field (Murphy & Wright, 1984). This raises a
rather difficult question in regard to measuring a cultural taxonomy. If

the taxonomies are dependent on the respondent's experience with and location in the institution, whose cognitive map should be considered as the cultural taxonomy of that institution? A Protestant outsider's, a seminary student's, or the Pope's?

CULTURAL TAXONOMIES AND SENSE OF CONTROL

The second set of questions considered by Dr. Heise is how cultural taxonomies might affect both the objective and the subjective control that people experience as they move through various roles. In my comments, I concentrate on the subjective side and explore the relationship between cultural taxonomies and a person's *sense of control*. This topic can be addressed by drawing upon concepts and research already available within social psychology, particularly from the study of social cognition. Here the concept of cultural taxonomies is similar to the more general concept of *schema*, which is a person's cognitive representation of conceptually related objects, situations, events, and sequences of events and actions (Markus & Zajonc, 1985). Schemas are people's subjective theories about how the world operates. Although there are several different ways that social psychologists label and categorize schemas, one classification seems particularly relevant to this discussion (Taylor & Crocker, 1981). Schemas can be classified in terms of their central focus as: (a) *Person schemas*, which are representations of oneself or other people (e.g., self-conceptions, implicit personality theories); (b) *role schemas*, which exist for social roles or social groups (e.g., stereotypes); and (c) *event schemas*, which contain beliefs and expectations about what is likely to transpire in a particular situation (e.g., the flow of interactions that comprise a conference).

Although role schemas are most obviously relevant to cultural taxonomies of careers, both person and event schemas are also of relevance. Dr. Heise's example of the Catholic Church shows that there are distinct representations (or role schemas) of the various roles in terms of their characteristics (i.e., power, prestige). Although his data do not touch on this point, it seems likely that people also hold beliefs about the personal characteristics of individuals (or person schemas) who occupy specific roles such as that of a priest. Similarly, beliefs about the Catholic Church as a social institution and about roles and role incumbents combine to provide beliefs and expectations (event schemas) about what will transpire during a Mass or a church picnic: For example, which actions will take place? In what sequence? And who will perform each act?

In short, cultural taxonomies of careers and their constituent roles are one kind of schema. This conceptual framework allows a reformulation of the question to be considered: Namely, how might schemas, especially culturally provided schemas, affect a person's sense of control?

A Model of Sense of Control

In order to consider this question, we need first to lay out a model of the components and their interrelationships that comprise sense of control. Figure 1 provides a schematic diagram of such a model, by synthesizing major strains in the current literature. In viewing this model, four points are noteworthy. First, it refers primarily to internal, cognitive structures and processes. That is, it conceptualizes control in terms of *subjective* experiences within a person's mind. It is not a model of actual control. (Although most elements are internal, a few presumed antecedents and consequences are external.) Second, sense of control is not a unitary concept, but is composed of multiple component beliefs and expectations regarding oneself and the environment. Third, the model postulates processes that are dynamic, and also dialectical: these processes include a feedback loop from "outcomes" back to the hypothesized antecedents of sense of control. This loop implies that accumulating experiences result in short-term changes in sense of control and longer term changes as a person undergoes development and aging. Last, the least elaborated or specified part of the diagram refers to the hypothesized antecedents of sense of control. Clearly, cultural beliefs, as discussed in Dr. Heise's chapter, are one such antecedent.

As schematized in Fig. 1, the model portrays the components of sense of control (shaded boxes) and their role in influencing whether a person will perform a particular behavior and how the results of that behavior feed back to affect the person's sense of control. A person's sense of control consists of beliefs and expectations about the *self* and about the *environment.* According to this model, a person's *self beliefs* about his or her own ability (e.g., skills) and capability (e.g., to exert effort) combine with *task beliefs* about the nature of the task (e.g., its difficulty) to produce his or her *self-efficacy expectations,* that is, a sense of whether he or she could successfully perform the behaviors needed to achieve the particular desired outcome (Bandura, 1977, 1982). The person's *beliefs about the causal nature of the environment* focus on whether he or she perceives the environment to be governed by "lawful" or "orderly" processes such that outcomes (e.g., "success" or "failure") are "contingent" upon people's behaviors as opposed to random forces (i.e., "noncontingent"). Believing that an environment is contingent does not necessarily mean that a person believes he or she has control, because his or her own outcomes may be

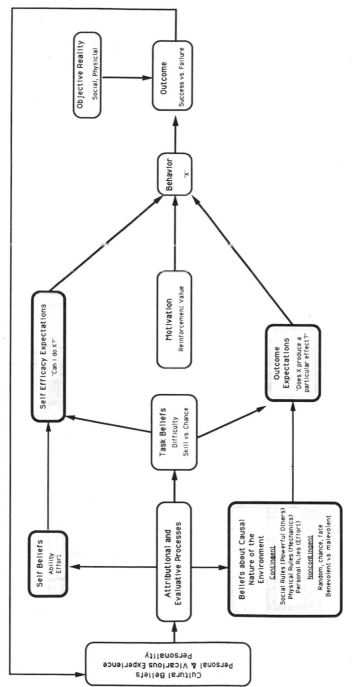

FIG. 1 A model of sense of control.

(perceived as) more contingent upon the behaviors of others than upon his or her own efforts. Beliefs about the causal nature of the environment also combine with task beliefs to produce *outcome expectations* (i.e., whether performing action X is generally likely to result in outcome Y). Thus, a person's sense of control consists of the complex interrelationships among his or her self-beliefs, self-efficacy expectations, beliefs about the causal nature of the environment, and outcome expectations.

Implicit in the model, of course, is the postulate that sense of control is modified by personal experience. It is presumed that a person assesses his or her own performance with reference to the reactions of others and to whether the desired outcome is obtained. Such evaluative and attributional processes may lead to adjustments in his or her sense of control through changes in beliefs and expectations about the self, the environment, or the task. Similarly, other people's experiences can affect a person's sense of control through social comparison and reference group processes. Furthermore, general cultural beliefs influence the beliefs and expectations constituting one's sense of control.

Cultural Schemas and Sense of Control

With this model in mind, it seems that culturally provided schemas (following Heise) could affect sense of control both before and after a particular role performance. As a concrete example arising from this conference, let us take serving as a discussant as the role and consider the related behaviors. *Before the role performance,* cultural schemas provide information about the environment, the task, and about one's self. Before even performing the role, the prospective discussant has a set of beliefs and expectations that are provided by cultural schemas that serve to guide behavior in this situation. In regard to beliefs about the causal nature of the environment and outcome expectations, cultural event schemas define conferences are generally contingent environments governed by universalistic norms. That is, in American culture, rewards and punishments are based on one's behaviors and not allocated by random processes. Moreover, they are based on merit or the quality of the person's performance. Indeed, cultural schemas may provide an "illusion of control" by instilling such beliefs (cf. Langer, 1975)! Similarly, role and event schemas in the culture define what it means to be a discussant at a conference by providing "scripts" that detail which actions are likely to take place (Schank & Abelson, 1977). In addition, culturally provided person schemas furnish beliefs about oneself in terms of which personal skills and abilities are relevant and about whether one is likely to possess the requisite skills and abilities. In part, whether a person believes that he or she possesses these or not may depend on cultural definitions of how similar to other roles the discussant role is. That is, cultural schemas define bounds within which skills are perceived as transferable from one role to the next. For example, the role of being a father and having obtained a certain age are not defined as relevant to the discussant role in America. However, in other cultures those roles might connote "wisdom," and incumbents might believe themselves to possess the required skills for performing the role of discussant.

After the role performance, culturally provided schemas can affect the evaluative and attributional processes in which a person engages by (a) influencing the availability and use of information and by (b) providing standards against which the role performance is judged. First of all, schemas may influence what information is attended to during a role performance and how it is encoded and organized. This, in turn, can affect the subsequent availability of information to be used in post-performance assessment (cf. Ostrom, Lingle, Pryor & Geva, 1980). For example, after performing the role of discussant and while subsequently recalling his or her performance, a person is likely to attend to and to recall only selected information about the audience's reactions (e.g., how many were asleep). Similarly, schemas have a selective influence on the retention, retrieval, and organization of information in memory. In general, schema-consistent information is remembered better than inconsistent information, although the latter is also likely to be recalled whenever it competes with information in the schema and the person is required to make use of it.

In still another respect, schemas may function as interpretive frameworks and thereby influence evaluations, judgments, and inferences. Person schemas provide implicit personality theories that can be employed to interpret one's own or others' behaviors; role schemas include standards against which the quality of a performance is judged; and event schemas define the situation in terms of environmental contingency versus noncontingency. For example, a conference is defined as involving contingent and universalistic norms, which make it more difficult for a person to attribute failure as a discussant to either a noncontingent environment (event schema) or a particularistic norms (role schema). This forces attention on one's own performance (person schema) as the basis for success or failure.

In summary, culturally provided schemas may influence the kind and amount of information available and how it is interpreted by a person during a post-performance assessment of his or her behavior. Thus, sense of control is maintained or altered through such attributional and evaluative processes.

RESEARCH IMPLICATIONS

Culturally provided schemas, including cultural taxonomies, provide a bridge between the culture and the person by serving as a mechanism that links societal-level processes and interpersonal transactions to individual-level, psychological processes (cf. Abeles, 1989; Abeles & Riley, 1987). These schema offer individuals cognitive maps that allow them to understand and construct "reality." This understanding and construction of reality is accomplished by the effect of the schemas on the person's beliefs, expectations, behaviors, as well as on the standards or values against which performance is judged. Although such schemas are potentially powerful, it should be re-emphasized that the flow of influence is not unidirectional. A person's experience may, in turn, influence the structure and content of schemas, including cultural taxonomies.

These are broad assertions that afford some understanding of a class of variables influencing a person's sense of control. Although assertions are easy to make, they are not easy to test empirically. The model presented in Fig. 1 lays out only in extremely broad strokes classes of variables and processes that presumably affect a person's sense of control as he or she moves through various roles and has particular experiences. Thus, it provides a large framework within which particular research objectives can be defined. However, the model does not specify how the life-long succession of cumulative experiences (both personal and vicarious) combine with other influences, such as cultural beliefs, to produce change or stability in sense of control as a person develops and ages.

A second ambiguity is implicit in—or rather implied by—the model of sense of control. The model refers to sense of control vis-à-vis a single behavior or domain of behaviors (e.g., performing the discussant role). Obviously, a person accumulates a wide variety of roles and performs an even more diversified set of behaviors as he or she moves through the life course. Does this mean that a person develops and retains a sense of control for each of his or her many significant roles or behavioral domains (e.g., as employee, parent, spouse) as opposed to a single, generalized sense of control? Certainly this is implied by the model and by research aimed at developing domain-specific measures of sense of control (Lefcourt, 1981). Thus, the second ambiguity is how are these multiple senses of control related to each other and how do they change and/or remain stable over the life course?

These two ambiguities (i.e., the global model vs. specific research questions; single behaviors vs. multiple, cumulative behaviors over the life course) reflect the current lack of research on how a person's sense of control is formed, maintained, and altered and with which consequences as he or she develops and ages (Rodin, 1986, 1987). These are but two of the key challenges facing research in this field (Abeles, 1987).

ACKNOWLEDGMENTS

The comments and advice of Matilda White Riley and Robin Barr on an earlier version of this discussion are gratefully acknowledged. The model, represented in Fig. 1, has benefited from the insightful and critical comments of several colleagues, but most especially from those of Margret Baltes and Ellen Skinner.

REFERENCES

Abeles, R. P. (1987). Introduction. In R. P. Abeles (Ed.), *Life-span perspectives and social psychology* (pp. 1–15). Hillsdale, NJ: Lawrence Erlbaum Associates.

Abeles, R. P. (1989). Social structure as a determinant of environmental experience. In K. W. Schaie & C. Schooler (Eds.), *Social structure and aging: Psychological processes* (pp. 149–153). Hillsdale, NJ: Lawrence Erlbaum Associates.

Abeles, R. P., & Riley, M. W. (1976–1977). A life-course perspective on the later years of life: Some implications for research. In *Social Science Research Council Annual Report* (pp. 1–16). New York: Social Science Research Council.

Abeles, R. P., & Riley, M. W. (1987). Longevity, social structure, and cognitive aging. In C. Schooler & K. W. Schaie (Eds.), *Cognitive functioning and social structure over the life course* (pp. 161–175). Norwood, NJ: Ablex.

Bandura, A. (1977). Self-efficacy: Toward a unifying theory of behavioral change. *Psychological Review, 84,* 191–125.

Bandura, A. (1982). Self-efficacy mechanism in human agency. *American Psychologist, 37*(2), 122–147.

Langer, E. (1975). The illusion of control. *Journal of Personality and Social Psychology, 32,* 311–328.

Lefcourt, H. M. (Ed.). (1981). *Research with the locus of control construct: Vol. 1. Assessment methods.* New York: Academic Press.

Markus, H., & Zajonc, R. B. (1985). The cognitive perspective in social psychology. In G. Lindzey & E. Aronson (Eds.), *Handbook of social psychology* (Vol. 1, 3rd ed., pp. 137–230). New York: Random House.

Murphy, G. L., & Wright, J. C. (1984). Changes in conceptual structure with expertise: Differences between real-world experts and novices. *Journal of Experimental Psychology: Learning, Memory, and Cognition, 10,* 144–155.

Ostrom, T. M., Lingle, J. H., Pryor, J., & Geva, N. (1980). Cognitive organization of person impressions. In R. Hastie, T. M. Ostrom, D. L. Hamilton, R. S. Wyer, E. Ebbeson, & D. Carlston (Eds.), *Person-memory: The cognitive basis of social perception.* Hillsdale, NJ: Lawrence Erlbaum Associates.

Rodin, J. (1986). Aging and health: Effects of the sense of control. *Science, 233,* 1271–1276.

Rodin, J. (1987). Personal control through the life course. In R. P. Abeles (Ed.), *Life-*

span perspectives and social psychology (pp. 103–120). Hillsdale, NJ: Lawrence Erlbaum Associates.

Schank, R. C., & Abelson, R. P. (1977). *Scripts, plans, goals, and understanding.* Hillsdale, NJ: Lawrence Erlbaum Associates.

Taylor, S. E., & Cocker, J. (1981). Schematic bases of social information processing. In E. T. Higgens, C. A. Harman, & M. A. Zanna (Eds.), *Social cognition: The Ontario symposium on personality and social psychology* (pp. 89–134). Hillsdale, NJ: Lawrence Erlbaum Associates.

Social Constraints on Self-Directedness Over the Life Course

Anne Foner
Rutgers University

The analysis of careers over the life course and the implications of these trajectories for opportunities for self-direction presents us with a conundrum. On the one hand, as Heise (this volume) notes, careers are governed by social rules, the very notion suggesting constraints. Indeed, even role definitions that require creativity and the exercise of independent judgment can be constraining. For example, in an ongoing study of mobility among 18th-century German musicians, Andrew Abbott notes that musicians in the courts of titled patrons were expected to compose new pieces often, sometimes weekly—hardly the autonomous conditions likely to encourage creativity. In fact, he suggests that the "new music" was often a recombination of other people's work. On the other hand, according to Heise, social systems may provide increasing opportunities to exercise self-direction to the extent that individuals move into many statuses and experience greater diversity in roles over the course of their lives. In short, social factors can both restrain individual autonomy and provide opportunities for self-direction.

In this discussion, I explore further various ways social factors influence the individual's chances to exercise self-direction. This discussion takes off from some of Heise's insights, particularly those focusing on self-realization. However, in contrast to Heise, who seems to accentuate the enhancement of opportunities to be self-directed and exercise choices over the course of people's various careers, the major thrust of my discussion is on the processes by which social factors limit individual flexibility, often in subtle and unexplored ways. My examples come primarily from the United States. However, I suggest ways that some of these social factors may vary across societies and thus have a differential impact on opportunities for self-realization.

MULTIPLE ROLES AND CAREER LINES

My first point concerns multiple roles and career lines. Heise notes that the notion of a career need not be narrowly applied to the individual's work life, but can apply to many institutional areas, with the individual thus having multiple career lines. According to Heise, there appears to be a liberating potential in this phenomenon. That is, the individual's array of role identities provides him or her with both personal and social capital that help the person to achieve goals and fulfill socioemotional needs. Over the life course a person's set of available statuses tends to get larger and more diverse and thus the more social resources the person has for attaining his or her goals.

I see another side of the coin: Holding multiple roles can create role strain and this can limit the person's ability to chart his or her course as he or she pleases. A familiar example these days is the working mother. The advertisements of a major magazine *(Redbook)* celebrate the way such a woman juggles career and family responsibilities. Perhaps this juggling sharpens her ingenuity. She may even attain high scores on Kohn and Schooler's (1983) measures of self-directedness: She may be relatively free from direct supervision, her tasks may involve only a moderate degree of repetitiveness, and the tasks, all told, are relatively complex. But she suffers from time constraints. Precisely because of these constraints, she does not have the autonomy to perform in some, perhaps all, of her roles as she might wish. We might explore whether in other countries with more extensive and socially supported child care, women are less likely to experience such overload and therefore are more likely to enjoy the self-realizing effects of diverse roles.

Or, consider the squeeze created by multiple roles within one institution, the family, where the middle-generation parent is torn among obligations to elderly parents, to spouse, and to offspring. Often the choices made about which obligations to honor are not guided by the parent's own wishes but by perceptions of societal expectations. This situation also occurs in preindustrial societies. For example, among the Kikuyu of Africa, the middle generation is often hard pressed by competing demands of offspring and elderly parents. In one situation where a younger man had limited resources but faced increased cash demands from his elderly parents, he is reported as saying: "It is a difficult job to look after them. They are often as unreasonable as children. They forget what it is like to have nine children and little land" (Cox & Mberia cited in Foner, 1984, p. 113).

Still another aspect of the potential limiting effects of multiple roles is suggested by Mortimer (1988). Her findings suggest that having autonomy in one role may not spill over to other roles and may even inhibit ability to exercise autonomy in other roles. In a longitudinal study following about 1,600 boys from 10th grade to 5 years beyond high school graduation, she noted that a great deal of autonomy at work when combined with long work hours interfered with school achievement among 11th-grade boys. It appears that spending extensive hours at work involving self-initiated planning and perceived as being very interesting lures adolescents in 11th grade away from school activities, thereby depressing academic achievement. Over the long run, this could affect the boys' chances of attaining work roles permitting the exercise of independent judgment.

SOCIAL NETWORKS AND COUNTERPART TRANSITIONS

Another important point that Heise makes is that the roles one fills and the way one fills them are affected by other people; these others may cast the person into roles with lower prestige or power; or the person may be obligated to offer others in complementary roles esteem or "trepidation"; such obligatory behavior is not self-directed.

I suggest that there is another way that others affect the person's freedom to act in a role: The individual's own career paths are affected by the career paths of other persons in his or her social network. This intermeshing can interfere with the individual's plans and can limit the person's ability to use time as he or she pleases. The retirement of the husband can reduce his wife's autonomy as is suggested by the well-known quip: "I married him for better or for worse but not for lunch." Or the divorce of children can refill the nest of the parents and subject the parents to new obligations. (For a further discussion of counterpart transitions among the old, see Foner, 1986.) Still another example is suggested by election-year campaigns where running for major office appears to constrain the autonomy of the candidate's spouse and children.

At the same time, I am not sure I would go so far as Heise has in saying that transitions are always the outcome of others' actions, that the person has to wait for others to act. Think of the situation of self-initiated transitions. SanGiovanni's (1978) study of ex-nuns is a particularly interesting example. To be sure, changes in the Catholic Church were the spur. As a result of Vatican Council II, religious orders were encouraged to assess their policies and structures and to renew themselves through critical examination. As a consequence, a good deal of questioning by nuns was taking place. But it was the individual who made the decision to leave the religious life; investiture into the lay life did not await the actions of others. According to SanGiovanni, the transition to lay life was shaped and controlled by the person herself; her passage was not formed by institutionalized rules, timetables, choices, and meanings (p. 147). What is interesting about this example is that although the individual nun exercised autonomy in making the transition, the exercise of self-direction in the new status was somewhat constrained by lack of resources. On the one hand, the ex-nuns were exercising self-determination as they wrote their own scripts, there being no role models for ex-nuns. But, on the other hand, they had no prior socialization for finding a job, opening a checking account, buying clothes, or going out on a date. Moreover, they experienced constraints in their new roles because they often violated other people's expectations. These others had not been socialized to deal with the new role of ex-nun.

There are undoubtedly other self-initiated transitions such as self-initiated separation from a spouse or the voluntary departure from a job. And these self-initiators too may find that they do not have the material or social resources to exercise self-direction in their new statuses (see, for example, Weitzman, 1985, on some economic consequences of divorce).

THE INFLUENCE OF SOCIAL IDENTITIES

The availability of social resources brings up another issue: how opportunities for self-direction over the life course are influenced by the person's age, class, gender, and race identities.

Consider first, age. From Heise's analysis, one could infer that as persons accumulate many roles over the life course, their opportunities for self-direction increase. He mentions that an older person is likely to be a person with a larger self (presumably someone with many statuses of great diversity). We know, of course, that in developed societies this is not generally the case. Rather the number and diversity of roles peaks among people in their middle years; among those in their 60s and older there is contraction in their roles with retirement, widowhood, and the empty nest (Riley & Foner, 1968).

It is not clear how we should interpret this contraction in roles with retirement and widowhood as it relates to self-direction. If I understand Heise correctly, such contraction means limits on the individual's autonomy. He suggests that confinement to a few statuses is likely to be frustrating because the individual may not have the best statuses for self-realization and has few opportunities for changing experience through personal choice. I would add that for some people the transition to retirement and certainly the transition to widowhood are not voluntary. Such involuntary transitions themselves are a challenge to self-directedness.

However, if I am correct about the constraints created by role overload, then for many people in their 60s and older, there may well be new-found freedoms as their roles contract. Thus many retirees report enjoying their unobligated time; parents with offspring out of the parental home are relieved that they no longer have to worry about setting an example for offspring, and even some widows appreciate the new friends and activities they have found on their own. Given the diversity in the older population (Dannefer, 1987), some segments of this older population are likely to experience constraints on opportunities for self-direction, in line with Heise's argument. But other older people may find more opportunities for self-realization. And social factors play a role in both outcomes: Social factors may help older people experience more freedoms or they may operate to constrain their choices. Among these social factors are the person's social locations in the class, race, or gender hierarchies and the attendant social resources available to the individual.

THE IMPACT OF CLASS AND OTHER SOCIAL LOCATIONS

Heise makes the important point that the self as represented in the body of one's current identities is a product of past decisions about institutional affiliations and careers and of others' activities as agents of status transitions. Here I want to emphasize that these past decisions of self and others are not randomly distributed but are affected by the person's class, gender, and race. As Dannefer (1987) has shown, there tends to be a cumulation of advantages or disadvantages over the life course. Such a pattern suggests that those starting out in the lower levels of various social hierarchies do not have the same freedom to make decisions about institutional affiliations and careers as those starting out at higher levels. For example, occupational sex segregation in the work force not only serves to distribute men and women into different occupations but limits the range of occupations that women in practice can choose (see England, 1981, for the persistence of occupational sex segregation). Similar constraints are experienced by minorities and by those at the bottom of the class system. Going beyond the the situation in the United States, if we think of an international stratification system, then people in the poorer countries generally will be more limited in the choices they can make about their careers than those in more prosperous countries.

CHANGING SOCIETIES AND SELF-DIRECTEDNESS

Just a word about change. Drawing charts about career patterns in different institutions and among different sections of the population can suggest a kind of stability and permanence in these various trajectories that in fact does not exist. The rhythm of individual change over the life course takes place against the background of societal change and these two kinds of change need not mesh (see, for example, Riley, Foner, & Waring, 1988). Such asychrony has implications for the exercise of self-direction.

Even within richer countries and among more advantaged strata, the person's exercise of self-direction can be thwarted by large-scale changes in the society as well as changes in the more immediate context of the roles he or she currently fills. Retirement is a case in point. Workers in their 50s or so are told to plan ahead for retirement in order to achieve the good life in retirement. Well and good, but their self-actualizing plans may be frustrated by large-scale and local changes. For example, economic changes such as inflation or new taxes, the character of their neighborhood changing around them as former residents move or die, new definitions for retirees that put pressure on people to retire at later ages, to say nothing about deterioration in their own or kin's health, can upset plans, and limit new choices. Among those still in the labor force, broad economic forces may lead to corporate buyouts that result in middle-level managers losing positions with a good deal of authority, and the political climate may lead to the imposition of restrictions on the autonomy of professions.

BRINGING PEOPLE BACK IN

All this said, I now want to reverse directions. I do not want to present a one-sided emphasis on the constraining influences of social structure. The self-directed actions of individuals also have an impact on their own lives, and in turn, these can act back on social institutions. According to Marx's well-known comment, people make history, but not exactly as they please. I would say rather that there is a reciprocal interaction between social influences and individual actions. But because I have already stressed the "not as they please" in Marx's aphorism, now I emphasize the way individuals' actions make a difference, even when they are in roles that seemingly offer little opportunity for self-direction or when they live in tradition bound societies.

One example comes from studies of industrial workers. Constrained by work rules and often having to meet production quotas, we learn that nevertheless they engage in self-directed activity. In Burawoy's (1979) study of a piecework machine shop, for example, workers established their own production goals within recognized limits and in the process subverted rules, created informal alliances with auxiliary workers, and made their own tools (p. 72). These activities arose from worker initiatives. True, Burawoy argued that such independent activities ultimately served the interests of their employers, but these activities also helped to make the work tolerable and exemplified aspects of self-direction.

Another example comes from age-set societies (Foner & Kertzer, 1978). These are small-scale, technologically undeveloped societal groups that utilize age as a major element in their social organization. For example, they are organized around named groupings of males based on age or generation; membership in these age sets is publicly recognized; duration of the age sets, once they are formed, lasts for the bulk of the life course; membership involves the allocation of significant social roles and social rewards; and age-set members move jointly from one age grade to the next. The timing of joint transitions from one age grade to the next was governed by rules, and these joint transitions were marked by public rituals. In many cases, however, individuals undertook activities associated with the next age grade prior to the publicly established time for transitions. Thus, in one age-set society, for example, those who wished to become elders as soon as possible generally tried to marry early and start to acquire the dignity of elder. Such individual flexibility contributed to the development of an informal set of rules side by side with the formal rule system.

Finally, consider the collective striving for autonomy among college youth of the 1960s and 1970s. Their challenges to and conflict with established authorities did result in changes in administrative procedures and gave students more opportunities for choice (Foner, 1974).

In such ways, individually or collectively, people exercise independent judgment and make their own choices; in doing so they help shape their own biographies and, in turn, help reshape social institutions and thus help make social history.

REFERENCES

Burawoy, M. (1979). *Manufacturing consent: Changes in the labor process under monopoly capitalism.* Chicago: University of Chicago Press.

Dannefer, D. (1987). Aging as intracohort differentiation: Accentuation, the Matthew effect, and the life course. *Sociological Forum, 2,* 211–236.

England, P. (1981). Assessing trends in occupational sex segregation, 1900–1976. In I. Berg (Ed.), *Sociological perspectives on labor markets* (pp. 273–295). New York: Academic Press.

Foner, A. (1974). Age stratification and age conflict in political life. *American Sociological Review, 39,* 187–196.

Foner, A. (1986). *Aging and old age: New perspectives.* Englewood Cliffs, NJ: Prentice-Hall.

Foner, A., & Kertzer, D. (1978). Transitions over the life course: Lessons from age-set societies. *American Journal of Sociology, 83,* 1081–1104.

Foner, N. (1984). *Ages in conflict: A cross-cultural perspective on inequality between old and young.* New York: Columbia University Press.

Kohn, M. L., & Schooler, C. (1983). *Work and personality: An inquiry into the impact of social stratification.* Norwood, NJ: Ablex.

Mortimer, J. T. (1988). Work experience and psychological change throughout the life course. In M. W. Riley, B. J. Huber, & B. B. Hess (Eds.), *Social structures and human lives: Vol. I. Social change and the life course* (pp. 267–284). Newbury Park, CA: Sage.

Riley, M. W., & Foner, A. (1968). *Aging and society: Vol. 1. An inventory of research findings.* New York: Russell Sage.

Riley, M. W., Foner, A., & Waring, J. (1988). Sociology of age. In N. J. Smelser (Ed.), *Handbook of sociology* (pp. 243–290). Newbury Park, CA: Sage.

SanGiovanni, L. (1978). *Ex-nuns: A study of emergent role passage.* Norwood, NJ: Ablex.

Weitzman, L. J. (1985). *The divorce revolution: The unexpected social and economic consequences for women and children in America.* New York: The Free Press.

Development of Control-Related Beliefs, Goals, and Styles in Childhood and Adolescence: A Clinical Perspective

John R. Weisz
University of North Carolina at Chapel Hill

Alli faces a "control dilemma." For weeks she has wanted to be included in a popular group of her junior high peers. She has made overtures, but the girls in the group have not shown much interest. What will she do now? In part, she may sort through her *beliefs* about her prospects for control in this situation: Is the outcome she intends (i.e., social acceptance by the high-status group) really contingent on the behavior of people like her? Some kids say that you have to be rich, or your parents have to be socially prominent, before you have a chance to be in the popular group. If these kids are right, then Alli has no chance. On the other hand, maybe being charming, or witty, or socially skilled can get you into the group; if so, Alli has to decide whether she has enough competence in those areas to succeed. A second part of the process for Alli may be *goal setting*. Perhaps she will decide, for example, to pursue the goal of getting into the popular group; or perhaps, instead, she will decide to find ways of appreciating her current social situation more; or perhaps she will simply give up and feel discouraged. A third aspect of Alli's response will be behavioral; she will adopt a certain *behavioral style* in the social context associated with her original control dilemma. In Alli's story can be found the three main elements of this chapter. We focus on the development and implications of control-related beliefs, goals, and behavioral styles.

Because I am interested in child and adolescent clinical psychology as well as developmental psychology, much of the research discussed here is noticeably clinical in its flavor. We focus on the public school age range (i.e., about 6–17 years). In what follows, we consider some of the findings, and some of the unanswered questions, in each of the three areas—

control-related beliefs, goals, and styles. In a concluding section, we focus on the insularity that I believe characterizes the three lines of research, and on the need to investigate possible connections among the three phenomena.

DEFINING CONTROL

For the purposes of this chapter, we define *control* as causing an intended event. Working from this definition, if we are to judge an individual's capacity for control we must gauge that individual's capacity to cause an event consistent with his or her intentions. This seemingly simple definition is designed to be at least roughly compatible with the perspectives of the Max Planck group (Skinner & Chapman, 1983), self-efficacy theory (Bandura, 1982), and the reformulated version of learned helplessness theory (Abramson, Seligman, & Teasdale, 1978).

Implicit within the definition are two important distinctions. First, control is distinguished from the likelihood of an intended event. An intended event may or may not be likely, quite independently of whether the individual plays a causal role; in the absence of a causal role, the individual does not exert control, even if the outcome eventually experienced is precisely what the individual intended. This brings us to a second distinction: Causality alone is also not control. Most "locus-of-control" questionnaires for adults and children focus in part or in full on judgments about the causality of events. In most such questionnaires, a judgment that one is the cause of unintended or undesirable outcomes (as well as intended or desirable outcomes) is classified as a sign of "internal" or "personal" control.

MAKING AN ACCURATE JUDGMENT ABOUT CONTROL

Real adaptive advantages may accrue to individuals who are able to make accurate judgments about their capacity for control, as we have defined it. Persistent pursuit of unattainable goals may carry such consequences as inefficient allocation of time and energy, inappropriate selection of school courses, unwise career choices, and possibly self-blame and depression. How may we make accurate assessments of our capacity for control? In my view, at least two issues need to be addressed in the process of making such assessments—issues of outcome contingency and of personal competence.

Contingency

Accurately judging the contingency of a target event can enhance one's ability to make a veridical control judgment. Contingency judgments may involve not only the gross distinction between totally noncontingent events (e.g., a snowstorm, or a roll of the dice) and those subject to some human influence, but also more refined distinctions about various levels of contingency. These more refined distinctions need to be made, of course, because within the realm of contingent outcomes the *degree* of contingency can vary widely, for example, from the extremely low level at which presidential election outcomes are contingent on each individual voter's behavior, to the extremely high level at which the volume of a stereo is contingent on the behavior of the individual whose hand is on the control knob.

Competence

Although event contingency has sometimes been treated as virtually synonymous with control in the psychological literature, an additional factor may need to be considered before an individual's level of control can be gauged accurately. We label that factor *competence*, and we define it as the individual's capacity to manifest the behavior on which the intended event is contingent. For events that are completely noncontingent, competence plays no role; one cannot be competent at, say, roulette or weather. However, for events that involve some degree of contingency, an individual's level of competence with respect to relevant behavior will determine the degree to which personal control can be manifest. (Whether the individual *will* exert control, and whether the individual experiences a subjective perception of control, also depends on the individual's probability of action, which may involve questions of motivation and values [Skinner, 1985]; but these matters do not concern us here because our discussion is focused on the individual's *capacity* to exert control.)

The Interplay of Contingency and Competence

I am suggesting (building on an earlier analysis, in Weisz & Stipek, 1982) that contingency and competence both need to be assessed if we are to judge accurately an individual's capacity to exert control. Contingency refers to the extent to which human attributes and behavior can influence an intended event; competence refers to the degree to which a particular individual can manifest the relevant attributes and behavior. Control is thus construed as a joint function of contingency and competence. The nature of this "joint function" is discussed in a later section.

Similar Notions From Other Control Theories

The notion that two factors such as contingency and competence are relevant to control achieves a kind of rough harmony with several other theoretical perspectives. Some of these perspectives are identified in Table 4.1.

None of the contrasts noted in the table maps perfectly onto the present distinction between contingency and competence. However, the rough convergence of these various perspectives suggests that a number of people who have thought about these matters believe that an understanding of control will require an understanding of (a) the susceptibility of intended events to human influence, and (b) the capacity of the individual to manifest the forms of behavior that are relevant.

TABLE 4.1
Conceptual Distinctions Similar to Contingency Versus
Competence

Control Theorists	Contingency-Related Concepts	Competence-Related Concepts
1. Crandall (1971)	Relationship between own behavior and unpleasant event	Competence to prevent failure
2. Bandura (1977)	Responsiveness of the environment	Efficacy in achieving the required behavior
3. Abramson et al. (1978)	Universal helplessness (i.e., no one's responses can produce the desired outcome)	Personal helplessness (i.e., others can generate the response needed to produce the desired outcome, but I cannot)
4. Gurin (1980)	Environmental responsiveness	Personal competence
5. Brim (1980)	Action-outcome expectancy	Sense of self-confidence
6. Skinner & Chapman (1983)	Causality beliefs	Agency beliefs

A Research Agenda

Much of the preceding discussion has focused on the question of the elements needed to make an *accurate* judgment about control. Such a discussion leads, quite naturally, to some potentially important empirical questions about the ways people actually do tend to make subjective judgments about control. These questions can be organized into an agenda for research on the developing person's developing understanding of control. The agenda involves a focus on three cognitive processes:

1. *Contingency judgment:* Judging the degree to which intended events are contingent upon variations in people's attributes and behavior.
2. *Competence judgment:* Judging the capacity of individuals to manifest attributes or behaviors on which intended outcomes are contingent.
3. *Integrating contingency and competence information:* Combining information about outcome contingency and personal competence in a manner that leads to judgments about control.

I summarize some of the developmental work done in these three areas. Then I turn to research on clinical correlates.

CONTROL-RELATED BELIEFS I: CONTINGENCY

In studying contingency beliefs, or contingency judgment, it is possible to focus on circumstances in which a variety of animate or situational factors limit actual contingency (e.g., Alloy & Abramson, 1979) or on conditions in which actual contingency is limited by chance or random factors (e.g., Langer, 1975). The research I discuss here deals with the second situation.

A Theoretical Perspective

Our thinking about chance-based noncontingency has profited considerably from the theoretical work of Piaget and his colleagues, particularly Barbel Inhelder (see, e.g., Piaget, 1930; Piaget & Inhelder, 1975). Their account depicts development as partly a process of dispensing with exaggerated perceptions of contingency through a stage-like developmental sequence. Experiments bearing on Piaget and Inhelder's notions have dealt primarily with probability concepts (e.g., Fischbein, 1975; Piaget & Inhelder, 1975). However, the Piagetian theorizing also seems related to the subject of interest here: Age differences in judgments about contingency between intended events on the one hand, and variations in people's attributes and behavior, on the other (see a relevant review by Sedlack & Kurtz, 1981).

Studies of Contingency Judgment

We carried out three studies of age differences in contingency judgment. In each study, we asked children to make judgments about totally noncontingent events. The questions were designed to assess whether the children accurately perceived the noncontingency of the events. For example, in one study (Weisz, 1980), children drew a card blindly from a deck; half the cards had a blue spot on the blind side, half had a yellow spot. Suppose the object is to draw a card that has a blue spot. Because the draw was completely blind, the outcome was entirely noncontingent. To determine whether children could detect this fact, we asked them to predict the level of success (e.g., how many blue spots out of five tries) that would be achieved by other children who differed in attributes or behavior that would be relevant to contingent outcomes but not noncontingent ones. For example, children predicted the likely winnings of "a smart kid" and one who was "not very smart," an older and a younger kid, and a kid who "got to practice lots of times before trying" and a kid who had no practice.

To illustrate the rationale for this and other studies on this topic, let us consider the familiar aphorism, "Practice makes perfect." A moment's thought reveals that the aphorism could only apply to contingent events. No amount of practice could make for perfect—or even improved—performance on activities involving totally noncontingent outcomes. Thus, if individuals are asked to predict the winnings (out of five tries) of a player who had practice and one who did not, a perception that the task is totally noncontingent should be reflected in predictions that practiced and unpracticed players will have equal winnings. Perceived contingency would be reflected by predictions that differ for practiced versus unpracticed players.

A primary finding of our studies can be summarized rather simply: Prediction patterns associated with perceived contingency were very common when children were confronted with *noncontingent* tasks. On the card task, with totally noncontingent outcomes, children in both kindergarten and fourth grade predicted that outcomes would be better for older than for younger players, better for smarter players than for those who were not very smart, better for those who tried hard than for those who did not, and better for those who practiced than for those who did not. Such predictions were almost universal among our kindergarten sample. Fourth graders were less likely to make such predictions than were kindergarteners, but perceived contingency responses still outnumbered perceived noncontingency responses even in this older group. Interestingly, such perceived contingency errors were common even among youngsters who explicitly identified outcomes as being determined by chance or "luck;" of the 17 children who made this identification, 16 made the perceived contingency error in at least one set of predictions. Similar results emerged from a second study (Weisz, 1981) in which youngsters (aged 6–10 and 11–14) made predictions about games of chance that they had just attempted at a state fair. In both studies, older subjects were slightly better than younger ones at recognizing noncontingency when they saw it, but illusory contingency was quite evident in both younger and older age groups.

The most complete picture of age trends emerged from a study in which we sampled kindergarteners, fourth graders, eighth graders, and college students (Weisz, Yeates, Robertson, & Beckham, 1982). Subjects at all four age levels were given the noncontingent card task just described and a skill version of the same task—a version in which memory and concentration could be used to determine which cards had a blue spot. We asked subjects to predict outcomes on both tasks, for players differing in age, intelligence, effort, and practice. With increasing age our subjects were increasingly likely to converge toward perceived noncontingency on the chance task but not on the still task. (But for an exception to this trend, see Weisz et al., 1982.)

One other important aspect of the findings should be noted: Despite age trends in the appropriate direction, a very substantial number of even the oldest subjects made errors in judging contingency. Suppose we classify as "logical" all those prediction patterns in which equal outcomes were predicted for players of differing attributes (e.g., smart vs. not smart) on the chance task, but different outcomes were predicted on the skill task. Suppose further that we omit predictions for the "older versus younger player" because of the problem noted in the preceding paragraph. Across the three remaining paired predictions, the mean percentage of logical prediction patterns was 0% for kindergarteners, 7% for fourth graders, 53% for eighth graders, and 53% for college students. This trend, like our other findings, suggests that whatever developmental differences in contingency reasoning were to be found in our sample were evident by early adolescence; no differences were evident between our eighth graders and our college students. Overall, the findings suggest that there are substantial gains in contingency reasoning as youngsters move into adolescence, but that errors in contingency judgment are quite prevalent even among college students.

CONTROL-RELATED BELIEFS II: COMPETENCE

We turn now to the development of competence beliefs and competence judgment. I touch lightly on the area; readers seeking more information on theory and evidence in the area would do well to see Harter (1982, 1983).

A Theoretical Perspective

Most of the theories bearing on the development of perceived competence appear to generate similar developmental predictions (see even the early hypothesis of Freud, 1957, and Piaget, 1960). Nicholls (1978, 1979), for example, suggested that the ability to assess one's competence relative to that of other persons requires (a) the ability to perform seriation, (b) the capacity to see one's performance and position from a detached perspective, and (c) the ability to relate temporally separate outcomes to one another. These abilities only emerge with development, and are evidently only consolidated during the elementary school years. For a different set of reasons, Bandura (1982) also suggested that "self-efficacy" estimates will grow more modest and more accurate through the childhood years.

Developmental Differences in the Magnitude and Accuracy of Competence Judgments

Thus far, cross-sectional evidence from the period of early through late childhood certainly suggests that levels of perceived competence grow increasingly modest with development. My first encounter with developmental differences of this sort came in unpublished parts of two studies of hypothesis-testing behavior (Weisz, 1977; Weisz & Achenbach, 1975). In both studies, children ranging in mental age from 5½ to 9½ years took part in a concept formation task in which prearranged feedback insured that all received exactly the same level of "success." The only competence-related differences in these studies involved children's use of hypotheses and strategies, and these differences, of course, showed the older children to be more competent. After completing "the game," each child was asked to move a sliding arrow along a scale to indicate how good he or she was at the game, "compared to other kids in your school." A rating at the top of the scale was said to mean "the best in your school." In both studies, there was a highly significant decline in self-ratings with increasing mental age. Children at the lowest mental age level gave themselves ratings near the top of the scale, whereas children at the upper mental age levels placed themselves about three fourths of the way up the scale, on the average. Developmental trends in magnitude of self-assessed competence within such noncognitive domains as sociometric status (Ausubel, Schiff, & Gasser, 1952) and physical strength (Goss, 1968) resemble the age-related declines found with the problem-solving tasks just described.

Nicholls (1978) collected self-ratings of competence more broadly defined than in the case of the preceding studies. He focused on children's assessments of their general reading ability. Nicholls showed children aged 5 through 13 an array of 30 line drawings of faces, arranged vertically on a sheet of paper. He told the subjects that these faces represented a rank ordering, with the top face representing the best reader in their class. He then asked the children, "Now, can you show me how good you are at reading? Which one is you?" Nicholls found that children's self-rated competence grew generally more modest as their age level increased. In fact, the mean rating of 13-year-olds was 15, precisely the mean that would be obtained if all children rated themselves accurately. To assess accuracy more directly, Nicholls calculated correlations between the 7- to 13-year-olds' own self-ratings and teacher ratings of the children's reading competence (no teacher ratings available for 5- and 6-year-olds). Self-ratings of children younger than 9 did not correlate significantly with teacher ratings; from age 9 onward, however, all teacher–child correlations were significant, and the correlations for 12- and 13-year-olds were remarkably high. The general direction of Nicholls' (1978) findings is roughly consistent with developmental trends found in studies of self-assessed strength (Goss, 1968), toughness (Freedman, 1975), social characteristics (Phillips, 1963), and sociometric status (Ausubel et al., 1952; for partially conflicting findings, see Harter, 1982).

A good deal has been written about the *determinants* of development in this area. Some of the research on this issue has been guided by theoretical perspectives like those of Nicholls (1978, 1979), who has attempted to identify specific cognitive activities necessary for accurate self-assessment. As noted earlier, Nicholls (1978) stressed the importance of the ability to seriate, to take a perspective outside of oneself, and to relate temporally separate outcomes to one another. More recently, Nicholls and Miller (1984) have focused on the role of developmental changes in the child's concept of ability. Ruble and her colleagues (e.g., Ruble, Boggiano, Feldman, & Loebl, 1980) have focused on developmental changes in social comparison processes. Taking a different tack, Stipek and her colleagues (e.g., Stipek, 1981, 1984; Stipek & Hoffman, 1980a, 1980b) have examined the role of developmental declines in cognitive egocentrism and in young children's tendency to confuse their desires (e.g., to be "the best") with reality. And Kun (1977) has described the tendency of younger children to use reasoning schemes with respect to ability that are the epitome of illogic from an adult perspective.

The overall impression that emerges from much of the literature in this area is that as in the case of contingency reasoning, certain cognitive developmental milestones may need to be attained in order to establish baseline conditions for accurate competence judgment. These cognitive developments, at least some of which seem to be in place by middle to late childhood, are apt to be necessary but not sufficient conditions for veridical judgment. Once the milestones have been attained, individual variations in veridicality may well be determined largely by a broad array of factors that are not, strictly speaking, cognitive–developmental in nature—factors so diverse as to include social stereotypes, vicarious experience (Bandura, 1977), susceptibility to beneffectance (Greenwald, 1980), and even affective state (Lewinsohn, Mischel, Chaplin, & Barton, 1980).

CONTROL-RELATED BELIEFS III: INTEGRATING CONTINGENCY AND COMPETENCE INFORMATION

Thus far I have argued that actual control is a function of contingency and competence, and that a veridical control judgment requires accurate information about both. Our discussion has focused on age differences in the ability to generate such information. Another important element in the research agenda is the study of how contingency and competence judgments relate to one another, and to judgments about control. Work in this domain is not central to the topic of this chapter, so I do not devote much space to it here. Interested readers may want to see a discussion of this work in Weisz (1986b).

Contingency, Competence, and Control Judgments by Children, Adolescents, and Young Adults

One of the few inquiries I have made into relations among contingency, competence, and control judgments was a study carried out during the mid-1980s, when the Pac Man video game craze swept the country (study described in Weisz, 1986b). Pac Man seemed an appropriate focus for the study because it was being played by people across a broad age range, its rules were identical for all ages, and it seemed to involve a combination of controllable (skill) and uncontrollable (chance) elements. The study focused on children (aged 6–10), adolescents (12–16), and young adults (18–25), all of whom had previously played Pac Man. All were interviewed about their control-related beliefs with respect to the game. The questions, all involving a 7-point Likert scale, included the following (plus comprehension checks that are not discussed here):

1. In Pac Man, how much does getting points depend on the players and what they do? (contingency)
2. How good do you think you are at Pac Man? (competence)
3. How much control do you have over getting points when you play Pac Man? (control)

We computed correlations among the ratings separately for the three age groups. The resulting coefficients, shown in Table 4.2, show that control ratings were significantly related to both the perceived contingency of the Pac Man game and the perceived competence of the inter-

TABLE 4.2
Pac Man Correlation Coefficients for Three Age Groups

	Age	Experience	Contingency	Competence	Control
			Ages 6–10 (N = 51)		
Experience	−.092				
Contingency	.022	−.117			
Competence	−.293*	.203	.469***		
Control	−.165	.022	.299*	.493***	
			Ages 12–16 (N = 44)		
Experience	.253				
Contingency	.102	.113			
Competence	−.098	.424**	.185		
Control	.013	.053	.645***	.482***	
			Ages 18–25 (N = 50)		
Experience	−.049				
Contingency	.018	.178			
Competence	.169	.229	.155		
Control	.073	.203	.346*	.579***	

*$p < .05$; **$p < .01$; ***$p < .001$

viewees, at all three age levels. The table reveals one other finding of interest: Among the youngest group only, contingency and competence ratings were significantly correlated. This suggests that the two concepts may not have been entirely distinguished from one another by the children in the youngest group, or possibly that these children were susceptible to a sort of "halo effect" in which high competence implies high contingency.

One other question was asked of the Pac Man data: Did the control judgments of subjects at any of the age levels appear to reflect contingency and competence information used in combination? One way to pose the question is to ask whether contingency and competence information together accounted for more of the variance in perceived control than did either factor alone. To find out, I squared the Pearson rs between contingency and control and between competence and control, then compared these r^2 values to the R^2 obtained by squaring the multiple correlation linking control to contingency and competence combined. The results showed that for both older groups, but not for the 6- to 11-year-olds, perceived control was better predicted by the combination of perceived contingency and perceived competence than by either factor alone. This is consistent with the notion that adolescents and young adults, but not children, use both the contingency and competence dimensions in reaching control judgments. The findings cannot be interpreted unambiguously, however; they are likely to have been due, in part, to the fact that perceived contingency and competence were correlated with one another at the youngest age level but uncorrelated at the two older levels.

In the future, researchers could contribute substantially to our understanding by addressing more directly the question of how (or whether) people at various ages use contingency and competence information to arrive at judgments about control. For example, respondents might be presented with various combinations of contingency and competence information regarding specific tasks, then asked to generate assessments of the prospects for control over task outcomes. As a possible stimulus for such work, I offer a heuristic model.

A Heuristic Theoretical Model

Figure 4.1 shows an idealized heuristic model for how contingency and competence information might be used by a logical person to form control judgments. The model, which involves additive effects of contingency and competence, certainly reflects only one of several possible ways the two kinds of information might be combined. To illustrate the process

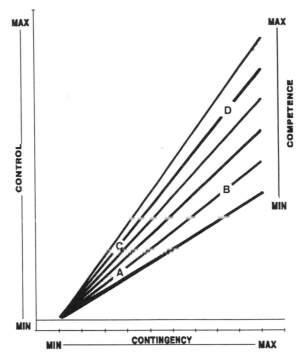

FIG. 4.1   A heuristic model for relations between perceived contingency and perceived competence, on the one hand, and perceived control, on the other.

represented in the model, suppose we imagine four possible situations for Alli in the social control dilemma outlined at the beginning of the chapter. In the situation marked A in the figure, the outcome Alli desires (i.e., entry into the high-status group) is not very contingent on the behavior of people like Alli; being witty and socially skilled may help a little, but not much, since group entry is largely reserved for children of wealthy and prominent families. Moreover, as A shows, Alli is not even very competent at the socially skilled behavior that *is slightly* relevant to group entry. In Situation B, group entry is highly contingent on socially skilled behavior, but Alli has the same low level of competence as in A. In C, Alli is very competent socially, but group entry is not very contingent for people like her. Finally, in D, group entry is highly contingent, and Alli is very competent. The multiplicative model shown in the figure generates the view that actual control will be lowest in situation A and highest in D. But what about judged control? Do people actually gauge control in a manner resembling either model? And do these judgmental processes differ with age? We have very little evidence on these questions.

Researchers could make a very useful contribution by tackling these questions directly.

CONTROL-RELATED BELIEFS IV: CLINICAL CORRELATES

We turn now to the question of clinical implications. Do beliefs about outcome contingency, personal competence, or one's prospects for control have significant correlates in the realm of mental health? My fellow researchers and I have recently begun to address this question, focusing on two kinds of mental health issues: child and adolescent depression and the effects of psychotherapy with children and adolescents.

Control-Related Beliefs and Child Depression

Are control-related beliefs involved in depression? Several theories of depression hold that the answer is yes. And research with adults has generated at least moderate support for the idea (see, e.g., Coyne & Gotlib, 1983; Peterson & Seligman, 1984). However, research with children (including adolescents) is not yet substantial enough to warrant conclusions. Depressed youngsters have been found to be more likely than their nondepressed peers to show self-blame for negative events (Moyal, 1977; Seligman et al., 1984); low self-esteem and negative self-assessments (Haley, Fine, Marriage, Moretti, & Freeman, 1985); a depressive attributional style that includes internal, stable, and global attributions for failure (Kaslow, Rehm, & Siegel, 1984; Seligman et al., 1984); and hopelessness regarding the future (Kazdin, French, Unis, Esveldt-Dawson, & Sherick, 1983). These findings suggest, indirectly, that depressed children may indeed perceive themselves as lacking in control. In more direct evidence, Moyal (1977) found that depressive symptoms were correlated with external locus of control among normal school children.

Such findings suggest that child depression may be negatively related to perceived control, construed globally. However, efforts to understand the etiology and dynamics of child depression, and to develop effective treatment strategies may require information about which *dimensions* of perceived control are most closely linked to child depression. This is a question that can be addressed from the perspective of the two-dimensional (contingency × competence) model previously detailed.

The two-dimensional model is particularly relevant to the reformulated learned helplessness model (Abramson et al., 1978), which focuses on control-related beliefs associated with depression. The reformulation distinguishes between *universal* and *personal* helplessness. In universal helplessness, perceived lack of control is attributed to a general noncontingency. Attributions are made to factors which are beyond the control of individuals like oneself—factors such as fate or luck. Individuals believe that neither they nor relevant others can exert control because outcomes occur noncontingently. By contrast, personal helplessness results when lack of control is attributed to factors inhering in the individual—factors such as inadequate ability. One's own actions are perceived as futile, but the individual believes that relevant others (e.g., "other kids") could be effective in the same situation (i.e., that others have the competence that is lacking in oneself). Thus, the kind of depression that involves universal helplessness appears to be associated with low levels of perceived contingency, and the kind of depression involving personal helplessness appears to be associated with low levels of perceived personal competence (see Weisz, 1986b; Weisz, Weiss, Wasserman, & Rintoul, 1987).

Given the apparent importance of perceived contingency and perceived competence to depression in theory, it seems appropriate to ask how the two are related to depression empirically. We have carried out three correlational studies designed to explore relations between these control-related beliefs and child depression. The three studies were similar in design, but different in the nature of their samples. The first involved a general sample of nonclinic, school-aged children; the second, samples from outpatient mental health clinics; the third, samples from inpatient mental health clinics.

Control-Related Beliefs and Depression in a General Population Sample. In one of the studies (Rintoul & Weisz, 1989), a self-report depression inventory and control-related belief measures were administered to a sample of fourth- through seventh-grade children. Children completed the Children's Depression Inventory (CDI; Kovacs & Beck, 1977) and a Perceived Contingency Scale for Children (Sample item: "Kids who do their work well get good grades"). To assess perceived competence, we administered Harter's (1985) Self-Perception Profile for Children. Finally, following Connell (1985), we administered a series of Contingency Unknown Probes (Sample item: "When other kids like me, a lot of times I can't figure out why." Correlations among the various scales are shown in Table 4.3. As the last column of the table shows, CDI scores were significantly correlated, and in plausible directions, with each measure except uncertainty about contingencies for failure.

Because some of the control-belief measures were correlated with one another, we carried out a stepwise multiple regression analysis, predicting

TABLE 4.3
Correlations Among Control Beliefs and Depression

	Cntg	Unc Pos	Unc Neg	CDI
Competence	.23*	−.37***	−.13	−.57***
	(n=191)	(n=188)	(n=188)	(n=190)
Contingency	—	−.24**	.13	−.26**
		(n=193)	(n=193)	(n=195)
Uncertain Positive	—	—	.12	.36***
			(n=193)	(n=192)
Uncertain Negative	—	—	—	.15
				(n=192)

*p < .01; **p < .001; ***p < .0001

children's depression scores from the three significant CDI correlates shown in the table: perceived competence, perceived contingency, and contingency unknown for success. We found that total perceived competence accounted for 32% of the variance in depression ($p < 0.0001$), and unknown success accounted for an additional 2% ($p = 0.01$). Perceived contingency did not add significantly to the model. Here and elsewhere where we report percentages of variance accounted for, a word of caution is in order. If one predictor variable, A, is better measured (i.e., contains less measurement error) than another, B, then (all other things being equal) A is apt to account for more variance in the criterion variable than will B. In other words, relative proportions of variance accounted for by two or more variables reflect more than simply the relative strength of relations between those variables and the criterion variable.

The findings among these school children suggested that depression in a nonclinic sample may be linked to some control-related beliefs but not to others. Perceived competence did appear to be related to child depression; but an apparent relationship between perceived noncontingency and depression appeared to be only an artifact of its covariance with perceived competence. When considered from the perspective of the reformulated learned helplessness theory, the findings suggest the possibility that child depression may be linked to "personal helplessness" but not to "universal helplessness."

One additional finding may prove to be important: Self-reported depression, although not related to perceived noncontingency, was related to reports that the causes of success were unknown. This suggests the possibility that child depression may not be so much related to a perception of *non*contingency as to a kind of *contingency uncertainty*.

Control-Related Beliefs and Depression in Outpatient and Inpatient Children. This possibility was explored further in two additional studies.

One of these (Weisz, Weiss, Wasserman & Rintoul, 1987) focused on three samples of youngsters aged 8–17 (with diverse diagnoses) who had been referred for treatment in outpatient mental health clinics. In the other study (Weisz, Stephens et al., 1989) we focused on three samples aged 8–17 (again with diverse diagnoses) from separate inpatient clinics. In both studies, we administered the CDI and Connell's (1985) Multidimensional Measure of Children's Perceptions of Control (MMCPC; it includes scales for "unknown success" and "unknown failure"). In addition, we administered Contingency, Competence, and Control (CCC) Probes designed to tap those three categories of control-related beliefs specifically with regard to solving problems at home and at school (because such problems were the cause of clinic referral for these youngsters).

Table 4.4 shows correlations of the various control-related belief measures with CDI scores in the three outpatient samples. As the table indicates, perceived contingency was not correlated with depression in any of the three samples. By contrast, in all three samples, perceived

TABLE 4.4
Control Belief Measures as Correlates of CDI Scores for Three
Outpatient Samples

	Sample A (N=77)	Sample B (N=57)	Sample C (N=52)
CCC Probes			
Contingency	−.11	−.14	−.27
Competence	−.38***	−.39**	−.29*
Control	−.32**	−.42***	−.38**
MMCPC Measures			
Internal success	−.41***	−.27*	−.41***
Internal failure	.19	−.04	.25
Other success	.23	.23	.23
Other failure	.34**	.12	.15
Unknown success	.31**	.34**	.37**
Unknown failure	.25*	.38**	.32*
Demographic Variables			
Age	.08	−.04	−.10
Sex[a]	.18	−.02	−.11

Note: CDI = Children's Depression; MMCPC = Multidimensional Measure of Children's Perceptions of Control

[a]Point-biserial correlation coefficients; 1 = male, 2 = female

*p < .05; **p < .01; ***p < .001

competence, perceived control, and internal attributions for success (on the MMCPC) were all negatively correlated with depression; and unknown success and failure were both positively correlated with depression.

We carried out three separate regression analyses, one for each sample, entering the five robust (i.e., significant across all three samples) correlates of CDI scores just listed as predictors of CDI. Only one predictor made significant contributions to the prediction of depression scores: perceived competence from the CCC Probes. In two of the samples, competence was joined by internal success; together the two predictors accounted for 23% of the variance in depression in one sample, and 28% in the other. In the third sample, competence was joined by perceived control and unknown failure, and together the three predictors accounted for 27% of the variance in depression.

Table 4.5 shows the correlations between the CDI scores and the various control-related belief scales, for the three inpatient samples. As the table reveals, only three of the belief scores were significantly correlated with depression across all three samples: perceived competence, perceived control, and unknown success. In multiple regression analyses, we entered the three robust correlates as predictors of CDI scores. As in

TABLE 4.5
Control Belief and Demographic Measures as Correlates of CDI
Scores for Three Inpatient Samples

	Sample A (N=70)	Sample B (N=76)	Sample C (N=37)
CCC Probe Measures			
Contingency	−.32**	−.33**	−.31
Competence	−.37**	−.48***	−.62***
Control	−.38***	−.66***	−.59***
MMCPC Measures			
Internal success	−.26	−.39***	−.58***
Internal failure	−.04	−.09	.13
Other success	.20	−.02	.08
Other failure	.26*	.16	.03
Unknown success	.44***	.39***	.54***
Unknown failure	.40***	.09	.34*
Demographic Variables			
Age	−.36**	−.17	.15
Sex[a]	.08	.03	.02

[a]Point-biserial correlation coefficients; 1 = male, 2 = female
*$p < 0.05$; **$p < 0.01$; ***$p < 0.001$

the outpatient study, the only predictor that contributed significantly in all three samples was perceived competence. In one sample, competence was joined by unknown success, and the two predictors accounted for 24% of the variance in depression. In a second sample, competence was joined by perceived control and unknown success, and the three predictors together accounted for 49% of the variance in depression. In the third sample, competence was joined by perceived control, and the two predictors accounted for 49% of the variance in depression.

In both the out- and inpatient studies, we tested whether the relates of depression were different at different ages. In both studies, we found that the relationships between CDI scores and the robust predictors remained significant with age (and sex) controlled.

Trends Across the Three Studies. Findings from the three depression studies show some interesting similarities. Low-perceived competence emerged as a significant correlate of depression across all seven samples of the three studies; perceived competence was also the only predictor of depression to contribute significantly in all seven multiple regression analyses. Perceived contingency, by contrast, showed little relationship to depression. As previously suggested, when these findings are considered from the perspective of reformulated learned helplessness theory, they suggest the possibility that child depression may be linked to "personal helplessness" but not to "universal helplessness." If true, this would have important implications for our understanding of the dynamics of childhood depression. It would suggest one potentially important distinction between the kinds of depression experienced by children and adolescents and the kinds that have been posited for adults (Abramson et al., 1978).

Another recurrent finding is the linkage between children's self-reported depression and uncertainty about the causes of their successes and/or failures. It may be that child depression is not so much a matter of believing that events are noncontingent (see Seligman, 1975) as of being unable to identify the contingencies associated with events. If this is the case, it might follow that clinical intervention with depressed youngsters will need to include efforts to help them clarify the contingencies associated with important outcomes in their lives, and even to identify those areas in which outcomes are in fact relatively noncontingent. Our data suggest that believing that outcomes are noncontingent is not nearly so likely to be associated with depression as is being uncertain about contingencies.

Control-Related Beliefs and Action: Psychotherapy Outcomes

The studies just reviewed failed to find a central role for perceived contingency in child depression. However, another study (Weisz, 1986a) in another domain, has found a potentially important correlate of perceived contingency in the clinical realm: Improvement during psychotherapy. Several lines of theory suggest that such control-related beliefs can mediate goal-directed action (see, e.g., Bandura, 1977; Chapman & Skinner, 1985a, 1985b; Dweck & Elliot, 1983). Causal analyses have indicated that perceived control can stimulate academic achievement (Calsyn, 1973; Stipek, 1980). Such theory and findings suggest the possibility that children's beliefs about the controllability of their problems may mediate their achievements during therapy for those problems. This may be especially true for children and adolescents (relative to adults), because they rarely refer themselves for therapy. Thus, any group of clinic-referred children is likely to include some youngsters who harbor serious doubts, or outright disbelief, that their problems can be controlled. Such youngsters may well show less effective problem resolution during therapy than children who perceive their problems as controllable. Thus, individual differences in control beliefs might be evidenced by differential rates of change in problem behavior during therapy, as children invest levels of energy in the therapeutic process commensurate with their beliefs about the controllability of their problems.

To explore this possibility, I arranged (Weisz, 1986a) for a sample of clinic-referred 8- to 17-year-olds to complete the CCC Probes at the time of their admission to outpatient therapy. As noted earlier, the Probes focused on the youngsters' contingency, competence, and control beliefs with respect to solving problems at home and at school. Children's actual problems at home and at school were assessed via parent reports on the Child Behavior Checklist at the outset of therapy, and then again 6 months later, when all the youngsters had completed therapy.

The results showed that improvement in the youngsters' total problem behavior over the 6 months spanned by the study was significantly correlated with their contingency beliefs ($r = 0.48$) and their control beliefs ($r = 0.41$), but not by their competence beliefs ($r = 0.07$). When contingency and control beliefs were entered into a regression equation, both contributed significantly to the prediction of improvement. Contingency was the strongest predictor, control added significantly to the prediction, and together the two predictors accounted for 26% of the variance in improvement scores.

One additional finding may prove to be important. As in the depression studies, I assessed whether findings for the sample as a whole were influenced by age of the youngsters. The only age effect indicated that competence beliefs, although not predicting significantly for the sample as a whole, did in fact predict improvement significantly for adolescents (ages 12–17; $r = 0.53$). This finding is reminiscent of Nicholls and Miller's (1984) development analysis of children's concepts of ability or competence. Those authors reported that children aged 7–9 are not likely to construe ability as capacity or to recognize it as a likely cause of outcomes. By ages 10–11, children have begun to construe ability as capacity, but they do not yet understand how levels of ability influence the likelihood of various outcomes. According to the Nicholls–Miller data, many children do not begin to reason about ability or competence in relatively adult-like ways until about age 12. Their data suggest an intriguing possibility relevant to the psychotherapy outcome data: Age differences in the predictive power of competence judgments may reflect developmental differences in children's understanding of competence and its implications.

The link between control-related beliefs (particularly perceived contingency and perceived control) may prove especially important in the realm of child psychotherapy. Because children rarely volunteer for therapy, they cannot be assumed to believe in its efficacy or in the controllability of their problems that stimulated the therapy. Consequently, there may be considerable variability in the control-related beliefs of any collection of children referred for therapy. The findings of the study suggest that this variability may provide some power in the prediction of therapeutic gains. The findings also suggest, indirectly, that there may be some value in making children's beliefs about the contingency and controllability of their problems a focus of the therapeutic process. Indeed, some researchers are already exploring the modifiability of control beliefs during child therapy (Omizo & Cubberly, 1984; Porter & Omizo, 1984). The study just reported suggests that such modification, if appropriately targeted, might enhance the prospect of therapeutic gains.

CONTROL-RELATED GOALS:
PRIMARY, SECONDARY, AND RELINQUISHED CONTROL

Thus far, we have focused on control-related beliefs and some of their clinical implications. We turn now to a less conventional perspective on control, one that several of us are now trying to nurture into empirical respectability, but that is still too embryonic to have stimulated much research to date. This embryonic perspective is the two-process model of control recently detailed by Rothbaum, Weisz, and Snyder (1982) and Weisz, Rothbaum, and Blackburn (1984a, 1984b).

Primary and Secondary Control

According to the model, there are two broad processes by which individuals may seek a sense of control. Individuals may pursue control by (a) attempting to change objective conditions so as to bring them into line with their wishes (a more or less traditional definition of control), or by (b) attempting to accommodate to objective conditions in order to effect a more satisfying fit with those conditions, and control their psychological impact. These two processes have been labeled *primary control* and *secondary control*, respectively. The two processes are described in overview form in Table 4.6. (For related perspectives, see Lazarus & Folkman, 1984, and Pearlin & Schooler, 1978.) Note that both primary and secondary control conform to the provisional definition given at the beginning of this chapter—that is, control means causing an intended event. In primary control, the intended event is some modification of objective conditions; in secondary control, the intended event is some modification of one's orientation toward those conditions—that is, internal change that affords control over the impact of objective conditions on the self while leaving those conditions unchanged.

According to our model, both primary and secondary control can assume varied forms. Some examples are shown in Table 4.7. As the table indicates, people may try to predict accurately, align themselves with powerful others, get into harmony with fate or chance, or interpret events, for reasons that we regard as reflecting primary control or for reasons we regard as reflecting secondary control. Thus assessing the reasons or goals underlying an individual's behavior is a crucial step in judging whether the behavior reflects a pursuit of primary or secondary control, or whether it actually represents relinquished control. This makes the assessment of primary, secondary, and relinquished control particularly difficult, because it means that reliable and valid classification will be difficult to achieve via direct observations or reports of behavior alone.

These difficulties notwithstanding, efforts to operationally define primary and secondary control may yet prove worthwhile. The two-process model may possibly have useful applications to the study of children's

TABLE 4.6
Primary and Secondary Control: An Overview
(Adapted from Weisz, Rothbaum, & Blackburn, 1984)

Type of Control and General Strategy	Typical Targets for Causal Influence	Overall Objective
Primary (influence objective conditions)	People, objects, events, circumstances, symptoms, problems	Enhance reward (or reduce punishment) by modifying objective conditions to fit self
Secondary (accommodate to objective conditions so as to influence their impact on self)	One's own expectations, wishes, goals, perceptions, attitudes	Enhance reward (or reduce punishment) by modifying oneself to fit objective conditions as they are

TABLE 4.7
Types of Primary and Secondary Control

Type of Control	Process	Description
Predictive	Primary	Attempts to accurately predict events and conditions so as to select strategies that are most likely to make objective conditions fit the self's needs, wishes, goals, etc.
	Secondary	Attempts to accurately predict events and conditions so as to control their impact on the self (e.g., to avoid uncertainty, anxiety, or future disappointment).
Illusory	Primary	Attempts to influence or capitalize on chance, so as to increase the likelihood that fate will fit one's needs, wishes, goals, etc. (e.g., riding a lucky streak).
	Secondary	Attempts to associate or "get into synchrony" with chance, so as to enhance comfort with and acceptance of one's fate.
Vicarious	Primary	Attempts to emulate the behavior, values, etc. of powerful individuals, groups, or institutions, so as to influence objective conditions as they do.
	Secondary	Attempts to associate or closely align oneself with other individuals, groups, or institutions, so as to share psychologically in the control they exert.
Interpretive	Primary	Attempts to understand or construe objective conditions so as to master them (e.g., figuring out the nature of a problem in order to solve it).
	Secondary	Attempts to understand or construe objective conditions so as to derive a sense of meaning or "purpose" from them, and thus enhance one's satisfaction with them.
Selective Attention	Primary	Attempts to focus attention on elements of a problem, so as to solve it.
	Secondary	Attempts to focus attention away from a problem area, so as to avoid or minimize the unpleasant thoughts and feelings associated with it.

stress coping behavior. We focus now on two studies that illustrate this possibility.

Control-Related Goals in a General Population Sample: Stress Coping

In one of these studies (Brotman-Band & Weisz, 1988), a semi-structured interview was used. The interviewer asked 6-, 9-, and 12-year-old children to describe stressful episodes they had experienced and their behavior and goals during those episodes. To enhance comparability of the situations, we asked children to focus on six domains of experience that previous literature suggested would be common to most children (e.g., "A time when another kid said mean things to you," and "Going to the doctor's office to get a shot"). We coded children's accounts of their behavior and goals in the various situations, using two layers of coding. The broadest layer involved coding for whether the goals the children articulated reflected primary, secondary, or relinquished control; independent coders achieved Kappas ranging from 0.82 to 0.91. The other layer (patterned after Lazarus & Folkman, 1984) involved coding the specific behaviors, or "ways of coping," the children described within each of the broad goal-oriented categories. For example, the broad primary control category included problem-focused aggression (e.g., hitting a child who has been teasing or taunting, to get him or her to stop), and the broad secondary control category included emotion-focused aggression (e.g., kicking a chair, after being embarrassed, just to let the feelings out); independent coders achieved Kappas ranging from 0.84 to 0.94 across the 10 ways of coping categories.

The findings are depicted in Fig. 4.2. A striking feature of our findings in preliminary analyses was the very low frequency of responses coded as relinquished control: 3.5%. Evidently, "giving up" was a rare response to stressful events in our sample (alternatively, it is a response to stress that children rarely remember, or are reluctant to report). One of our central findings was an overall age effect: Reports of secondary control coping (alone or in combination with primary control coping) increased

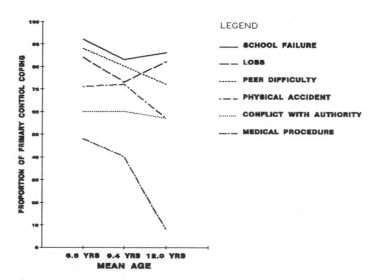

FIG. 4.2 Developmental differences in mean proportion of primary control coping in six situational contexts.

with age, whereas reports involving only the use of primary coping declined with age. Both age effects were accounted for by differences between 6-year-olds and the two older age groups (which did not differ from one another).

This main effect was qualified by an age × situation interaction: The age-related decline in exclusively primary control coping and increase in secondary control coping was accounted for primarily by responses in the medical stress situation (i.e., "getting a shot"). This makes good sense. In the medical situation, more than any of the others, primary control efforts (e.g., attempts to avoid going to the doctor's office, or avoid getting the shot once there) are not likely to be productive, whereas secondary control coping (e.g., thinking about a pet puppy to distract oneself from noticing the shot) may have beneficial effects. In the other five situations, there may often be very real adaptive advantages to the pursuit of primary control. Indeed, we also found a highly significant main effect of situation, with the school failure situation evoking high levels of primary coping, as contrasted with the medical situation that evoked high levels of secondary coping overall. (Readers interested in situational differences in coping styles among different groups of adults should see a thoughtful analysis of coping among 18- to 65-year-olds, carried out by Pearlin & Schooler, 1978.)

There may be adaptive advantages in the preference of our youngest subjects for primary control goals. When we had independent judges rate the likely effectiveness of the coping strategies described by each child for each situation, we found that among the 6-year-olds, but not among the two older groups, primary control coping strategies were rated as significantly more efficacious than secondary control strategies. In other words, children in our youngest group appeared to be better at generating effective primary control strategies. Thus, it could be argued that the tendency of 6-year-olds in our sample to rely on primary control goals was appropriate for them given the fact that the secondary control strategies they did generate were relatively ineffective.

Overall, our findings suggested that children's coping goals may be influenced by both situational constraints and developmental level. We suspect that secondary control responses may emerge somewhat later in development than primary control responses, and that this may be partly due to the relatively greater subtlety, indirectness, and unobservability of the secondary control objective. We return to these possibilities at the end of this section.

Control-Related Goals Among Children With Juvenile Diabetes

Eve Brotman-Band's (in press) dissertation built on the medical situation findings of Brotman-Band and Weisz (1988) by focusing on the control-related coping goals of children suffering from juvenile diabetes. This focus seems especially appropriate for a study of primary and secondary control coping goals. Children with juvenile diabetes are confronted with an array of adaptive challenges, some of which appear to call for primary control goals (e.g., regulating the disease by monitoring and controlling diet, administering insulin injections, etc.) and some of which appear to call for secondary control goals (e.g., accepting the unalterable fact that one has the disease and must live a different lifestyle than others who are not diabetic).

In an effort to differentiate different levels of cognitive development (not just age), Brotman-Band administered Piagetian tests to her diabetic subjects. She thus formed two groups: a formal operational group averaging 14 years of age, and a pre-formal group averaging 8 years. The two groups were taken through semi-structured interviews patterned after those used by Brotman-Band and Weisz (1988), but focused specifically on stressors and coping challenges associated with juvenile diabetes. Examples include having to eat differently from other kids, getting insulin shots, having a reaction to insulin or low blood sugar. The coding system was similar in form to that used by Brotman-Band and Weisz, with general categories for primary, secondary, and relinquished control coping goals, and fine-grained ways of coping categories within the general categories. However, relinquished control was rare, and the nonrelinquishing responses were ultimately coded along a 5-point scale reflecting the relative degree of primary versus secondary control reflected in the respondents' goals. A rating of "1" was assigned to responses reflecting only primary control goals, "3" reflected equal primary and secondary control, and "5" reflected all secondary control. (The interjudge Kappa for this system was 0.95.)

Using this 5-point scale, Brotman-Band found a highly significant difference between the two cognitive developmental level groups. The preformal group's coping scores (M = 1.53) reflected a much more exclusive reliance on primary control goals than did the formal operational group's scores (M = 2.60). Lest it be assumed that this was entirely good news for the parents of the formal operational group, I should note one other significant finding: Over the full sample, and particularly among the formal operational group, scores reflecting greater reliance on secondary control goals were associated with *poorer* physicians' ratings of medical adjustment. Evidently, extensive use of secondary control can be associated with reductions in appropriate primary control—such as strict adherence to an acceptable diet and the prescribed medical regimen. Thus, although the study revealed striking differences between the two cognitive developmental groups in self-reported alliance on primary versus secondary control goals, it also provided a reminder that either type of goal may be maladaptive in certain situations.

Age Trends Across the Two Studies, and Some Possible Reasons. Combining evidence across the two interview studies helps us to generate a preliminary picture of developmental trends with regard to primary, secondary, and relinquished control goals. Relinquished control goals seem rare at each of the age levels sampled. Most subjects at the age levels we have studied appear to favor some form of active coping in most of the stressful circumstances we have surveyed. Whether this active coping is aimed at primary or secondary control goals may be a function of both situation and the developmental level of the individuals involved. Our evidence suggests the possibility that secondary control goals may be more likely to be included among coping objectives (a) when the individuals doing the coping are relatively mature cognitively, (b) when the stressful situations involved place limits on the possibility of primary control, and (c) particularly when both a and b hold true. For example, all three of the interview studies showed developmental increments in self-reports of secondary control goals in medical situations where the prospects for primary control were limited.

Why might there be a developmental delay in the use of secondary control coping? Several possible explanations should be considered. It is possible that secondary control coping develops more slowly than primary control because it is more often hidden from view (e.g., in the form of cognitions) and thus more difficult to learn through observation of parents, siblings, peers, and others. It is also possible that secondary control results from efforts to provide some measure of control when primary control efforts have failed or are judged to be unworkable. If this is the case, then it may be that development is associated with increased use of secondary control because it is only with development that children come to appreciate the unworkability of the primary control attempts in some situations (e.g., the medical situations covered here). This would be consistent with some of the data reviewed earlier on illusions of controllability and contingency that appear to be harbored by children well into the elementary school years. Finally, it is possible that secondary control coping is more difficult to describe verbally than primary control coping, and that the developmental trends discussed here are artifacts of developmental increments in children's verbal facility. To rule out this possibility, and generally to assess the robustness of the findings reported here, we need to apply a diversity of assessment methods and research strategies.

CONTROL-RELATED STYLES:
OVERCONTROLLED AND UNDERCONTROLLED BEHAVIOR

We turn now to the topic of control-related styles. Of our three primary topics, this one is the most closely and immediately linked to clinical manifestations in children. In fact, the two behavioral styles on which we focus—overcontrolled and undercontrolled—have, in at least one stream of research, been identified through the study of children's behavior problems. It is this stream of research and my own extensions of it into cross-cultural study, that constitute the basis for what I present here. In the process, I omit discussion of a very important and seemingly related conceptualization: Block and Block (e.g., 1980), in developing their concepts of *ego control* and *ego resiliency*, advanced a fourfold classification involving brittle overcontrollers, brittle undercontrollers, resilient overcontrollers, and resilient undercontrollers. The reader interested in over- and undercontrolled behavior would do well to examine that important work.

Factor analytic studies of child behavior problems have identified two broad-band "syndromes" of child problem behavior—sets of behavior problems that are often found to co-occur. These are overcontrolled behavior (e.g., fearfulness, sleep problems, headaches, social inhibition, sadness, and worry) and undercontrolled behavior (e.g., disobedience, fighting, swearing, impulsivity, arguing). The term *overcontrolled* reflects the view that stimulation and distress tend to be controlled, and excessively so, through internalization within the child. The term *undercontrolled* reflects the view that stimulation and distress are not sufficiently controlled by the child. The two syndromes, which could also be construed as behavioral "styles" have emerged in more than a dozen independent factor analytic studies of child behavior problems (see Achenbach & Edelbrock, 1978) and in research not only with Americans (e.g., Achenbach, 1978; Achenbach & Edelbrock, 1978, 1979), but also with British (e.g., Collins, Maxwell, & Cameron, 1962); Sicilians (Peterson, 1965); Japanese (Hayashi, Toyama, & Quay, 1976); and Greeks, Finns, and Iranians (Quay & Parskeuopoulos, 1972). The over- and undercontrolled syndromes or styles thus appear to have considerable generality.

When the two styles are assessed via problem reports (e.g., on child problems checklists filled in by parents or teachers), they tend to be significantly correlated with one another. This has given rise to the notion that there is a general "problem" factor, such that children who have problems of one kind tend to have problems of other kinds as well. Indeed, there is some evidence that children who show high levels of both behavioral styles (e.g., aggressive loners) are particularly at risk for later substance abuse and delinquency (see Kellam, 1987). However, there are certainly many children who are more prone to show overcontrolled than undercontrolled problems, and many children for whom the reverse is true. What causes these tendencies? Why are some children more susceptible to one behavioral style than the other? I suspect that genetic and constitutional factors often play a significant role, and that a number of additional factors may also be involved. Over the past few years, several colleagues and I have focused our research on one factor that we suspect may play a role in the process: culture.

In brief, we have been exploring the prevalence of over- and undercontrolled behavior in two cultures—Thailand and the United States—whose values and socialization patterns are different in ways that would seem to be directly relevant to the two control-related behavioral styles. Thai culture is unusually homogeneous in a number of ways that set it apart from American culture. Approximately 95% of the population subscribe to Thai Buddhism, a variant of the Therevada school, and their temples, or *wats*, dot the landscape. Within this Buddhist tradition, and in Thai society generally, prohibitions against aggression, cruelty, and other forms of undercontrolled behavior are quite strong, relative to U.S. traditions. Thai parents and other adults are very intolerant of aggressive, abusive, disrespectful, or other kinds of uncontrolled behavior in children (Gardiner & Suttipan, 1977; Moore, 1974; Suvannathat, 1979). Instead, children are taught a blend of peacefulness, politeness, and deference. A Thai ideal, stressed from early childhood on, is *krengchai,* an attitude of modesty and deference that aims to avoid disturbing others (Phillips, 1965; Suvannathat, 1979). In American culture, by contrast, there seems to be a higher level of tolerance for a certain amount of rudeness, independence, and brashness in children and adolescents. Thai social values also discourage strong overt expression of emotion, and encourage outward displays of self-control and unemotionality (see National Identity Office, 1984). Several researchers (e.g., Boesch, 1977; Sangsingkeo, 1969) have argued that this orientation may foster child problems involving excessive inhibition; by contrast, American children are often encouraged—by parents, teachers, and clinicians—to label, describe, and express their feelings to others.

Thai culture, compared to U.S. culture, thus appears to be less tolerant of undercontrolled behavior and more tolerant of overcontrolled behavior. If this is true, one important result may be differences in the prevalence of the two behavioral styles in the general population, and perhaps in the clinical settings, of Thailand and the United States. Although more than one model of cultural influence might be envisioned and tested (as we have done—e.g., Weisz, Suwanlert, Chaiyasit, Weiss, Walter, & Anderson, 1988), we focus here on a problem suppression–facilitation model. Following this model, the cultural patterns described earlier might directly affect the incidence of over- and undercontrolled behavior, with the former especially prevalent in Thai clinics, the latter in U.S. clinics. This would be consistent with Draguns' (1973) suggestion that, within a given culture, psychopathology may be "an exaggeration or a caricature of the socially shared and prevalent patterns of adaptation" (p. 33).

Over- and Undercontrolled Behavior in Thai and American Children

We have explored this possibility in a series of studies. In one (Weisz, Suwanlert, Chaiyasit, Weiss, Achenbach, & Walter, 1987), we collected parent reports of child problem behavior in general population samples of Thai and American children aged 6–11 ($N = 960$). In another study (Weisz, Suwanlert, Chaiyasit, Weiss, Achenbach, & Travathan, 1989) we obtained teacher reports for similar general population samples ($N = 945$). In both studies we found that overcontrolled behavior was reported significantly more often for Thai than American children, consistent with the notion that socialization within Thai culture is associated with a special susceptibility to overcontrolled problems. However, in neither study did we find reliable cross-national differences in undercontrolled problems. One possible artifactual reason for this finding in both studies is that Thai adults, because their standards are different from American standards, may tend to report a given pattern of child behavior as more undercontrolled than do American adults. On the other hand, it is possible that the finding is not artifactual at all; perhaps Thai children have more overcontrolled behavior than American youngsters without the compensating benefit of being less undercontrolled.

In a third study (Weisz, Suwanlert, Chaiyasit, & Walter, 1987), we compared the kinds of problems noted by parents of Thai and American children when they took their youngsters to mental health or child guidance clinics for help from specialists. This provided information on youngsters whose behavior was extreme enough to have stimulated special attention by parents and mental health professionals. Our procedure involved recording all behavior problems noted by parents in both countries ($N = 760$) when discussing their children with clinicians at the time of clinic admission. These referral problems were then coded for whether they matched problems which loaded on the empirically derived over- or undercontrolled syndrome. When we analyzed composite overcontrolled and undercontrolled scores, we found results quite consistent with the direction of the literature reviewed earlier: Overcontrolled problems were reported much more often for Thai than American youngsters;

undercontrolled problems were reported much more often for American than Thai youngsters. Table 4.8 illustrates these differences by displaying the 12 most common referral problems in each national sample. Note that all 12 in the U.S. list are undercontrolled, whereas 7 in the Thai list are overcontrolled.

Summary: Culture, Development, and Over- Versus Undercontrolled Behavioral Style

The findings of the three studies conducted thus far do not present a uniform or final picture. The one finding consistent across all three studies was that overcontrolled behavior was more often reported for Thai than American youngsters. Only one of the three studies supported the possibility that undercontrolled behavior might be more prevalent in American youngsters than their Thai counterparts, and that study involved a sample of clinic-referred youngsters, not typical of the general population. Hearing of these findings, some clinicians and at least one researcher have told me that it would not be surprising to them if the patterns of socialization associated with growing up in Thailand might produce overcontrolled behavior; but, they have suggested, even very strong cultural prohibitions might fail to inhibit undercontrolled behavior because it is stimulated by such basic tendencies toward self-expression and perhaps even aggression. The suggestion is that Thai rearing practices may lead children to try to inhibit undercontrolled behavior, but that they are unlikely to succeed. I am not qualified to evaluate such speculation. However, I can comfortably say that our research thus far has not resolved any major issues. What it has done is to suggest the possibility that tendencies toward undercontrolled or overcontrolled styles may be shaped in rather complex ways. Among the forces that our data (not all of it reviewed here) suggest as possible contributions are culture, sex, age, and the interplay of the three. To understand the role of such forces will certainly require substantial further study.

CONTROL-RELATED BELIEFS, GOALS, AND STYLES: TOWARD LINKAGE

Thus far we have reviewed theory and research on control-related beliefs, goals, and styles, in a somewhat insular fashion. There is a good reason for this fact: The three lines of theory and research, have also been carried on in rather insular fashion. In the early stages of this work there

TABLE 4.8
Twelve Most Common Referral Problems in Thailand and the U.S.

	Type[a]	U.S. %	Thai %	X^2	p-value
Most Common in U.S. Sample					
1. Poor school work	U	33.9%	35.9%	.4	ns
2. Disobedient at home	U	19.3%	6.1%	29.5	<.001
3. Temper tantrums, hot temper	U	15.4%	11.7%	2.2	ns
4. Gets into fights	U	14.3%	.8%	49.3	<.001
5. Disobedient at school	U	14.1%	2.9%	30.3	<.001
6. Physically attacks people	U	12.5%	7.4%	5.4	<.05
7. Lying or cheating	U	11.5%	3.5%	17.5	<.001
8. Steals outside the home	U	10.4%	4.5%	9.5	<.005
9. Can't concentrate, pay attention	U	10.2%	6.4%	3.6	<.10
10. Argues a lot	U	9.9%	3.2%	13.8	<.001
11. Demands attention	U	8.9%	1.1%	24.3	<.001
12. Can't sit still, hyperactive	U	8.6%	5.6%	2.6	ns
Most Common in Thai Sample					
1. Poor school work	U	33.9%	35.9%	.4	ns
2. Somatic problems (esp. headaches) with no known physical cause	O	6.3%	29.3%	69.3	<.001
3. Absentminded, forgets easily	N	2.6%	17.0%	44.4	<.001
4. Fearful or anxious	O	3.4%	12.8%	22.6	<.001
5. Lacks motivation to study/ learn	N	4.7%	12.0%	13.2	<.001
6. Sleep problems	O	1.0%	11.7%	36.5	<.001
7. Underactive, lacks energy	O	.5%	11.7%	41.6	<.001
8. Temper tantrums, hot temper	U	15.4%	11.7%	2.2	ns
9. Stubborn, sullen, irritable	M	4.7%	9.8%	7.5	<.01
10. Nervous movements, twitching	O	2.1%	9.0%	17.6	<.001
11. Strange behavior	O	1.0%	9.0%	25.6	<.001
12. Worrying	O	2.6%	7.4%	9.4	<.005

Note: Table shows the 12 most common referral problems in the United States and Thai samples, respectively, listed in descending order of frequency. Columns show the percentage of youngsters in the United States and Thai samples, respectively, for whom each problem was reported, and results of chi-square tests comparing the U.S. and Thai figures.

[a]Type of problem, as determined by factor analyses of the CBCL. U=loads exclusively or predominantly on the Undercontrolled syndrome; O=loads exclusively or predominantly on the Overcontrolled syndrome; M=loads on both syndromes with about equal frequency across various age by sex groups; N=not included in factor analysis, because not listed on CBCL.

may be value in such an approach. Certainly the somewhat isolated work within each area has generated some potentially useful findings, some involving developmental differences, and some involving clinically significant relationships.

What I suggest in this concluding section is that there may also be value in efforts to probe for linkage among control-related beliefs, goals, and styles. At a rather simple-minded level, it seems likely that our beliefs may influence the goals we set, and that our goals may, in turn, influence our patterns of behavior. Thus, it seems worthwhile to explore the extent to which such causal connections obtain when the phenomena under study are linked to issues of control. For heuristic purposes, let us speculate a bit about some of the forms such causal connections may take. To do so, we return to the example of Alli, with which we began this chapter.

Alli's Control Dilemma

When we left Alli, she was coping with her strong desire to be a part of a popular group at school, juxtaposed against her uncertainty about whether "getting in" was, for her, a controllable event. To summarize Alli's options within the framework of this chapter, one might construe her as having to (a) decide on her control-related beliefs with regard to the desired outcome (e.g., the extent to which the outcome is contingent and the extent to which she is competent to perform outcome relevant behavior); (b) select her control-related goals (e.g., the primary control goal of modifying the group's composition so that it will include her, or the secondary control goal of modifying her own perspective on the current situation, perhaps by finding more to appreciate in her current friends); and (c) manifest some pattern of control-related behavior (e.g., tending toward overcontrol or undercontrol). Here we consider whether these three steps occur independently of one another or might to some degree be linked.

Belief-to-Goal Sequences

To consider the possibility of causal links, let us focus on Fig. 4.3, and consider some of the possible consequences if Alli's beliefs fall into each of the four positions—A, B, C, and D—shown in the figure.

A: Low Contingency, Low Competence.   A shows a particularly low level of perceived control, involving low levels of perceived event contingency and a low level of perceived competence. In Alli's dilemma, this might

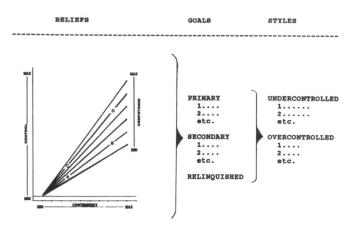

FIG. 4.3 Contemplating a possible linkage among control-related beliefs, goals, and styles.

involve a belief that there is very little that kids like Alli (not rich, parents not socially prominent) can do to be accepted by the high status group and that even the few things that may have a slight impact on the group are not even things that Alli is very good at doing (e.g., being witty and charming). Under such circumstances, there would seem to be two rather appropriate options among the control-related goals we have discussed: relinquished control and secondary control. Relinquished control, giving up, with no attempt to enhance the rewardingness of Alli's situation, does not seem a very happy option; it certainly may be selected by children in a variety of situations, but, our evidence thus far suggests, not often. Secondary control might offer a means of making Alli the master of her situation, at least psychologically. For example, success at the selective attention form of secondary control might mean that she is able to focus her attention away from the issue of her relationship to the high status group. And success at interpretive secondary control might mean that Alli achieves an understanding of her situation in ways that make it less painful and more rewarding for her; for example, she might recognize that her nonacceptance by the high-status group is due to such "outside" factors as her parents' income, and thus "not her fault," and she might begin to appreciate the value of her current friends who are not so hung up on superficialities like money and social standing.

B: High Contingency, Low Competence. Position B might represent Alli's belief that acceptance by the high-status group is highly contingent on the behavior of people like her (e.g., that wit and charm can be the ticket of admission) but that she is not particularly good at being witty and charming. Under this set of beliefs, two rather different control-related goals might be appropriate, depending on Alli's beliefs about the nature of her competence. If Alli subscribes to what Dweck and Elliot (1983) have called an *entity model,* she might believe that her competence in the areas of wit and charm is a relatively fixed factor in her calculations, and that she must set goals that do not require more competence than she currently possesses (note that Dweck & Elliot, 1983, discuss the possibility that entity models can lead to relinquished control, and helpless behavior). Following an entity model, Alli might opt for a secondary control goal, one involving acceptance of the status quo. On the other hand, if Alli subscribes to an *incremental model* (Dweck & Elliot, 1983), she might anticipate that her levels of wit and charm are improvable, indeed, likely to improve with effort on her part. Following this model, Alli might well adopt a primary control goal of entry into the high-status group, working from the assumption that if she tries she can develop the necessary competence. What this discussion suggests is that predicting which goals people will adopt, based on their control-related beliefs, may require a rather rich knowledge of their related cognitions about those beliefs (e.g., whether they subscribe to entity or incremental models of competence).

C: Low Contingency, High Competence. The same point applies when we consider Position C in the figure. Here we might imagine that Alli believes group entry is relatively noncontingent on the behavior of kids like her, but that she is very good at the kinds of behavior that may have a slight impact. A crucial cognitive issue in this situation may be Alli's component beliefs about the stability of the contingencies that currently prevail. If the low level of contingency is viewed as fixed and immutable, then secondary control goals may be the most reasonable options for Alli. However, if the current low level of contingency is seen as quite variable, (e.g., dependent on changeable whims of the group members, or on the presence of one or two members who are often absent from the group), then a primary control goal may be reasonable. Here, as in the previous situation, one would need to know more than simply current levels of perceived contingency and perceived competence in order to make an enlightened prediction about which control-related goals might be adopted.

D: High Contingency, High Competence. Finally, we consider a situation in which Alli believes that group entry is highly contingent on the behavior of kids like her, and that she is very good at the relevant kinds of behavior. Here, a primary control goal would seem to be a more logically obvious choice than in any of the three preceding situations.

However, we should note, following the discussion in the preceding two paragraphs, that Alli might hesitate to adopt such a goal if she believes that (a) the contingencies are highly variable from one time to another, and/or (b) her level of competence is unsteady and might decline, say, under the pressure of trying to "do well" with the high status group.

Goal-to-Style Sequences

We turn now to the question of how the control-related goals that people adopt may be related to their control-related behavioral styles. In this area, I think informed speculation is extremely difficult, because our knowledge base is so thin and because the control-related behavioral categories considered here are so gross. The broad categories of overcontrolled and undercontrolled behavior almost certainly encompass a rich array of specific behavioral styles (indicated by numbers in the figure) too subtle to be detected in a factor analysis. Moreover, the fact that the over- and undercontrolled styles have been identified primarily through analyses of children's behavior problems may mean that they do not capture important aspects of adaptive behavior. It is true that the over- and undercontrolled styles have been linked to the constructs of introversion and extraversion (see Achenbach & Eldebrock, 1978), but those constructs, too, emerged at least in part from the study of maladaptive behavior.

A very simple-minded analysis might suggest that secondary control goals would be more likely to lead to overcontrolled behavior than would primary control goals, and that primary control goals would be more likely than secondary goals to stimulate undercontrolled behavior. However, I think that even this general statement ventures onto thinner ice than I am willing to tread. I do believe that people's behavioral styles are related to their goals, but our cross-cultural research also leads me to suspect that socialization can influence the styles individuals employ in the pursuit of their goals. Some Americans have been reared to believe that assertiveness and clear statements of one's wishes are the best way to achieve primary control of various kinds. Some Thai people, by contrast, have been reared to believe that deference, politeness, and the preservation of social harmony provide the best means of satisfying primary control goals. Thus, very similar goals may be pursued via very dissimilar behavioral styles, styles developed partly through socialization experiences within one's culture.

Given these complexities, I am inclined to avoid predictions about which control-related goals will lead to which behavioral styles. Instead, I suggest that the study of causal connections between control-related goals and behavioral styles could contribute importantly to our understanding. The enterprise will be challenging indeed, because it is apt to involve an expansion of the array of goals and styles that need to be considered, and it is apt to lead into research on underlying assumptions (induced partly through socialization) about optimum means of achieving various goals.

Some Left-Over Issues and Problems

Finally, I want to outline a few issues and problems that we have not tackled in the preceding discussion. Each of these may need to be confronted by researchers who probe connections among control-related beliefs, goals, and styles.

Choosing Secondary Versus Relinquished Control. According to our conceptual analysis of the various control-related goals, individuals who believe that their prospects for primary control are at a minimum would be better off shifting to the pursuit of secondary control goals than relinquishing control. Yet, in the samples we have obtained thus far, small subsamples report having simply given up. We need to understand more about the beliefs, or other factors, that stimulate such a seemingly maladaptive choice. One possibility is that the pursuit of secondary control options requires a certain level of energy, and that people whose lack of primary control has sapped their energy tend to opt for the no-energy option of relinquished control. Our developmental findings suggest another possibility: Identifying secondary control options may be a skill, one that requires some cognitive development and some learning. Youngsters who relinquish control may tend to be those who have had insufficient cognitive development, or insufficient learning opportunities, to permit ready identification of secondary control goals or even to recognize the potential satisfactions such goals might afford.

The Role of Motives, Impulses, and Other Noncognitive Processes. Any purely cognitive analysis is likely to bypass much of the fuel that energizes human behavior. To illustrate this point, we need only to return to the case of Alli and imagine that entry into the high-status group is her grandest dream, the most important goal in her hierarchy, and the object of nearly all her fantasy life. Under these conditions, even if Alli believes that outcome contingency and her personal competence are both at very low levels, she might nonetheless pursue the primary control goal of group entry. As another example, it should be noted that children's overcontrolled and undercontrolled behavior sometimes appears to be almost reflexive, not stimulated by beliefs or goals so much as by a burst of energy or an unconstrained impulse—as when a child gets fidgety and climbs on top of his or her desk, or blurts out an inappropriate comment in class. I am not suggesting that investigators interested in cognitive processes like those discussed in this chapter should also study motivational factors. What I am recommending is modesty, a recognition that the cognitive factors can only account for part of the variance in goal selection and behavioral style. In essence, I am cautioning against overcognizing.

Multiple Goals. The last issue is another complicating factor that I have artfully avoided until now: Most people are capable of adopting multiple goals. This means that on some (perhaps even most) occasions, whatever people's control-related beliefs, they may select one or more primary control goals and/or one or more secondary control goals; in some cases, people may also hold in mind the fall-back option of relinquishing control if nothing primary or secondary seems to work. I do suspect that people tend to organize their goals into hierarchies, such that we might speak of a person's "principal goal" in a given situation. However, we may also need to recognize that adopting multiple goals can represent a kind of maximizing strategy that could have real adaptive advantages.

To illustrate, I close with a story told by a Thai government official in a discussion of differences between Thai and American approaches to coping with stress. It seems that two experienced hikers, a Thai man and an American man, were hiking in the woods and got lost. The longer they searched for a way out, the darker and deeper the woods seemed to get. In the midst of the search, the Thai man broke into a grin, then began to laugh out loud, at the silly predicament these two seasoned hikers had gotten themselves into. The American turned to him and said, "Why are you laughing? Don't you see how lost we are?" The Thai hiker replied, "Oh—if I stop laughing will we find our way out?" As I interpret the story, the Thai hiker was maximizing, seeking primary control (getting out) and secondary control (a changed perspective, finding the humor in the situation) at the same time. He was only willing to give up the secondary if that would increase his prospects for primary control, which of course it would not.

As the story suggests, maximizing by adopting multiple control-related goals may be a particularly useful stress-coping device. Perhaps the phenomenon bears study in its own right.

ACKNOWLEDGMENTS

The research reported here was supported by grants from the National Institute of Mental Health (#1-R01-MH34210, 1-R03-MH38450, and 5-R01-MH38240), which I gratefully acknowledge. I also acknowledge with thanks the contributions of my primary collaborators in much of the work reported here: Eve Brotman-Band, Wanchai Chaiyasit, Somsong Suwanlert, Betty Rintoul, Bernadette Walter, Aviva Wasserman, and Bahr Weiss.

REFERENCES

Abramson, L. Y., Seligman, M. E. P., & Teasdale, J. D. (1978). Learned helplessness in humans: Critique and reformulation. *Journal of Abnormal Psychology, 87*, 49–74.

Achenbach, T. M. (1978). The Child Behavior Profile, I: Boys aged 6–11. *Journal of Consulting and Clinical Psychology, 46*, 478–488.

Achenbach, T. M., & Edelbrock, C. S. (1978). The classification of child psychopathology. A review and analysis of empirical efforts. *Psychological Bulletin, 85*, 1275–1301.

Achenbach, T. M., & Edelbrock, C. S. (1979). The Child Behavior Profile, II: Boys aged 12–16 and girls 6–11 and 12–16. *Journal of Consulting and Clinical Psychology, 47*, 223–233.

Alloy, L. B., & Abramson, L. Y. (1979). Judgment of contingency in depressed and nondepressed college students: Sadder but wiser. *Journal of Experimental Psychology: General, 108*, 441–485.

Ausubel, D. P., Schiff, H. M., & Gasser, E. B. (1952). A preliminary study of developmental trends in socioempathy: Accuracy of perception of own and others sociometric status. *Child Development, 23*, 111–128.

Bandura, A. (1977). Self-efficacy: Toward a unifying theory of behavioral change. *Psychological Review, 84*, 191–215.

Bandura, A. (1982). Self-efficacy mechanism in human agency. *American Psychologist, 37*, 122–147.

Block, J. H., & Block, J. (1980). The role of ego control and ego resiliency in the organization of behavior. In W. A. Collins (Ed.), *Minnesota Symposia on Child Psychology* (Vol. 13, pp. 39–101). Hillsdale, N.J.: Erlbaum.

Boesch, E. (1977). Authority and work attitude of Thais. In K. Wenk & K. Rosenburg (Eds.), *Thai in German eyes* (pp. 176–231). Bangkok: Kledthai.

Brim, O. G. (1980, May). *How a person controls the sense of efficacy through the life span.* Paper presented at the Social Science Research Council Conference on the Self and Perceived Personal Control Through the Life Span, New York.

Brotman-Band, E. (in press). Stress-coping among children with diabetes. *Journal of Pediatric Psychology.*

Brotman-Band, E., & Weisz, J. R. (1988). How to feel better when it feels bad: Children's perspectives on coping with everyday stress. *Developmental Psychology, 24*, 247–253.

Calsyn, R. (1973). *The causal relationship between self-esteem, locus of control, and achievement: A cross-legged panel analysis.* Unpublished doctoral dissertation, Northwestern University, Chicago, IL.

Chapman, M., & Skinner, E. A. (1985a). Action in development—development in action. In M. Frese & J. Sabini (Eds.), *Goal directed behavior: Psychological theory and research on action* (pp. 200–221). Hillsdale, NJ: Lawrence Erlbaum Associates.

Chapman, M., & Skinner, E. A. (1985b, April). *Children's cognitive performance as influenced by beliefs about control.* Paper presented at the meeting of the Society for Research in Child Development, Toronto, Ontario, Canada.

Collins, L. F., Maxwell, A. E., & Cameron, A. (1962). A factor analysis of some child psychiatric data. *Journal of Mental Science, 108*, 274–285.

Connell, J. P. (1985). A new multidimensional measure of children's perception of control. *Child Development, 56,* 1018–1041.

Coyne, J. C., & Gotlib, I. H. (1983). The role of cognition in depression: A critical appraisal. *Psychological Bulletin, 94,* 472–505.

Crandall, V. C. (1971, August). *Discussant's comments.* Presented at the symposium on developmental aspects of locus of control expectancies, at the Annual Convention of the American Psychological Association, Washington, DC.

Draguns, J. G. (1973). Comparison of psychopathology across cultures: Issues, findings, directions. *Journal of Cross-Cultural Psychology, 4,* 9–47.

Dweck, S. C., & Elliot, E. S. (1983). Achievement motivation. In P. Mussen & E. M. Hetherington (Eds.), *Handbook of child psychology* (Vol. 4, pp. 643–691). New York: Wiley.

Fischbein, E. (1975). *The intuitive sources of probabilistic thinking in children.* Boston: Reidel.

Freedman, D. G. (1975). The development of social hierarchies. In L. Levi (Ed.), *Society, stress, and disease: Vol. 2. Childhood and adolescence.* London: Oxford University Press.

Freud, S. (1957). On narcissism: An introduction. In *Collected Papers* (Vol. 14). London: Hogarth.

Gardiner, H. W., & Suttipan, C. S. (1977). Parental tolerance of aggression: Perceptions of preadolescents in Thailand. *Psychologia, 20,* 28–32.

Goss, A. M. (1968). Estimated versus actual physical strength in three ethnic groups. *Child Development, 39,* 283–290.

Greenwald, A. G. (1980). The totalitarian ego: Fabrication and revision of personal history. *American Psychologist, 35,* 603–618.

Gurin, P. (1980, May). *The situation and other neglected issues in personal causation.* Reported in Thematic Minutes V of the Social Science Research Council Conference on the Self and Perceived Personal Control Through the Life Span, New York.

Haley, G. T., Fine, S., Marriage, K., Moretti, M. M., & Freeman, R. J. (1985). Cognitive bias and depression in psychiatrically disturbed children and adolescents. *Journal of Consulting and Clinical Psychology, 53,* 535–537.

Harter, S. (1982). The perceived competence scale for children. *Child Development, 53,* 87–97.

Harter, S. (1983). Developmental perspectives on the self-system. In P. H. Mussen (Ed.), *Handbook of child psychology* (Vol. IV, pp. 275–386). New York: Wiley.

Harter, S. (1985). *Manual for the self-perception profile for children.* Denver, CO: University of Denver.

Hayashi, K., Toyama, B., & Quay, H. C. (1976). A cross-cultural study concerned with differential behavioral classification: 1. The Behavior Checklist. *Japanese Journal of Criminal Psychology, 2,* 21–28.

Kazdin, A. E., French, N. H., Unis, A. S., Esveldt-Dawson, K., & Sherick, R. B. (1983). Hopelessness, depression, and suicidal intent among psychiatrically disturbed inpatient children. *Journal of Consulting and Clinical Psychology, 51,* 504–510.

Kaslow, N. J., Rehm, L. P., & Siegel, A. W. (1984). Social-cognitive correlates of depression in children. *Journal of Abnormal Child Psychology, 12,* 605–620.

Kellam, S. G. (1987). A developmental epidemiological perspective on social adaptation and cognitive function. In C. Schooler & K. W. Schaie (Eds.), *Cognitive functioning and social structure over the life course* (pp. 230–246). Norwood, NJ: Ablex.

Kovacs, M., & Beck, A. T. (1977). An empirical-clinical approach toward a definition of childhood depression. In J. G. Schulterbrandt & A. Raskin (Eds.), *Depression in childhood: Diagnosis, treatment, and conceptual models* (pp. 1–25). New York: Raven Press.

Kun, A. (1977). Development of the magnitude-covariation and compensation schemata in ability and effort attributions of performance. *Child Development, 48,* 862–873.

Langer, E. J. (1975). The illusion of control. *Journal of Personality and Social Psychology, 32*, 311–328.

Lazarus, R. S., & Folkman, S. (1984). Coping and adaptation. In W. D. Gentry (Ed.), *Handbook of behavioral medicine* (pp. 282–325). New York: Guilford Press.

Lewinsohn, P., Mischel, W., Chaplin, W., & Barton, R. (1980). Social competence and depression: The role of illusory self-perceptions. *Journal of Abnormal Psychology, 89*, 203–212.

Moore, F. J. (1974). *Thailand: Its people, its society, its culture.* New Haven, CT: Hraf Press.

Moyal, B. R. (1977). Locus of control, self-esteem, stimulus appraisal, and depressive symptoms in children. *Journal of Consulting and Clinical Psychology, 45*, 951–952.

National Identity Office (Kingdom of Thailand) (1984). *Thailand in the 80s.* Bangkok: Muang Boran Publishing House.

Nicholls, J. G. (1978). The development of the concepts of effort and ability, perception of academic attainment, and the understanding that difficult tasks require more ability. *Child Development, 49*, 800–814.

Nicholls, J. (1979). *The development of perception of own attainment and causal attributions for success and failure in reading.* Unpublished manuscript, Victoria University, Wellington, New Zealand.

Nicholls, J. G., & Miller, A. T. (1984). Development and its discontents: The differentiation of the concept of ability. In J. G. Nicholls (Ed.), *The development of achievement motivation* (pp. 185–218). Greenwich, CT: JAI Press.

Omizo, M. M., & Cubberly, W. E. (1984). The effects of group counseling on self-concept and locus of control among learning disabled children. *Journal of Humanistic Education and Development, 23*, 69–79.

Pearlin, L. I., & Schooler, C. (1978). The structure of coping. *Journal of Health and Behavior, 19*, 2–21.

Peterson, C., & Seligman, M. E. P. (1984). Causal explanations as a risk factor for depression: Theory and evidence. *Psychological Review, 91*, 347–374.

Peterson, D. R. (1965). Structural congruence and metric variability in a cross-cultural study of children's behavior problems. *Archivo di Psychologia, Neurologia, e Psichiatrica, 2*, 174–187.

Phillips, B. N. (1963). Age changes in accuracy of self-perceptions. *Child Development, 34*, 1041–1046.

Phillips, H. P. (1965). *Thai peasant personality: The patterning of interpersonal behavior in the village of Bang Chan.* Berkeley, CA: University of California Press.

Piaget, J. (1930). *The child's conception of physical causality.* London: Routledge & Kegan Paul.

Piaget, J. (1960). *The child's conception of the world.* Totowa, NJ: Littlefield, Adams.

Piaget, J., & Inhelder, B. (1975). *The origin of the idea of chance.* New York: Norton.

Porter, S. S., & Omizo, M. M. (1984). The effects of group relaxation training/large muscle exercise, and parental involvement on attention to task, impulsivity, and locus of control among hyperactive boys. *Exceptional Child, 31*, 54–64.

Quay, H. C., & Parskeuopoulos, I. N. (1972, August). *Dimensions of problem behavior in elementary school children in Greece, Iran, and Finland.* Paper presented at the 20th International Congress of Psychology, Tokyo, Japan.

Rintoul, B., & Weisz, J. R. (1989). *Control beliefs and depression among school-aged children.* Manuscript submitted for publication.

Rothbaum, F., Weisz, J. R., & Snyder, S. (1982). Changing the world and changing the self: A two-process model of perceived control. *Journal of Personality and Social Psychology, 42*, 5–37.

Ruble, D. N., Boggiano, A. K., Feldman, N. S., & Loebl, J. H. (1980). Developmental analysis of the role of social comparison in self-evaluation. *Developmental Psychology, 16*, 105–115.

Sangsingkeo, P. (1969). Buddhism and some effects on the rearing of children in Thailand. In W. Caudill & T. Y. Lin (Eds.), *Mental health research in Asia and the Pacific* (pp. 286–295). Honolulu: East–West Center Press.

Sedlack, A. J., & Kurtz, S. T. (1981). Review of children's use of causal inference principles. *Child Development, 52,* 750–784.

Seligman, M. E. P. (1975). *Helplessness: On depression, development, and death.* San Francisco: Freeman.

Seligman, M. E. P., Peterson, C., Kaslow, N. J., Tanenbaum, R. L., Alloy, L. B., & Abramson, L. Y. (1984). Attributional style and depressive symptoms among children. *Journal of Abnormal Psychology, 93,* 235–238.

Skinner, E. A. (1985). Action, control judgments, and the structure of control experience. *Psychological Review, 92,* 39–58.

Skinner, E. A., & Chapman, M. (1983, April). *Control beliefs in an action perspective.* Paper presented at the biennial meeting of the Society for Research in Child Development, Detroit, MI.

Stipek, D. J. (1980). A causal analysis of the relationship between locus of control and academic achievement in first grade. *Contemporary Educational Psychology, 5,* 90–99.

Stipek, D. J. (1981). Children's perceptions of their own and their classmates' ability. *Journal of Educational Psychology, 73,* 404–410.

Stipek, D. J. (1984). Young children's performance expectations: Logical analysis or wishful thinking? In J. Nicholls (Ed.), *The development of achievement motivation* (pp. 33–56). Greenwich, CT: JAI Press.

Stipek, D. J., & Hoffman, J. M. (1980a). Children's achievement-related expectancies as a function of academic performance histories and sex. *Journal of Educational Psychology, 72,* 861–865.

Stipek, D. J., & Hoffman, J. M. (1980b). Development of children's performance-related judgments. *Child Development, 51,* 912–914.

Suvannathat, C. (1979). The inculcation of values in Thai children. *International Social Science Journal, 31,* 477–485.

Weisz, J. R. (1977). A follow-up developmental study of hypothesis behavior among retarded and nonretarded children. *Journal of Experimental Child Psychology, 24,* 108–122.

Weisz, J. R. (1980). Developmental change in perceived control: Recognizing noncontingency in the laboratory and perceiving it in the world. *Developmental Psychology, 16,* 385–390.

Weisz, J. R. (1981). Illusory contingency in children at the state fair. *Developmental Psychology, 17,* 481–489.

Weisz, J. R. (1986a). Contingency and control beliefs as predictors of psychotherapy outcomes among children and adolescents. *Journal of Consulting and Clinical Psychology, 54,* 789–795.

Weisz, J. R. (1986b). Understanding the developing understanding of control. In M. Perlmutter (Ed.), *Social cognition: Minnesota symposia on child psychology* (Vol. 18, pp. 219–278). Hillsdale, NJ: Lawrence Erlbaum Associates.

Weisz, J. R., & Achenbach, T. M. (1975). The effects of IQ and MA on hypothesis behavior in normal and retarded children. *Developmental Psychology, 11,* 304–310.

Weisz, J. R., Rothbaum, F. M., & Blackburn, T. C. (1984a). Standing out and standing in: The psychology of control in America and Japan. *American Psychologist, 39,* 955–969.

Weisz, J. R., Rothbaum, F. M., & Blackburn, T. C. (1984b). Swapping recipes for control. *American Psychologist, 39,* 974–975.

Weisz, J. R., Stephens, J., Curry, J. F., Cohen, R., Craighead, W. E., Burlingame, W. V., Smith, A., Weiss, B., & Parmelee, D. X. (1989). Control-related beliefs and depression among inpatient children and adolescents. *Journal of the American Academy of Child and Adolescent Psychiatry, 28,* 358–363.

Weisz, J. R., & Stipek, D. J. (1982). Competence, contingency, and the development of perceived control. *Human Development, 25,* 250–281.

Weisz, J. R., Suwanlert, S., Chaiyasit, W., Walter, B. R. (1987). Over- and undercontrolled problems among Thai and American children and adolescents: The *wat* and *wai* of cultural differences. *Journal of Consulting and Clinical Psychology, 55,* 719–726.

Weisz, J. R., Suwanlert, S., Chaiyasit, W., Weiss, B., Achenbach, T. M., & Trevathan, D. (1989). Epidemiology of behavioral and emotional problems among Thai and American children: Teacher reports for ages 6–11. *Journal of Child Psychology and Psychiatry, 30,* 471–484.

Weisz, J. R., Suwanlert, S., Chaiyasit, W., Weiss, B., Achenbach, T. M., & Walter, B. R. (1987). Epidemiology of behavioral and emotional problems among Thai and American children: Parent reports for ages 6–11. *Journal of the American Academy of Child and Adolescent Psychiatry, 26,* 890–898.

Weisz, J. R., Suwanlert, S., Chaiyasit, W., Weiss, B., Walter, B. R., & Anderson, W.W. (1988). Thai and American perspectives on over- and undercontrolled child behavior problems: Exploring the threshold model among parents, teachers, and psychologists. *Journal of Consulting and Clinical Psychology, 56,* 601–609.

Weisz, J. R., Weiss, B., Wasserman, A. A., & Rintoul, B. (1987). Control-related beliefs and depression among clinic-referred children and adolescents. *Journal of Abnormal Psychology, 96,* 58–63.

Weisz, J. R., Yeates, K. O., Robertson, D., & Beckham, J. C. (1982). Perceived contingency of skill and chance events: A developmental analysis. *Developmental Psychology, 18,* 898–905.

Control of Environment
and Control of Self

Morris Rosenberg
University of Maryland

One of the most impressive features of Weisz' research on the beliefs, goals, and styles of control is that it successfully integrates a broad range of concepts—locus of control, self-efficacy, learned helplessness, mastery, powerlessness, and so on—that have often been treated separately in the literature. Furthermore, it has moved this field forward by developing a program of research that is cumulative, theoretically informed, and well-executed.

TWO-PROCESS MODEL OF CONTROL

In this discussion, I limit my comments to two points. The first deals with Weisz' two-process model of control. The first process, called *primary control,* involves the effort to act on the environment in order to produce desired outcomes. The second process, called *secondary control,* is an attempt "to accommodate to objective conditions in order to effect a more satisfying fit with those conditions."

Although there are many reasons why people wish to exercise control, I focus on the exercise of control as a way of dealing with problems. In the stress literature, these methods of control are usually referred to as *coping devices.* Weisz sees primary and secondary control as illustrations of Lazarus and Folkman's (1984) problem-focused and emotion-focused methods of coping. Primary control—the attempt to bring about changes in objective conditions as a way of solving one's problems—is a form of

147

problem-focused control. Secondary control—an effort to control the psychological impact of the objective conditions—is a form of emotion-focused control. As Weisz observes:

> In primary control, the intended event is some modification of objective conditions; in secondary control, the intended event is some modification of one's orientation toward those conditions—that is, internal change that affords control over the impact of objective conditions on the self while leaving those conditions unchanged.

Schulz (1982) argued that one of the fundamental human motives is the wish to experience desirable emotions. Desirability, of course, is not restricted to hedonic emotions. Some emotions may be desirable because we consider them to be socially appropriate (e.g., feeling sad at a funeral or observing other "feeling rules," to use Hochschild's, 1983, expression); others because they serve certain goals or objectives (remaining calm in a crisis); and so on. But certainly one of the major desires of human beings is to maximize hedonically satisfying emotional experiences. Although there are many exceptions, it is apparent that people usually prefer to be happy rather than sad, contented rather than annoyed, calm rather than nervous, and so on.

Emotions, however, are peculiar in one particular respect. Although we often have clear emotional preferences, we have little or no direct control over our emotions. Emotions appear to be rooted in the involuntary nervous system.

The involuntary character of the emotions, it may be noted, applies generally to emotional *experience,* not to emotional *display.* Emotional display is largely under the control of the voluntary nervous system. On the other hand, we cannot, through force of will, make ourselves feel calm, enthusiastic, sad, and so on.

Human beings are thus confronted with a serious and pervasive problem, namely, that one of their chief life objectives—the wish to experience hedonically satisfying emotions—is largely outside their voluntary control. What, then, do they do?

I suggest that people attempt to control their emotional experiences, not by acting on the emotions, but by acting on the *causes* of the emotions. Human beings are aware that certain stimuli or events characteristically produce certain emotional states. They thus attempt to control these stimuli or events as a way of arousing the desired emotions.

Where are the causes of the emotions to be found? In terms of proximate influence, most people recognize that the causes of the emotions are to be found in two places. The first is in the mind, the second, in the body.

In this discussion, I limit my comments to the control of the mind. Most people recognize that a major cause of the internal state of physiological arousal that is the foundation of the emotion is the operation of the mind. The reason I feel good is that I have just encountered a delightful friend. The reason I feel angry is that I have just witnessed a cruel injustice. The reason I feel excited is that I have just watched my team score a touchdown. I recognize that the feeling is a consequence of the cognitive event.

One might contend, of course, that the cause of the emotion lies in the external stimulus—the good friend, the act of injustice, the football game. But that is the distal, not the proximal, cause. This explanation is incomplete because it leaves out an important intervening event—the mental operations brought to bear on the external stimulus. How else can one explain the fact that the same stimulus so often gives rise to radically different emotional responses? The cruel and unjust act that arouses in me feelings of indignation and fury has no such effect on the perpetrator of the act. The movie climax that fills me with such excitement arouses nothing but boredom in my companion. It is not simply the external event but the *interpretation* of the event that arouses the emotion. As Epstein (1973) said:

> Thus if I make the interpretation that someone has wronged me and deserves to be punished, I feel anger. If I interpret the situation as one that is threatening, and that I would like to escape from, I feel fear. If I make the interpretation that I am deprived of love or some other need vital to my happiness, and have no hope that it will ever be fulfilled, I feel depressed . . . each emotion implies an underlying cognition. (p. 411)

Although we usually cannot exercise control over our emotions directly, we can exercise a substantial amount of control over the thoughts that, we believe, arouse them. Let me mention some of the forms that cognitive self-regulation may take. One of the chief devices used by people to control their emotions is to tell themselves what and how to think.

Pearlin and Schooler's (1978) study of stress and coping presents some interesting examples of these cognitive processes. Pearlin and Schooler were interested in the question of how people dealt with four major recurrent role-related life stresses: marriage, parenting, work, and finances. One device used was *selective ignoring* (e.g., "try to ignore difficulties by looking only at good things"). Another was *positive comparisons* (e.g., thinking of others who are worse off than themselves). A third device was *selective valuation* (e.g., deciding that "financial success does not interest me"). A fourth device was alteration of one's time frame (e.g., redirecting attention from the bleak present to a hopefully brighter future). And so on.

A good example of such cognitive self-regulation appears in Weisz' discussion of selective attention. Selective attention, Weisz notes, is a cognitive process intended to control internal states. These internal states, I suspect, usually involve emotional experiences. For example, if I have just suffered a severe disappointment, I may focus my attention on an entertaining novel. The reason I do so is that, because I am unable to eliminate the disappointment directly, I attempt to drive out of my mind those thoughts that arouse disappointment and supplant them with thoughts that, I believe, will arouse feelings of contentment and pleasure. Selective attention, then, is a purposive device chosen by the individual, based on a clear cause and effect theory. This theory, furthermore, may be entirely conscious. People may be fully aware of what they are doing and why they are doing it. They know that they are reading the light novel both to extrude those thoughts that arouse painful emotions and to insert those thoughts that generate pleasurable emotions. Selective attention, then, is one of a large number of cognitive devices that individuals use to manipulate their emotions.

PURPOSES OF PRIMARY AND SECONDARY CONTROL

Because primary control is intended to produce effects on the environment whereas secondary control is intended to produce effects upon the self, it might appear that they are intended to serve different objectives. I want to suggest that this is not necessarily so—that they are often alternative devices for achieving the same objective. Although it is certainly not the only reason, I believe that one of the main reasons for attempting to produce effects on the environment is *in order to feel good inside.* It is difficult to argue with Schulz' (1982) contention "that most persons desire to maximize positive and minimize negative feelings" (p. 82). Why, for example, does Alli, the adolescent discussed by Weisz, want to join the high-status group? Although she may have several objectives in mind, surely one of the most important of these is the expectation that she will feel happier as a result. But this is the very same reason why secondary control (for example, deciding that she is proud not to be a member of such a snobbish, pretentious group) may be utilized.

Primary and secondary control may thus be alternative ways of producing the same intended effects. Furthermore, they both represent efforts to produce intended effects on one's own mind. For example, assume that disappointment at failure is painful to me, and that I must take a test that threatens to arouse this unpleasant feeling. There are two possible ways to deal with this problem. One involves primary control. I study, do homework, or do whatever else is necessary to obtain a passing grade. My aim is to avoid perceiving myself as a failure, a thought that I know will arouse in me painful feelings.

But I may achieve the same objective by means of secondary control. One way to do so is to utilize selective attribution (Kelley, 1967; Wortman, Costanzo, & Witt, 1973). Faced with the fact of poor performance, one tactic I might use (indeed, the tactic that most people actually use) is to attribute the poor performance to external rather than to internal causes. I may decide that the test was unfair, the instructions were confusing, the room was too hot, the planets were in the wrong alignment, and so on. If I can convince myself of the truth of these causal attributions, I can achieve the same desired outcome without the strenuous effort of mastering the course material.

The recognition that primary and secondary control may be alternative ways of achieving desired emotional outcomes is deeply embedded in our cultural tradition. Take the fable of the fox and the grapes. Finding that the method of primary control (reaching the grapes) is ineffective, the fox resorts to secondary control (deciding they are sour) as a way of mitigating its disappointment.

It is probably pointless to ask whether people are generally more likely to use primary or secondary control as a way of generating the desired emotional states. It is plausible to think that they will use primary control when the environment is relatively malleable and the costs are relatively small and secondary control when they are not. It is of more than passing interest to note that, in the Pearlin and Schooler (1978) study described earlier, the authors were surprised by how rarely people dealt with the role-related stresses of daily life by confronting their problems directly (primary control). Far more often they dealt with them by attempting to produce effects on their cognitive processes (secondary control). However, the type of coping mechanism employed in part depended on the nature of the problem. External control mechanisms were more likely to be employed when dealing with family problems, because the actor could potentially produce effects in this context, than in work environments, where matters were less readily controlled.

To readers sensitive to the operation of defense mechanisms, such devices may appear to be ineffective and self-defeating. They might argue that, underneath, the fox really is disappointed at its failure to obtain the grapes. Not being an expert in fox phenomenology, I would rather not venture an opinion on the subject. I would, however, direct attention to two facts. The first is the evidence (Taylor & Brown, 1988) that, in a number of cases, self-deception does succeed in generating more satisfying feelings. The second is the finding reported by Weisz that the use of primary control tends to be associated with feelings of sadness and anxiety. If this is so, then emotional self-regulation may be achieved more effectively by the sly manipulation of one's thoughts than by the honest effort to do something about the objective situation.

Is the evasion of reality a sign of psychological immaturity? Perhaps so, but it is noteworthy that, according to Weisz, it is not a sign of chronological immaturity. Weisz reports that younger children are more apt to try to do something about their problems (primary control) whereas older children give more thought to ways of minimizing the emotional distress associated with them (secondary control). As far as these data are concerned, maturity appears to be associated with a stronger tendency to *evade* reality.

DEVELOPMENTAL TRENDS

Why is there an increasing reliance on secondary control as children grow older? Weisz has speculated on some of the possible reasons for this developmental trend. First, he suggests, secondary control may develop more slowly because it is more often hidden from view in the form of cognitions. Second, secondary control may be used when primary efforts fail. Finally, Weisz raises the possibility that younger children may actually exercise secondary control but lack the verbal facility to express it.

In the same spirit of speculation that animates Weisz' discussion, let me offer an alternative view.

In conducting research on self-concept development (Rosenberg, 1986), I was struck by the degree to which younger children tend to conceptualize the self as a social exterior, whereas older children are more likely to conceptualize it as a psychological interior. Asked to tell us what they are really like deep down inside, the younger children tend to describe themselves in terms of visible, public, overt features. They tell us how they look, where they live, what school they attend, what games they play, what possessions they own, what their family is like, how they behave, and so on. If one asks an early elementary school child what he or she is like, the child is apt to say such things as that he or she is 7 years old, has brown hair, has a dog named Ruff, has an uncle who is almost 7-feet tall, plays marbles, likes grilled cheese sandwiches, and is a good speller. The self-concept of the young child, then, consists largely of physical features, social identity elements, territorial location, material possessions, characteristic activities, and abilities and talents. These are mostly visible features of the self (Montemayor & Eisen, 1977; Rosenberg, 1986).

It is relevant to note that these ways of conceptualizing the self are not essentially different from ways of conceptualizing other people. Speaking of the development of the perception of others in children, Shantz (1975) observed that "There is a developmental trend toward conceiving of people less in terms of their surface appearance, possessions, and motor behavior and more in terms of an underlying reality" (p. 314). Changes in self-perception, then, show a striking similarity to changes in person–perception processes (Tagiuri, 1969) generally (Livesley & Bromley, 1973).

Although adolescents also include a number of visible elements in their self-descriptions, they are much more apt to assign a prominent role to internal features as well. These may include their attitudes, beliefs, opinions, values, hopes, traits, emotional dispositions, and so on. In contrast to the younger child, the older child incorporates into his or her self-concept a rich internal world of thoughts and feelings.

Why these different modes of self-conceptualization? One important reason, I believe, is that the young child has not fully developed the ability to take the role of the other (Mead, 1934). The young child, as Piaget (1951) has shown, is egocentric, seeing the world almost exclusively from his or her own, rather than from other people's, point of view (Flavell, Fry, Wright, & Jarvis, 1968; Selman, 1980). It is not until children have developed an awareness and interest in the internal thoughts and feelings of others that they are able to become detached and interested observers of their own internal processes.

One reason that the younger children may be less likely to exercise secondary control, then, is that they have not developed the tendency to direct their attention to an internal world of thoughts and feelings. As Piaget (1951) said, ". . . in virtue of his very ego-centrism, the child is not conscious of his own thought . . ." (p. 179). If this is so, then the disposition to manipulate their own thoughts as a way of determining their own feelings is likely to be underdeveloped. I believe that it is only when youngsters become attentive to an internal world of experience (their own or other people's) that they come to recognize that one way to deal with their problems is to attempt to regulate their own thoughts in ways that will maximize hedonic emotions. Younger children, not yet able to adopt this strategy, have no option but to attempt to deal with the world directly. It must be a source of considerable frustration that the younger children, who are in fact those least competent to produce the intended effects on the external environment, are precisely those who are most dependent on this method of attaining their objectives.

ACKNOWLEDGMENTS

Preparation of this discussion was facilitated by the award of a Guggenheim Fellowship.

REFERENCES

Epstein, S. (1973). The self-concept revisited, or a theory of a theory. *American Psychologist, 28,* 404–416.

Flavell, J. H., Fry, C., Wright, J., & Jarvis, P. (1968). *The development of role-taking and communication skills in children.* New York: Wiley.

Hochschild, A. (1983). *The managed heart.* Berkeley: University of California Press.

Kelley, H. (1967). Attribution theory in social psychology. In D. Levine (Ed.), *Nebraska Symposium on Motivation* (Vol. 15, pp. 192–258). Lincoln, NE: University of Nebraska.

Lazarus, R. S., & Folkman, S. (1984). *Stress, appraisal, and coping.* New York: Springer.

Livesley, W. J., & Bromley, D. B. (1973) *Person perception in childhood and adolescence.* New York: Wiley.

Mead, G. H. (1934). *Mind, self, and society.* Chicago: University of Chicago.

Montemayor, R., & Eisen, M. (1977). The development of self-conceptions from childhood to adolescence. *Developmental Psychology, 13,* 314–319.

Pearlin, L. I., & Schooler, C. (1978). The structure of coping. *Journal of Health and Social Behavior, 19,* 2–21.

Piaget, J. (1951). *Judgment and reasoning in the child.* London: Routledge & Kegan Paul.

Rosenberg, M. (1986). *Conceiving the self.* Malabar, FL: Krieger.

Schulz, R. (1982). Emotionality and aging. In K. R. Blankstein & J. Polivy (Eds.), *Self-control and self-modification of emotional behavior* (pp. 71–100). New York: Plenum.

Selman, R. (1980). *The growth of interpersonal understanding.* New York: Academic Press.

Shantz, C. (1975). The development of social cognition. In E. M. Hetherington (Ed.), *Review of child development theory and research* (Vol. 5, pp. 257–323). Chicago: University of Chicago.

Tagiuri, R. (1969). Person perception. In G. Lindzey & E. Aronson (Eds.), *The handbook of social psychology* (Vol. 3, 2nd ed., pp. 395–449). Reading, MA: Addison-Wesley.

Taylor, S. E., & Brown, J. (1988). Illusion and well-being: A social psychological perspective on mental health. *Psychological Bulletin, 103,* 193–210.

Wortman, C. B., Costanzo, P. R., & Witt, T. R. (1973). Effect of anticipated performance on the attributions of causality to self and others. *Journal of Personality and Social Psychology, 27,* 372–81.

What Is Intellectual Efficacy Over the Life Course?: Using Adults' Conceptions to Address the Question

Cynthia A. Berg
University of Utah

Imagine the following statement made by an older adult: "You're young; that's an advantage." This statement aptly summarizes much of the previous research on measured intellectual efficacy during adulthood. Regardless of the theoretical orientation adopted by cognitive aging researchers (i.e., Piagetian, neo-Piagetian, psychometric, or information processing), there are data that support intellectual advantages for the young adult, when examining performance on intelligence tests across the adult life span (e.g., Papalia, 1972; Salthouse, 1982; Schaie, 1979). In fact, much of the research in the cognitive aging literature has been aimed at discovering when the young are at an advantage over the old and when they are not (see Botwinick, 1977, for a review).

The prominence in cognitive aging research given to measured cognitive and intellectual skills has diverted attention away from questions regarding whether older adults believe that the young hold an intellectual advantage over the old. Only recently has research addressed older adults' beliefs and attitudes about their cognitive and intellectual abilities and what happens to these abilities throughout their life span (e.g., Cornelius & Caspi, 1986; Lachman, 1986a). These beliefs and attitudes about intellectual aging are important as they may impact current and future intellectual performances. The research on perceived intellectual efficacy borrows many ideas of what defines intellectual efficacy from the work on measured intellectual efficacy. How relevant the wealth of data from the cognitive aging literature is in addressing older adults' beliefs about their cognitive and intellectual efficacy, however, is not clear. Primarily, it is not obvious that the kind of intellectual abilities that cognitive aging researchers have investigated are the abilities that older adults would agree constitute intelligence. I argue in this chapter that work on measured and perceived intellectual efficacy during adulthood will benefit from an examination of what adults mean by intellectual efficacy.

The primary goal of this chapter is to demonstrate that adults' conceptions of intellectual efficacy may be useful in extending and supplementing current models of measured and perceived intellectual efficacy and in building contextual models of intelligence. The model that results from merging adults' and theorists' conceptions of intellectual efficacy may require that work in intellectual efficacy cross traditional boundaries in psychology (e.g., cognitive, social, clinical, etc.). The model that results, however, may better represent the types of components involved in effective adult intellectual functioning, particularly functioning that occurs in adults' everyday lives.

This chapter reviews some of the recent work on measured intellectual efficacy and perceived intellectual efficacy during adulthood, to illustrate how the question of what is intellectual efficacy has been answered differently in these literatures. As there is not consistent agreement in these two literatures on what defines intellectual efficacy, we may wonder to which conception of intellectual efficacy adults prescribe. Unfortunately how adults define intellectual efficacy has not been addressed.

Second, I provide a brief introduction to the contextual perspective, a relatively new conceptual and theoretical approach to cognitive and intellectual development during adulthood. The contextual approach is used to examine the question of "What is intellectual efficacy during the adult life span?" (e.g., Baltes, Dittmann-Kohli, & Dixon, 1984; Berg & Sternberg, 1985a; Lerner, Hultsch, & Dixon, 1983; Lerner & Kauffman, 1985). Third, I present data on adults' own beliefs about what constitutes intelligent functioning across the life span and describe how such beliefs may be used in building a framework for what defines intellectual efficacy. Fourth, using this initial framework for intellectual efficacy, I present data that address adults' perceptions of the developmental course of self-efficacy for different intellectual abilities. Finally, I focus on one ability that individuals perceive constitute intelligent functioning, namely, everyday problem solving. Data on what adults perceive to underlie efficacy in everyday problem solving are used to examine what kinds of intellectual abilities will lead to an understanding of everyday intellectual skills.

RESEARCH ON INTELLECTUAL EFFICACY

Measured Intellectual Efficacy

Research on measured intellectual efficacy and aging has predominantly used psychometric (i.e., paper and pencil) measures of intelligence to measure intellectual efficacy. This literature contains numerous studies, which show (a) differential patterns of change (e.g., decline, stability, or improvement) with age for different intellectual abilities (see Baltes et al., 1984, for a review), (b) large variability between individuals in the course of their intellectual development (e.g., Schaie, 1983, for a review), and (c) modifiability of intelligence within a given individual (e.g., Baltes, Dittmann Kohli & Kleigl, 1985, Baltes & Willis, 1982). In the last two decades, theories of cognitive aging have focused on ways to explain why certain cognitive abilities show differential functions of decline, stability, or improvement throughout the adult life span.

One such theory is Horn and Cattell's (1967) theory of fluid and crystallized intelligence. Fluid intelligence is represented by tasks that require adjusting to novel problems, problems for which prior education and experience provide little advantage (e.g., number series, spatial problem solving, etc.). Crystallized intelligence is best measured by tasks for which prior education, acculturation, and experience provide one with an advantage for solving the problems (e.g., vocabulary test, arithmetic test, etc.). Research on intellectual development throughout the life span demonstrates that performance on measures of fluid intelligence begins to decline early in adulthood, whereas performance on measures of crystallized intelligence is relatively stable throughout the adult life span (Horn & Cattell, 1967; Schaie, 1979).

Nancy Denney (1982, 1984) has advanced a similar distinction between exercised and unexercised cognitive abilities to describe why some abilities remain stable and others decline across the adult life span. Exercised ability is the ability an individual exhibits when performance on the ability has been well-trained or highly practiced (e.g., measures of crystallized intelligence). Unexercised ability is the ability an individual exhibits when performance involves no prior training or practice (e.g., measures of fluid intelligence).

These two theories of adult intelligence have been helpful in understanding how performance on psychometric tests differs between the young and the older adult. However, skepticism has been expressed throughout the years as to the relevance of psychometric tests for measuring adult intelligence (e.g., Baltes et al., 1984; Labouvie-Vief, 1980; Labouvie-Vief & Chandler, 1978). Psychometric tests were originally designed to predict success in school and are moderately correlated (rs = .4−.7) with various measures of school achievement (Carroll, 1982). Correlations between psychometric test performance and measures of real-world intellectual efficacy such as occupational success (Wigdor & Garner, 1982) and complex decision making skills (e.g., Ceci & Liker, 1986) are often quite small and insignificant. Correlations between psychometric measures of fluid and crystallized intelligence and psychometric measures of practical intelligence (e.g., the Educational Testing Service Basic Skills Test), however, have been found to be much larger (see Willis & Schaie, 1986).

By relying on psychometric intelligence tests, work on measured intellectual efficacy has largely defined intellectual efficacy for adults as the same as it is for school-aged children, "academic forms of intelligence." This definition is in contrast to theorists who argue that intellectual efficacy becomes less tied to academic forms and more tied to pragmatic forms of intelligence during middle and late adulthood (e.g., Baltes et al., 1984; Cavanaugh, Kramer, Sinnott, Camp, & Markley, 1985; Labouvie-Vief, 1982). A slightly different view of intellectual efficacy comes from work on perceived intellectual efficacy.

Perceived Intellectual Efficacy

Research on perceived efficacy and cognitive aging comes from two different traditions (Lachman, 1986b). The tradition of metacognition in cognitive aging (e.g., Cavanaugh & Perlmutter, 1982; Dixon & Hultsch, 1983; Herrmann, this volume; Perlmutter, 1978) has primarily focused on memory, examining the knowledge individuals have of their own memory (i.e., how many items an individual can remember, strategies that will be useful in remembering, etc.) and how this knowledge relates to actual memory performance. A second tradition comes out of Bandura's social-learning theory (e.g., Bandura, 1982) and examines how perceptions of intellectual efficacy may change throughout the life span and influence and be influenced by specific cognitive performances (e.g., Cornelius & Caspi, 1986; Lachman, 1986a; Lachman & Jelalian, 1984). I focus here on work that comes from Bandura's tradition and limit my discussion to work on intellectual efficacy and aging.

Perceived self-efficacy has been defined by Bandura (1982) as "concerned with judgments of how well one can execute courses of action required to deal with prospective situations" (p. 122). Self-efficacy judgments have been found to impact a number of performance measures: (a) an individual's willingness to engage in certain kinds of activities, (b) an individual's expenditure of effort in a given task, and (c) an individual's emotional reaction to an activity (see Bandura, 1986, for a review). Perceived self-efficacy may be important for understanding cognitive decline in older subjects as cognitive performance is said to vary as a function of perceived efficacy. That is, some of the performance decrements seen in older adults, may be a consequence of expectations of intellectual decline in older adults.

Lachman and her colleagues have conducted much of the research on perceived intellectual efficacy in older adults. Lachman, Baltes, Nesselroade, and Willis (1982) developed a multidimensional inventory that assesses beliefs and feelings of intellectual efficacy. In particular, their measure consists of scales that assess perceptions of intellectual control (internal, chance, and powerful others), achievement motivation, anxiety about intellectual aging, and attitudes towards one's own intellectual aging. In general, Lachman et al.'s inventory assesses these beliefs with everyday intellectual behaviors such as studying a map, ("If I studied a map carefully, I could figure out how to get around in a strange place"), doing crossword puzzles ("My crossword puzzle skills will go downhill even if I keep doing puzzles"), and writing letters ("It means a lot to me to be able to write coherent letters to my friends"). However, she used measures of fluid and crystallized intelligence to assess measured intellectual efficacy (e.g., measures of general reasoning, memory span, etc.).

Lachman et al. found that these self-perceptions of intellectual efficacy were related moderately (rs ranging from −.54 to .40) to a wide range of measures of intelligence (i.e., measures of general reasoning, memory span, crystallized knowledge, and perceptual speed). An internal locus of control, high-achievement motivation, and a positive attitude toward one's own aging were associated with high scores on measures of intelligence, whereas other orientations to control (i.e., chance and powerful others) and anxiety toward one's own aging were associated with low scores on measures of intelligence. Lachman et al.'s research demonstrates that perceived intellectual efficacy is related to measured intelligence in older adults.

Cornelius and Caspi (1986) administered Lachman et al.'s intellectual efficacy questionnaire to middle-aged and older individuals to examine possible age differences in perceived intellectual efficacy. They found that intellectual efficacy remained stable during the middle-aged years, but declined between ages 60 and 75. However, concern about intellectual efficacy remained stable during the middle-aged years and increased between ages 60 and 75. These changes in perceived intellectual efficacy might lead to declines in measured intellectual efficacy or might be the result of declines in measured intellectual performance throughout the life span.

Lachman et al. (1986) addressed the question of causal directions between perceived intellectual efficacy and measured intellectual performance via a cognitive training study designed to improve performance on measures of attention, figural relations, and induction. Although the cognitive training improved performance on some of the specific cognitive measures, training did not change individuals' beliefs regarding their intellectual self-efficacy.

Lachman (1986a) suggested that one reason for the lack of change in perceived intellectual efficacy is that perceived intellectual efficacy and measured intellectual efficacy were assessed by different kinds of mental abilities. That is, the intellectual efficacy questionnaire assesses a wide range of intellectual behaviors, largely those engaged in in everyday life, while the psychometric measures of intelligence used in such studies include academic abilities such as vocabulary and abstract reasoning. Thus, although individuals may have perceived gains in academic cognitive performance, these gains did not translate to increased feelings of intellectual efficacy on a wide range of everyday behaviors. The lack of relation between improvement in intellectual performance and perceived intellectual efficacy points out how older adults may perceive that academic intellectual abilities (e.g., attention, spatial problem solving, and abstract problem solving) are quite unrelated to their ability to execute everyday intellectual behaviors.

In sum, researchers investigating perceived intellectual efficacy have been defining intellectual efficacy in two different ways. They have been measuring perceived intellectual efficacy via everyday intellectual behaviors (e.g., studying a map, doing crossword puzzles), while assessing intellectual performance via psychometric intelligence tests that have been used traditionally to measure the academic success of students in school. It seems clear from the research that adults view these two kinds of intellectual behaviors as somewhat distinct (see also Williams, Denney, & Schadler, 1983). Which kind of intellectual behaviors, "academic" or "everyday," better represent an adult's view of what constitutes intellectual efficacy is unknown. A relatively new approach to cognitive and intellectual development, a contextual approach, will be used to define the scope of what constitutes intellectual efficacy and to suggest methods for investigating the nature of intelligence throughout the adult life span (e.g., Baltes et al., 1984; Berg & Sternberg, 1985a; Lerner et al., 1983; Lerner & Kauffman, 1985).

CONTEXTUAL PERSPECTIVE

Contextual perspectives to intelligence and cognition have historically been associated with the cross-cultural literature that has examined how different cultural contexts contribute to differences in people's intellectual performance (Berry, 1974; Laboratory of Comparative Human Cognition, 1982). Recent contextual models of intellectual development share the notion that intelligence is concerned with the mental activity involved in providing an optimal fit between the individual and the demands of the individual's context (e.g., Baltes et al., 1984; Berg & Sternberg, 1985a; Rogoff, 1982). The individual's context is described as multifaceted, consisting of biological, sociocultural, environmental, and historical elements (Lerner & Kauffman, 1985).

The contextual approach ties intelligence to the specific environment in which intellectual behavior is exhibited and suggests that what constitutes "intelligence" may change with environmental variations. The contexts of adults have been described as differing in a variety of ways throughout the life span. For instance, Havighurst (1972) and Neugarten, Moore, and Lowe (1968) characterized adulthood as involving different developmental life tasks that are most appropriately accomplished at a certain time in the life span. For example, starting a family and an occupation have been characterized as relevant life tasks during young adulthood and adjusting to impairments of health and to retirement as relevant life tasks during late adulthood. Congruent with the work on life tasks, work in stress and coping finds that adults differ in the kinds of major and daily life stressors they report (e.g., Folkman, Lazarus, Pimley, & Novacek, 1987; Lazarus & DeLongis, 1983), differences that may arise from adults' different developmental life tasks. Young adults typically report more hassles dealing with finances, work, and family and friends; whereas older adults report more hassles dealing with health and home maintenance. The contexts of adults also differ throughout the life span in terms of biology (e.g., Finch & Schneider, 1985), and often the physical environment (e.g. Scheidt & Windley, 1985). As the contexts of adults differ throughout the life span in such a multifaceted way, so may changes occur in the kinds of activities it takes to adapt to these contexts (see Folkman et al., 1987, for a demonstration of the different kinds of coping mechanisms used by young and older adults).

Contextual perspectives to adult intellectual development emphasize that many aspects of an individual's context change throughout the adult life span. Baltes and his colleagues (e.g., Baltes et al., 1984; Dittmann-Kohli & Baltes, 1984; Smith, Dixon, & Baltes, 1985) emphasized that early in development many of the environments to which individuals must adapt are shared in common and consist of predominantly "academic" tasks. In adult development, however, the environments to which individuals must adapt become increasingly specialized and vary across individuals, with the kinds of tasks that individuals hold in common consisting of more "everyday" sorts of tasks. Berg and Sternberg (1985a) also argued that the environmental demands to which older individuals must adapt (e.g., death of a spouse, chronic illness, retirement, etc.)

differ, often substantially, from the environmental demands to which younger individuals must adapt (e.g., different job, marriage, birth of child, etc.). As changes occur in a person's context with development, the mental activity it takes to adapt to these contexts may also change.

One criticism that can be raised against contextual perspectives to intellectual development is that they do not represent a well-articulated view of intelligence as adaptation, but simply the broad strokes by which intelligence can be understood. The specific details for determining which aspects of adaptive behavior should be considered as "intelligent" are typically missing. For instance, although we know from work on stress and coping that stressors dealing with the household and personal concerns are relevant features of an adult's context, we do not understand how such features of the context should be incorporated into models of intelligence. One way in which to uncover what can be considered adaptive intelligent behavior is to examine the beliefs that adults of various ages hold about intelligence as it is manifested at various points in the life span.

People's views regarding what defines intellectual efficacy are important from a contextual perspective for two reasons. First, Neisser (1979) and others (e.g., Sternberg, 1984) argued that intelligence is to some extent a cultural invention, or at least a construct based on consensual agreement. That is, a person's intelligence is the degree to which the person corresponds to his or her culture's prototype of an exceptionally intelligent individual. The measures of intelligence that we use today are simply those that correspond with our culture's view of an exceptionally intelligent individual (i.e., someone who excels in school) and are, in some sense, based on the intuitive notions of researchers who study intelligence. Second, as intelligence is defined within the contextual perspective as the mental activity it takes to adapt to a particular context, it makes sense to ask those who occupy that context what mental abilities they are using to adapt to their context. I now present preliminary research that explores people's conceptions of intelligence across the adult life span and demonstrate how these conceptions may be useful in building a framework for what may be considered relevant for intellectual efficacy across the life span.

BUILDING A FRAMEWORK FOR INTELLECTUAL EFFICACY DURING ADULTHOOD

In order to examine people's conceptions of intelligence during adulthood, Berg and Sternberg (1985b) explored people's prototypes of intelligent individuals during early adulthood, middle-aged adulthood, and late adulthood. To understand the range of behaviors that individuals believe constitute an intelligent adult, Berg and Sternberg (1985b) asked 141 individuals ranging in age from 20 to 83 years to list behaviors that they viewed as characteristic of an exceptionally intelligent individual and an exceptionally unintelligent individual of either 30, 50, or 70 years of age. A subset of these behaviors, identified by a group of adults of various ages as important in characterizing intelligent individuals at these ages, was then given to a new group of young, middle-aged, and older individuals. This group consisted of 69 individuals: 21 young (mean age = 34.8, range 26–40), 26 middle-aged (mean age = 48.6, range 41–59) and 22 older (mean age = 67.6, range 61–85) individuals. (Note, this work is currently being extended with a much larger sample of individuals.) These subjects rated how likely it would be for individuals of average intelligence and individuals of exceptional intelligence at 30, 50, and 70 years of age to be engaged in these behaviors. The variable of interest in the rating questionnaire was the difference between ratings of the individual of exceptional intelligence and the individual of average intelligence. This difference variable reflected the degree to which a particular behavior was perceived as able to discriminate between individuals of average intelligence and individuals of exceptional intelligence at any particular age level.

These difference variables then were factor analyzed via principal component factor analyses with a varimax rotation separately for the intelligent characteristics at 30, 50, and 70 years of age. The three major factors obtained for the ratings of what characterizes intelligence at 30 years of age were (a) solving novel problems, (b) crystallized intelligence, and (c) everyday competence; for the ratings of what characterizes intelligence at 50 years of age the factors were (a) solving novel problems, (b) everyday competence, and (c) social competence; for the ratings of what characterizes intelligence at 70 years of age the factors were (a) composite fluid and crystallized intelligence, (b) everyday competence, and (c) cognitive investment. (See Table 5.1 for a list of the factors and representative behaviors that had loadings on these factors of .6 or above.)

In order to determine if there were individual differences in people's intuitive notions of intelligence as a function of age, factor scores, representing how much the participant valued the specific factor, were correlated with the age of the participant. Significant positive correlations were found between the age of the participant and the importance given to some of the nontraditional intellectual characteristics. In particular, age was found to correlate positively with everyday competence for the 30-year-old prototype ($r = .33$, $p < .01$), with knowledge and responsibility for the 50-year-old prototype ($r = .31$, $p < .01$) and with cognitive investment ($r = .35$, $p < .01$) for the 70-year-old prototype. It appears,

TABLE 5.1
Components of Intelligence According to Adults

Factor

30-year-old

I. Novelty in Problem Solving
   Is interested in gaining knowledge and learning new things.
   Reasons logically and well.
   Displays curiosity.
   Is able to perceive and store new information.
   Solves problems well.
   Is able to learn and reason with new kinds of concepts.
II. Knowledge and Verbal Intelligence
   Is experienced in one's field.
   Is competent in career choice.
   Is able to draw conclusions from information given.
   Is well educated in career choice.
   Displays clarity of speech.
III. Everyday Competence
   Displays good common sense.
   Adjusts to life situations.
   Is able to adapt to disastrous life situations.
   Is interested in one's family and home life.
   Deals effectively with problems and stress.

50-year-old

I. Novelty in Problem Solving
   Is able to analyze topics in new and original ways.
   Is able to perceive and store new information.
   Is able to learn and reason with new kinds of concepts.
   Is able to integrate and compare information.
   Displays curiosity.
II. Everyday Competence
   Adjusts to life situations.
   Is perceptive about people and things.
   Is open-minded about new ideas and trends.
   Is able to adapt to disastrous life situations.
   Deals effectively with problems and stress.
   Is able to adapt well to one's environment.
   Thinks before acting or speaking.
III. Social Competence
   Acts in a mature manner.
   Has high moral values.
   Is interested in one's family and home life.
   Displays good common sense.

(continued)

TABLE 5.1
(continued)

Factor

70-year-old

I. Composite Fluid and Crystallized Intelligence
Displays a good vocabulary.
Reads widely.
Is able to perceive and store new information.
Discovers new ideas.
Is able to draw conclusions from information given.
Solves problems well.
Is able to learn and reason with new kinds of concepts.
Is well educated in career choice.

II. Everyday Competence
Displays wisdom in actions and thoughts.
Is perceptive about people and things.
Thinks before acting or speaking.
Is able to adapt to disastrous life situations.
Adjusts to life situations.
Reasons logically and well.
Is aware of what is going on around him or her.
Displays good common sense.
Is able to adapt well to one's environment.

III. Cognitive Investment
Displays curiosity
Appreciates young and old individuals.
Is interested in one's family and home life.

---

then, that older individuals believe that nontraditional intellectual abilities are more important than do younger individuals in characterizing intelligence.

Support for the increasing importance of nonacademic abilities in characterizing intelligence across the adult life span comes from other data gathered in the Berg and Sternberg study. In addition to rating the behaviors just described, individuals were asked various questions regarding their beliefs about intelligence. One such question was whether individuals believed that intelligence tests that were used for measuring the intelligence of individuals in high school were appropriate for measuring the intelligence of middle aged and older adults and why or why not. Eighty-two percent of the individuals answered that intelligence tests used with high school students were not appropriate for measuring intelligence during middle and late adulthood, with individuals indicating that life experience and maturity must be considered and that intelligence tests should be geared on the practical as opposed to the academic realm.

The beginning framework for components of intellectual efficacy that results from this study includes verbal intelligence, solving novel problems, everyday competence, motivation and personal investment, and social competence. This framework illustrates that laypeople view the realm of intellectual behavior as encompassing more everyday intellectual skills than are studied by researchers in adult intelligence. Researchers and laypeople are in agreement that novelty in problem solving and verbal intelligence are important aspects of intelligence (e.g., Horn & Cattell, 1967; Thurstone, 1960). However, abilities such as everyday competence have only recently been addressed by researchers in cognitive aging (e.g., Cornelius & Caspi, 1987; Denney & Palmer, 1981; Willis & Schaie, 1986). Competencies such as social competence and motivation, however, have rarely been examined in the cognitive aging field (e.g., Kramer, 1986; Lachman, 1986b).

The study suggests that similarities do exist in the types of behaviors that are considered to be adaptive and reflective of intelligent behavior at different adult ages. However, the perceived rank or importance of these adaptive behaviors in characterizing intelligence seems to differ from one age to the next. For instance, older individuals viewed nonacademic intellectual abilities as better able to discriminate between individuals of exceptional and average intelligence of nearly all ages than did younger individuals. This perceived salience of everyday competence in the later years is in agreement with many researchers who emphasize the importance of practical intellectual abilities during the middle and late adult years (e.g., Baltes et al., 1984; Labouvie-Vief & Chandler, 1978).

The approach used here to help define intellectual efficacy, namely using people's conceptions of what comprises intelligence, is not without its limitations. First, this particular study is based on a relatively small sample size and current research in progress is needed to determine whether such beliefs about intelligence extend to larger and more divergent samples of adults. Second, the view of intelligence represented by such beliefs may not generalize to another point in history or to another culture or subculture. If intelligence is viewed in its context, then behaviors that are adaptive intellectually at one point in time or for one culture may not be adaptive during another point in time or for another culture (e.g., Horn, 1979; Laboratory of Comparative Human Cognition, 1982).

Perhaps most importantly, the framework for intellectual efficacy that results from work on people's conceptions of intelligence may potentially be incorrect or incomplete in some respects. People's conceptions of intelligence should not be used exclusively to build a framework for what defines intellectual efficacy, just as experts' conceptions of intelligence should not be used exclusively. Rather, people's conceptions set the scope for what might be investigated in intellectual research and must be validated against actual measures of intellectual functioning. For instance, I am piloting a study in a retirement center where individuals are nominated by their peers as highly intelligent and then examined on a broad array of psychometric intelligence tests and observed in their functioning on several everyday life tasks (e.g., social competence, motivation, ability to cope with life situations, etc.). The framework that resulted from the work on people's conceptions of intelligence led me to broaden the kinds of intellectual behaviors that I investigated as representative of intelligence beyond psychometric measures of intelligence. People's conceptions of intelligence, however, should not replace actual behavioral measurements of intellectual functioning.

In summary, this sample of adults perceives that intellectual efficacy includes abilities that have traditionally been measured in intellectual aging (e.g., fluid intelligence and crystallized intelligence) and abilities that have until recently been outside the scope of intelligence testing (e.g., everyday competence, social competence). Research on measured intellectual efficacy shows that measures of some of these specific abilities show differential functions of decline, increase, and stability across development. Work on perceived intellectual efficacy would predict correspondences between the developmental functions of measured intellectual efficacy and perceived intellectual efficacy. Whether developmental functions of measured intellectual efficacy are accompanied by similar functions of perceived intellectual efficacy was the primary question of the next study.

Beliefs About the Developmental Course of Intellectual Self-Efficacy

Given the framework described earlier on what constitutes the scope of intellectual efficacy, the following study examined people's beliefs about what happens to these abilities throughout their life span. The participants were 75 community-residing individuals ranging in age from 20 to 87 years of age: 19 young (mean age = 31.7, range 20–39), 37 middle-aged (mean age = 49.1, range 40–59), and 19 older adults (mean age = 69.9, range 60–87). Participants were first given two tests from Thurstone's Primary Mental Abilities Test (1960): Number Series, to tap fluid intelligence and Verbal Meaning, to tap crystallized intelligence.

Participants were then asked to complete a questionnaire regarding self-perceptions of intellectual abilities. Participants were asked to rate during their own adult life span (age 20 to age 90) their own past, current, and future ability on a 1 (exceptionally bad) to 9 (exceptionally good) rating scale with 5 (representing average ability) as the midpoint. For instance, a 50-year-old individual reflected on the developmental course of his abilities prior to 50, rated his present ability, and predicted his future ability in the years past 50. Participants made ratings for five different abilities that the previous study on people's intuitive notions of intelligence indicated were factors comprising intelligence during adulthood: (a) solving novel problems such as the number series task, (b) vocabulary skills such as the verbal meaning task, (c) everyday competence such as dealing with everyday problems, (d) the ability to be motivated and interested in a variety of things, and (e) social competence such as the ability to communicate with other people.

A repeated measures analysis of variance was used to determine the effect of ability (e.g., novel problem solving, verbal, etc.), the effect of decade year (i.e., ratings for 20, 30, 40, etc.), and the effect of the age group of the participants (young, middle-aged, and older) on these ratings. The results (as displayed in Fig. 5.1) indicated that, in general, people perceived marked differences between the developmental course of novel problem solving and all other intellectual skills throughout their life span. There were significant differences in the level of functioning achieved in these abilities F (4, 256) = 5.87, $p < .01$, with people indicating that their level of novel problem solving was much lower than their level of vocabulary, everyday problem solving, motivation, and social competence.

In addition, there was a significant decade year × abilities interaction F (28, 56) = 5.17, $p < .01$, indicating that participants' perceived level of novel problem solving declined more markedly and somewhat earlier than their perceived level of the other abilities (i.e., vocabulary, everyday problem solving, motivation, and social competence). This distinction between the level and developmental function of perceived novel problem solving and the other intellectual abilities held when examining the perceptions of young, middle-aged, and older adults separately, as there was no significant abilities × decade year × age group interaction.

These beliefs regarding intellectual efficacy were accompanied by similar developmental functions of measured ability for the two abilities that were assessed, number series and vocabulary performance. An ANOVA on the Number Series Test indicated a significant effect of age F (2, 72) = 14.90, $p < .01$, with Scheffé multiple comparisons revealing that older individuals ($M = 4.9$ correct) performed significantly worse than middle-aged ($M = 10$ correct) and young individuals ($M = 12.3$), who did not differ from each other. An ANOVA on the Verbal Meaning Test revealed no significant effect of age ($M = 48.5$, 49.8 and 45.2 correct for the young, middle-aged, and older individuals, respectively).

There was a fair amount of agreement between people's perceived ability to solve novel problems and measured number series performance

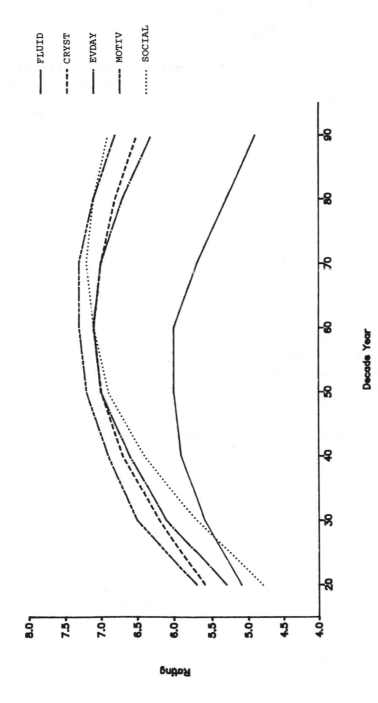

FIG. 5.1   Perceived intellectual efficacy by ability.

169

and perceived vocabulary ability and measured vocabulary performance (see Table 5.2 for the correlations). These correlations indicate that individuals were fairly accurate in their perceptions of academic skills and thus may be accurate in their perceptions of their everyday competence, social competence, and motivation. Self-perceptions of the other intellectual abilities were not related to measures of number series nor vocabulary. From these correlations, it seems that psychometric measures of fluid and crystallized ability may not be extremely useful in measuring what people *perceive* as their everyday competence, motivation, and social competence.

The similarity in perceived developmental functions among vocabulary ability and other nontraditional intellectual abilities (e.g., everyday competence, motivation, and social competence) and the dissimilarity between these abilities and novel problem solving is quite consistent with research on the developmental functions of measured intellectual abilities (e.g., Cornelius & Caspi, 1987; Horn & Cattell, 1967). Cornelius and Caspi, for example, measured everyday problem-solving ability, and performance on the verbal meaning and letter series tests of Thurstone's Primary Mental Abilities Test. They found that the developmental functions of measured vocabulary and everyday problem solving were very similar, increasing until age 70, whereas the developmental function of measured letter series performance increased until age 40 and decreased sharply from age 50. Whether self-perceptions of intellectual efficacy for these different abilities lead to different developmental functions of measured intellectual efficacy, or vice versa, needs to be addressed in future research.

Additional research is needed to determine what differentiates these abilities in the minds of adults. Some research suggests that measures of fluid intelligence are often abilities that (a) older individuals perceive as unfamiliar, difficult, and effortful (Cornelius, 1984); (b) adults of all ages perceive as related more to "academic" types of skills, rather than

TABLE 5.2
Correlations Between Perceived and Measured Intellectual Abilities

Perceived Ability	Measured Performance	
	Number Series	Vocabulary
Novelty in problem solving	.45**	.28*
Vocabulary	.05	.43**
Everyday competence	.05	.20
Motivation	.16	.21
Social competence	−.25	−.06

*$p<.05$; **$p<.01$

"everyday" skills (Cornelius, Kenny, & Caspi, 1985); and (c) many individuals perceive as of limited use for measuring the intelligence of adults (e.g., Berg & Sternberg, 1985b). Other dimensions that may be useful in differentiating such abilities include the actual and perceived amount of control an individual has over the developmental course of the ability (e.g., Harter & Connell, 1984, Rodin, chapter 1, this volume), the importance an individual gives to the ability (e.g., Harter, 1983), and the kinds of contexts in which the individual exhibits the ability (Bronfenbrenner, 1977).

In summary, this study on perceived intellectual efficacy illustrates the importance of looking at perceived intellectual efficacy on specific intellectual abilities, rather than measuring perceived intellectual efficacy in a molar fashion. This study suggests that people's perceptions of their own intellectual abilities differ both in level and in developmental trajectory, depending on the ability. If perceived intellectual efficacy were assessed in a more specific fashion, it may be possible to get a better idea of how increases in measured ability achieved through training result in changes in one's perceived intellectual efficacy. Research by Dittmann-Kohli, Baltes, and Kliegl (1983) indicates that assessing perceived intellectual efficacy in a more specific fashion yields better relations to actual gains in measured intellectual functioning achieved through training, than Lachman demonstrated. That is, gains on traditional measures of intelligence achieved through training were related to perceived intellectual efficacy for training relevant tasks, but not to perceived intellectual efficacy for everyday tasks.

In addition, psychometric measures of fluid and crystallized intelligence may not provide us with much guidance in measuring what people perceive to be their everyday competence, motivation, and social competence. If traditional measures of intelligence will not be useful in assessing these abilities that laypeople perceive as important in the assessment of intelligence, then what measures will be?

UNCOVERING EFFICACY IN EVERYDAY COMPETENCE

I have recently begun a large-scale project investigating contextual features of people's everyday experiences and problems throughout the life span with Carol Sansone, that is helpful in addressing what individuals perceive as constituting efficacy in everyday competence. We are examining the dimensions that individuals use to describe their everyday experiences and problems in six different domains and how these dimensions may be influenced by global contextual features (e.g., domain of problem, developmental demands) and by features of the individual (e.g., experience, age, gender, etc.). Six different domains (school, work, health, leisure, friends, family, and an open domain) were chosen for examining how people describe their experiences and problems. These domains were chosen as they arise as relevant domains for children and adults in many different literatures: planning (e.g., Kreitler & Kreitler, 1987), stress and coping (e.g., Compas, 1987; Folkman et al., 1987) and practical problem solving (Cornelius & Caspi, 1987; Spivack & Shure, 1982).

Preliminary coding of these open-ended descriptions of experiences and problems indicates that many different kinds of dimensions are represented in these descriptions. These dimensions describe many features of the experience or problem: when and where it took place, emotional aspects, interpersonal exchanges, actions (both physical and verbal), cognitive aspects, physical state of the person, evaluations of self and other, and so on. In addition to having individuals describe their experiences and problems, individuals indicate how they dealt with the problem, how they felt about what they did in response to the problem, and what they would do in the future to avoid the problem, among other questions. We currently have data on 125 young adults and 40 older adults, with data collection with children and middle-aged adults, in process.

Most pertinent to the question framed at the beginning of this section "What kinds of abilities will be useful in understanding efficacy in everyday competence?", we asked participants to describe the individual that they felt would best have been able to solve the problem (i.e., abilities, personality, talents, etc.). This question was designed to uncover abilities that individuals perceive as characterizing efficacy in everyday problem solving in these six specific domains. We have now coded all of the young adults' data and some of the older adults' data on such efficacy questions. Some of our preliminary data are presented here to illustrate how people's perceptions of efficacy for everyday problem solving extend beyond the cognitive realm.

Table 5.3 lists our current coding scheme for these dimensions of efficacy which include achievement motivation (e.g., drive toward success, highly motivated, hard working, drive), personality characteristics (extroverted, neurotic, and open to experience), dimensions of affect (both expression of affect and control of affect), social skills (e.g., getting along with others, skilled in communication), and cognition (e.g., intelligence, creativity, logic, insight), among others. As one can see from Table 5.3, cognitive characteristics were only one component of efficacy among many components. Not only were cognitive characteristics only one component of efficacy, but their mention in these problems was quite infrequent.

TABLE 5.3
Behaviors Mentioned as Characterizing Efficacy in Everyday
Problem Solving

Efficacy Component	Description
Achievement motivation	Attributes associated with a drive toward success (e.g., dedicated, determined, drive, hard working, motivated, etc.).
Affect	Emotional reactions to events (e.g., fear, angry, hostile, etc.).
Controlled affect	Being in control of emotions (e.g., calm, cool, collected, etc.).
Cognition	Skills related to thinking (e.g., intelligence, creativity, logical, insightful).
Time management	Ability to plan ahead (e.g., doesn't procrastinate).
Experience	Attributes associated with experience in a particular domain (e.g., experienced, knowledgeable, well-trained, etc.).
Extroverted personality	(e.g., outgoing, assertive, aggressive, fun loving, adventurous, self-assured.)
Neurotic personality	Characterized by moodiness and anxiety.
Openness to experience	Similar to Costa and McCrae's factor of personality (e.g., open-minded, curious, personally aware).
Personal integrity	Being truthful, honest, having good morals.
Physical	Use of physical skills to solve the problem (e.g., athletic skills, high pain threshold, physical health).
Social skills	Getting along with others, skilled in communication, etc.
Inappropriate skills	Being harsh, verbally abusive, a good liar.
Change in environment	Making one's environment more stable, more financially stable.
Humor	Jokes about problem, lighthearted.
Use of other people	Uses friends, relationships, and other intermediaries.
Nothing as alternative	Avoided the problem, helpless to change anything about the problem.
Nothing as best course of action	Lassez-faire approach as letting the problem solve itself is best course of action.

For instance, on one section of the questionnaire we asked individuals to describe a recent problem, without specifying a specific domain of the problem. The frequency with which components of efficacy were mentioned by both young and older individuals are listed in Table 5.4. First, notice that cognitive characteristics were mentioned fairly infrequently by both young (11.5%) and older individuals (7.9%). Second, notice that there was a great deal of similarity in the kinds of characteristics that young and older adults saw as comprising efficacy for solving

TABLE 5.4
Percent Mentions of Components of Efficacy in Everyday Problem:
Open Domain

Efficacy Component	Young	Older
Achievement motivation	11.5	13.2
Affect	1.3	0
Controlled affect	10.2	6.6
Cognition	11.5	7.9
Time management	1.8	0
Experience	5.8	17.1
Extroverted personality	15.9	18.4
Neurotic personality	.4	0
Open to experience personality	8.8	2.6
Personal integrity	1.3	1.3
Physical	5.3	0
Social skills	16.4	23.7
Inappropriate skills	2.7	1.3
Change in environments	1.8	0
Humor	1.3	0
Other people	2.2	5.3
Nothing as alternative	.4	1.3
Nothing as best course of action	0	1.3

their everyday problems. For instance, both groups mentioned that efficacy in everyday problem solving would include social skills, achievement motivation, and extroverted personality characteristics. There may, however, be slight differences in the frequency with which behaviors were mentioned by young and older adults: Older individuals mentioned the use of experience more than younger individuals, whereas younger individuals mentioned controlling affect and cognition slightly more than older individuals.

In order to get a preliminary sense of domain differences in the kinds of characteristics perceived to comprise efficacy in these domains, we examined the mention of these behaviors by the domain of everyday problem for young adults (see Table 5.5). It appears that certain characteristics may be perceived as differentially effective to use when solving problems that occur in a certain domain. For instance, social skills were perceived as extremely effective when solving problems with friends, controlling one's affect was perceived as differentially effective when solving problems that occur during work or with one's family, and cognitive skills were viewed as most effective when solving school-related problems. As we gather more data on older individuals, we will be able to determine whether there are age differences as well as domain differences in what is considered efficacy for everyday problems.

This work on perceived efficacy in everyday problem solving demon-

TABLE 5.5
Percent Mentions of Components of Efficacy by Domain of
Everyday Problem: College Students

Efficacy Component	Domain					
	Work	Health	Leisure	Friends	Family	School
Achievement motivation	11.8	25.0	19.6	4.5	0	18.4
Affect	0	0	0	0	3.2	2.6
Lack of affect	19.6	5.0	2.2	13.6	22.6	5.3
Cognition	9.8	2.5	4.3	6.8	6.5	21.1
Experience	7.8	5.0	8.7	9.1	0	2.6
Extroversion	19.6	10.0	19.6	13.6	22.6	18.4
Openness to experience	7.8	15.0	8.7	4.5	16.1	0
Physical skills	5.9	10.0	10.9	11.4	0	5.3
Social skills	13.7	2.5	6.5	31.8	12.9	23.7
Nothing	0	5.0	2.2	0	0	0

strates that if we are to expand our definition of intelligence to encompass everyday competence (as adults perceive is necessary) and capture what adults perceive as efficacy in everyday competence, the domain of skills relevant for intellectual efficacy must be greatly enlarged. These skills largely consist of skills that researchers outside of the field of intelligence testing investigate and consist of personality characteristics, motivation, social skills, and affect. In order to capture what adults perceive as efficacy in everyday competence, researchers must be willing to incorporate such skills into models that describe everyday performance (e.g., Cornelius & Caspi, 1986; Lachman, 1986b). Adults may, however, be wrong in what they perceive as defining efficacy in everyday competence, and thus such perceptions of efficacy must be validated against behavioral measures of everyday competence. Some research on everyday competence also points to the importance of skills other than cognitive ones in everyday competence as measures of cognitive abilities do not explain much of the variability in measures of everyday competence (e.g., Berg, 1989; Cornelius & Caspi, 1987).

Although preliminary at this point, there was some suggestion that age differences may exist in the perceived importance of components of efficacy for solving everyday problems. This difference is consistent with a contextual perspective to intelligence, as older adults are perhaps solving different kinds of problems than younger adults. The stress and coping literature, discussed earlier, indicates that although young and older adults deal with similar kinds of stressors, they do differ in the frequency with which they experience certain kinds of stressors (e.g.,

Folkman et al., 1987). Other characteristics of individuals that may be important in determining what components are deemed most effective such as experience and gender are currently being investigated. There was also some suggestion that components of efficacy may differ somewhat by domain, in that certain components were viewed as differentially effective in specific domains. This research suggests a very complex interaction between features of the individual (e.g., age and experience) and features of the context (e.g., domain of the problem) that impact efficacy in everyday problem solving. It may be that a small number of components may not be maximally effective in solving a wide range of everyday problems for all individuals (see also Berg, 1989; Mischel, 1984) as the context of the problem and the individual may require different components.

SUMMARY AND CONCLUSIONS

To conclude, I have argued that an understanding of measured intellectual efficacy and perceived intellectual efficacy during adulthood will benefit from an examination of adults' conceptions of what defines intellectual efficacy. A contextual theoretical perspective to intellectual development was used to examine the question of "What is intellectual efficacy during the adult life span?". Using this perspective, a beginning framework for what constitutes intellectual efficacy across the life span was proposed that uses people's own beliefs regarding what constitutes intelligent functioning across the life span. This framework included novelty in problem solving, vocabulary, everyday competence, motivation, and social competence. This view of intellectual efficacy is, in fact, consistent with what other theorists suggest is important for intellectual development during adulthood (e.g., Baltes et al., 1984; Berg & Sternberg, 1985a; Labouvie-Vief & Chandler, 1978).

Using this framework for what characterizes intelligence, a study was presented that examined the congruence between the developmental course of perceived intellectual efficacy and measured intellectual efficacy for different abilities. In this study, differences in perceived intellectual efficacy were found between novel problem solving and all other intellectual abilities, such that novel problem solving was perceived to decline much earlier and more markedly in the adult life span than other abilities. In addition, psychometric measures of fluid and crystallized intelligence were not predictive of people's self-perceptions of nontraditional intellectual skills such as everyday competence, social competence, and motivation. The differential functions of perceived intellectual efficacy for novel problem solving and the other intellectual abilities are consistent with research on the developmental functions of measured intellectual abilities (e.g., Cornelius & Caspi, 1987; Schaie, 1979). Research is needed to ascertain whether these differential functions of perceived efficacy produce differential functions of measured intellectual efficacy or are a product of such differential functions.

Finally, research was presented that begins to investigate a nontraditional measure of intelligence, namely, everyday problem solving, and what comprises efficacy for solving everyday problems. This research indicates that cognitive components may be only one of many components (e.g., personality, achievement motivation, and expressions of affect) involved in effectively solving everyday problems. By looking at nontraditional measures of intelligence such as everyday problem solving, the field of intellectual aging will begin to intersect with many fields outside of intelligence testing: stress and coping (e.g., see Evans, this volume; Folkman et al., 1987), personality development (Costa & Mc-Crae, 1980; Lachman, 1986b), and interpersonal problem solving (e.g., Spivack & Shure, 1982).

The major limitation in building a model of intellectual efficacy based on adults' perceptions of intelligence is that adults may be incorrect. I have argued that peoples' perceptions of intellectual efficacy should set the scope for what we consider as constituting intelligence, just as experts' conceptions should also set the scope. Neither the conceptions of laypeople nor experts should provide the final "truth" regarding what constitutes intelligence. These conceptions must be validated against behavioral measures of intelligence and adaptation in order to be certain that these perceptions provide an accurate basis for a model of intellectual efficacy. The advantage of including laypeople's conceptions is that they may elucidate elements of intelligence that have previously been missing in the literature. In fact, the studies reported in this paper indicate that researchers may be missing intelligent behaviors that are representative of everyday competence.

The research presented here, although preliminary in nature, points out how research framed within a contextual position to intelligence may benefit from what researchers from fields other than intellectual and cognitive aging know about adaptation to environments across the life span (e.g., stress and coping, interpersonal problem solving, motivation, etc.). Although such an approach to intellectual aging will cross diverse literatures and boundaries within developmental psychology, such complexity may be critical in defining a contextual position to intelligence.

ACKNOWLEDGMENTS

I would like to thank Debra Doyle, Christopher Layne, and Joel Richards for their help in various phases of data preparation. I would also like to thank Warner Schaie and Carmi Schooler for their helpful comments on an earlier draft of this chapter. This research was supported, in part, by a Biomedical Research Support Grant (S07RR07092) from NIH and a grant from the University Research Committee at the University of Utah.

REFERENCES

Baltes, P. B., Dittmann-Kohli, F., & Dixon, R. A. (1984). New perspectives on the development of intelligence in adulthood: Toward a dual-process conception and a model of selective optimization with compensation. In P. B. Baltes & O. G. Brim, Jr. (Eds.), *Life-span development and behavior* (Vol. 6, pp. 33–76). New York: Academic Press.

Baltes, P. B., Dittmann-Kohli, F., & Kliegl, R. (1985). *Reserve capacity of the elderly in aging-sensitive tests of fluid intelligence: Replication and extension.* Unpublished manuscript, Max Planck Institute for Human Development and Education, Berlin, FRG.

Baltes, P. B., & Willis, S. L. (1982). Plasticity and enhancement of intellectual functioning in old age: Penn State's adult development and enrichment program (ADEPT). In F. I. M. Craik & S. E. Trehub (Eds.), *Aging and cognitive processes* (pp. 353–389). New York: Plenum.

Bandura, A. (1982). Self-efficacy in human agency. *American Psychologist, 37,* 122–147.

Bandura, A. (1986). *Social foundations of thought and action: A social cognitive theory.* Englewood Cliffs, NJ: Prentice-Hall.

Berg, C. A. (1989). Knowledge of strategies for dealing with everyday problems from childhood through adolescence. *Developmental Psychology, 25,* 607–618.

Berg, C. A., & Sternberg, R. J. (1985a). A triarchic theory of intellectual development during adulthood. *Developmental Review, 5,* 334–370.

Berg, C. A., & Sternberg, R. J. (1985b). *Implicit theories of intelligence across the adult life span.* Unpublished manuscript. Department of Psychology, Yale University, New Haven, CT.

Berry, J. W. (1974). Radical cultural relativism and the concept of intelligence. In J. W. Berry & P. R. Dasen (Eds.), *Culture and cognition: Readings in cross-cultural psychology* (pp. 225–230). London: Methuen.

Botwinick, J. (1977). Intellectual abilities. In J. E. Birren & K. W. Schaie (Eds.), *Handbook of the psychology of aging* (pp. 580–605). New York: Van Nostrand.

Bronfenbrenner, U. (1977). Toward an experimental ecology of human development. *American Psychologist, 32,* 513–531.

Carroll, J. B. (1982). The measurement of intelligence. In R. J. Sternberg (Eds.), *Handbook of human intelligence* (pp. 29–120). New York: Cambridge University Press.

Cavanaugh, J. D., Kramer, D. A., Sinnott, J. D., Camp, C. J., & Markley, R. P. (1985). On missing links and such: Interfaces between cognitive research and everyday problem solving. *Human Development, 28,* 146–168.

Cavanaugh, J. C., & Perlmutter, M. (1982). Metamemory: A critical examination. *Child Development, 53,* 11–28.

Ceci, S. J., & Liker, J. (1986). Academic and nonacademic intelligence: An experimental separation. In R. J. Sternberg & R. K. Wagner (Eds.), *Practical intelligence: Nature and origins of competence in the everyday world* (pp. 119–142). New York: Cambridge University Press.

Compas, B. E. (1987). Stress and life events during childhood and adolescence. *Clinical Psychology Review, 7,* 1–28.

Cornelius, S. W. (1984). Classic pattern of intellectual aging: Test familiarity, difficulty, and performance. *Journal of Gerontology, 39,* 201–206.

Cornelius, S. W., & Caspi, A. (1986). Self-perceptions of intellectual control and aging. *Educational Gerontology, 12,* 345–357.

Cornelius, S. W., & Caspi, A. (1987). Everyday problem solving in adulthood and old age. *Psychology and Aging, 2,* 144–153.

Cornelius, S. W., Kenny, S., & Caspi, (1985). *Academic and everyday intelligence in adulthood: Conceptions of self and ability traits.* Unpublished manuscript, Department of Psychology, Cornell University, Ithaca. NY.

Costa, P., & McCrae, R. (1980). Still stable after all these years: Personality as a key to some issues in adulthood and old age. In P. B. Baltes & O. Brim (Eds.), *Life-span development and behavior* (Vol. 3, pp. 65–102). New York: Academic Press.

Denney, N. W. (1982). Aging and cognitive changes. In B. B. Wolman & G. Stricker (Eds.), *Handbook of developmental psychology* (pp. 807–827). Englewood Cliffs, NJ: Prentice-Hall.

Denney, N. W. (1984). A model of cognitive development across the life span. *Developmental Review, 4,* 171–191.

Denney, N. W., & Palmer, A. M. (1981). Adult age differences on traditional and practical problem-solving measures. *Journal of Gerontology, 36,* 323–328.

Dittmann-Kohli, F., & Baltes, P. B. (1984). *Towards an action-theoretical and pragmatic conception of intelligence during adulthood and old age.* Unpublished manuscript, Max Planck Institute, Berlin, FRG.

Dittmann-Kohli, F., Baltes, P. B., & Kliegl, R. (1983, November). *Cognitive training and self-efficacy in the elderly.* Poster presented at the meeting of the Gerontological Society of America, San Francisco, CA.

Dixon, R. A., & Hultsch, D. F. (1983). Metamemory and memory for text relationships in adulthood: A cross validation study. *Journal of Gerontology, 38,* 687–694.

Finch, C. E., & Schneider, E. L. (Eds.) (1985). *The handbook of the biology of aging.* New York: Van Nostrand.

Folkman, S., Lazarus, R. S., Pimley, S., & Novacek, J. (1987). Age differences in stress and coping processes. *Psychology and Aging, 2,* 171–184.

Harter, S. (1983). The development of the self-system. In M. Hetherington (Ed.), *Carmichael's manual of child psychology: Socialization, personality, and social development* (Vol. 4, pp. 275–385). New York: Wiley.

Harter, S., & Connell, J. P. (1984). A model of children's achievement and related self-perceptions of competence, control, and motivational orientation. In M. Mayer (Ed.) *Advances in motivation and achievement* (Vol. 3, pp. 219–250). Greenwich, CT: JAI Press.

Havighurst, R. (1972). *Developmental tasks and education.* New York: Van Nostrand.

Horn, J. L. (1979). Trends in the measurement of intelligence. In R. J. Sternberg & D. Detterman (Eds.), *Human Intelligence: Perspectives on its theory and measurement* (pp. 191–201). Norwood, NJ: Ablex.

Horn, J. L., & Cattell, R. B. (1967). Age differences in fluid and crystallized intelligence. *Acta Psychologia, 26,* 107–129.

Kramer, D. A. (1986). A life-span view of social cognition. *Educational Gerontology, 12,* 277–289.

Kreitler, S., & Kreitler, H. (1987). Conceptions and processes of planning: The developmental perspective. In S. L. Friedman, E. K. Scholnick, & R. R. Cocking (Eds.), *Blueprints for thinking* (pp. 110–178). New York: Cambridge University Press.

Laboratory of Comparative Human Cognition. (1982). Culture and intelligence. In R. J.

Sternberg (Ed.), *Handbook of human intelligence* (pp. 642–722). New York: Cambridge University Press.

Labouvie-Vief, G. (1980). Adaptive dimensions of adult cognition. In N. Datan & N. Lohmann (Eds.), *Transitions of aging* (pp. 3–26). New York: Academic Press.

Labouvie-Vief, G. (1982). Dynamic development and mature autonomy: A theoretical prologue. *Human Development, 25*, 161–191.

Labouvie-Vief, G., & Chandler, M. J. (1978). Cognitive development and life-span developmental theory: Idealistic versus contextual perspectives. In P. B. Baltes (Ed.), *Life-span development and behavior* (Vol. 1, pp. 181–210). New York: Academic Press.

Lachman, M. E. (1986a). Personal control in later life: Stability, change, and cognitive correlates. In M. M. Baltes & P. B. Baltes (Eds.), *The psychology of control and aging* (pp. 207–236). Hillsdale, NJ: Lawrence Erlbaum Associates.

Lachman, M. E. (1986b). The role of personality and social factors in intellectual aging. *Educational Gerontology, 12*, 339–344.

Lachman, M. E., Baltes, P. B., Nesselroade, J. R., & Willis, S. L. (1982). Examination of personality-ability relationships in the elderly: The role of the contextual (interface) assessment mode. *Journal of Research in Personality, 16*, 485–501.

Lachman, M. E., Baltes, P. B., Nesselroade, J. R., & Willis, S. L. (1986). *Cognitive training with elderly adults: Effects on personality and ethical issues.* Unpublished manuscript, Brandeis University, Department of Psychology, Waltham, MA.

Lachman, M. E., & Jelalian, E. (1984). Self-efficacy and attributions for intellectual performance in young and elderly adults. *Journal of Gerontology, 39*, 577–582.

Lazarus, R. S., & DeLongis, A. (1983). Psychological stress and coping in aging. *American Psychologist, 40*, 770–779.

Lerner, R. M., Hultsch, D. F., & Dixon, R. A. (1983). Contextualism and the character of developmental psychology in the 1970s. *Annals of the New York Academy of Sciences, 412*, 101–128.

Lerner, R. M., & Kauffman, M. B. (1985). The concept of development in contextualism. *Developmental Review, 5*, 309–333.

Mischel, W. (1984). Convergences and challenges in the search for consistency. *American Psychologist, 39*, 351–364.

Neisser, U. (1979). The concept of intelligence. In R. J. Sternberg & D. K. Detterman (Eds.), *Human intelligence: Perspectives on its theory and measurement* (pp. 179–189). Norwood, NJ: Ablex.

Neugarten, B. L., Moore, J. W., & Lowe, J. C. (1968). Age norms, age constraints, and adult socialization. In B. L. Neugarten (Ed.), *Middle age and aging* (pp. 22–28). Chicago, IL: University of Chicago Press.

Papalia, D. E. (1972). The status of several conservation abilities across the life span. *Human Development, 15*, 229–243.

Perlmutter, M. (1978). What is memory aging the aging of? *Developmental Psychology, 14*, 330–345.

Rogoff, B. (1982). Integrating context and cognitive development. In M. E. Lamb & A. L. Brown (Eds.), *Advances in developmental psychology* (Vol. 2, pp. 125–170). Hillsdale, NJ: Lawrence Erlbaum Associates.

Salthouse, T. A. (1982). *Adult cognition.* New York: Springer-Verlag.

Schaie, K. W. (1979). The primary mental abilities in adulthood: An exploration in the development of psychometric intelligence. In P. B. Baltes & O. G. Brim, Jr. (Eds.), *Life-span development and behavior* (Vol. 2, pp. 67–115). New York: Academic Press.

Schaie, K. W. (Ed.). (1983). *Longitudinal studies of adult psychological development.* New York: Guilford Press.

Scheidt, R. J., & Windley, P. G. (1985). The ecology of aging. In J. E. Birren & K. W. Schaie

(Eds.), *The handbook of the psychology of aging* (Vol. 2, pp. 245–260). New York: Van Nostrand.

Smith, J., Dixon, R. A., & Baltes, P. B. (1985). *Expertise in life planning: A new research approach to investigating aspects of wisdom.* Unpublished manuscript, Max Planck Institute for Human Development and Education, Berlin, FRG.

Spivack, G., & Shure, M. B. (1982). The cognition of social adjustment: Interpersonal cognitive problem solving thinking. In B. Lahey & A. E. Kazdin (Eds.), *Advances in clinical child psychology* (Vol. 5, pp. 323–372). New York: Plenum.

Sternberg, R. J. (1984). A contextual view of the nature of intelligence. *International Journal of Psychology.*

Thurstone, L. L. (1960). *Primary mental abilities.* Chicago: University of Chicago Press.

Wigdor, A. K., & Garner, W. R. (Eds.). (1982). *Ability testing: Uses, consequences, and controversies.* Washington, DC: National Academy Press.

Williams, S. A., Denney, N. W., & Schadler, M. (1983). Elderly adults' perception of their own cognitive development during the adult years. *International Journal of Aging and Human Development, 16,* 147–158.

Willis, S. L., & Schaie, K. W. (1986). Practical intelligence in later adulthood. In R. J. Sternberg & R. K. Wagner (Eds.), *Practical intelligence: Nature and origins of competence in the everyday world* (pp. 236–268). New York: Cambridge University Press.

The Role of Adaptive Processes in Intellectual Functioning Among Older Adults

Gary W. Evans
Megan A. Lewis
University of California, Irvine

According to Berg, intelligence should be examined from within a contextual perspective. This means that intellectual functioning is a dynamic, evolving process that changes both with alterations in cognitive aptitude and with shifts in adaptive demands placed on the individual by the world around him or her. One can best appreciate the true meaning of intelligent human functioning by analyzing everyday problem solving. In addition, individual beliefs about what intelligence is and self-assessments of one's capability to enact intelligent responses constitute a critical aspect of intellectual functioning, especially during late adulthood.

In our comments on Berg's chapter we do two things. First, we offer some criticisms of Berg's preliminary work on intellectual functioning across the life span. Second, we examine some of the salient, adaptive tasks that confront aging individuals along with their coping resources for dealing with them.

CRITICAL COMMENTS ON BERG'S ANALYSIS

We share Berg's positive inclination toward a contextual perspective for understanding intellectual functioning. There are a few aspects of her research, however, that may not do full justice to the contextual perspective. First, we should not only ask people about their beliefs in intellectual self-efficacy through self-report measures; but additional methodological approaches should be used. More thinking is needed about how to measure actual, everyday problem solving as it unfolds naturalistically or in response to experimental dilemmas and problems posed to research subjects. Perhaps one initial strategy would be to compare individuals who appear to be particularly adept and particularly inept in intellectual functioning as they are confronted with identical problem solving demands that are age-appropriate and socioculturally realistic. As a specific example, two groups of older adults (high vs. low in intellectual functioning) could be compared as they attempt to solve problems. To be classified as high in intellectual functioning both self-beliefs and two other observers would have to rate the individual as high in intellectual functioning. A similar strategy would be used to rate persons as low in intellectual functioning. These two groups would then be given a series of problems to solve. Several strategies might be employed to analyze their responses to the problems. A few examples include thinking aloud, probes at set points about what/how the person is trying to do, utilization of provided resources that vary in utility for solving the problem, or tracking of queries made by the participants from a knowledgeable confederate whom they can work with.

It might also prove valuable to simply ask people why they believe certain individuals, generally viewed as intelligent, are judged in that way. Researchers could also interview people and those around them as they are confronted with actual, real-world problems. Just what do people do when forced to cope with having to relocate their residence, change their jobs or retire, when facing a major medical procedure, or when grieving for a lost friend or spouse? We believe that more in depth observation of actual everyday problem-solving behavior, in conjunction with the kinds of research Berg and her colleagues are conducting, may increase our understanding of intellectual functioning. As in Herman's comments in the discussion following this one, we are concerned about the tendency to rely on individual's self-reports of intellectual functioning. On the other hand, we acknowledge that it is difficult to develop systematic, scientifically valid approaches for measuring everyday problem solving.

A second criticism of Berg's work is that her definitions of context as reflected for example in the column headings in Table 5.5 (work, health, leisure, friends, family) may not be the best way to define context. The divisions strike us as too broad. Perhaps more fine-grained descriptions of context are in order. This might further our understanding of the possible connections between environmental demands and efficacious intellectual functioning among older adults. For example, work could be subdivided into several dimensions that a priori seem pertinent to everyday problem solving. These subdivisions might include task demands and resources for the major job required, interpersonal relationships at work, suboptimal physical features at work (e.g., climate, temperature, workspace design), or clarity of role functions. Another example of a more fine-grained analysis of ecological context has been offered by Lawton (1982). He suggested that dimensions of the physical environment such as novelty, crowdedness, or complexity, can be categorized into phenomenal, consensual, or explicit environmental factors. Phenomenal physical dimensions refer to aspects of the physical environment that are idiosyncratic such as familiarity. Consensual elements are features of the physical environment that tend to be experienced by most people in the same respect, for example, climate. Explicit factors are those that can be measured in objective units such as volume, or area.

Third, we offer a general caveat about the major thrust of this book. An underlying premise throughout is that greater self-efficacy is a good thing. Major impediments to optimal human functioning in old age are created by physical and psychosocial barriers to self-efficacy. This may be a deceptively simple presumption about self-efficacy. In a thought-provoking article on aging and personal control, Rodin (1986) reminded us that control is not always good. Demands or expectations for control and the exercise of self-efficacy may exceed the abilities and/or desires of individuals to enact the behaviors required. Brennan, Moos, and Lemke (in press), for example, found that gerontologists overestimated the amount of personal control and decision-making ability that elderly residents wanted in congregate housing. Incongruence between person and environment can occur both with provision of too little control or with the provision of behavioral options that exceed the older person's ability to take advantage of them (Lawton, 1980).

With control also comes responsibility and thus the potential for feelings of guilt and self-blame when negative things do occur. If the negative outcomes are particularly important and/or longlasting, negative impacts on self-esteem may occur as well. Karuza, Rabinowitz, and Zevon (1986) distinguished between feelings of responsibility and control over the cause of a problem, and having responsibility and control over the solution to a problem. Through a reattribution intervention with older adults, Rodin and Langer (1980) decreased feelings of responsibility for the cause of a problem. This in turn increased activity and sociability. Although retaining responsibility for causing problems may provide the older adult with a sense of meaning for a negative event (Taylor, 1983), retaining responsibility may cause anger, embarrassment, or shame. Maintaining the responsibility for the solution to a problem can have benefits and costs as well. Retaining responsibility can increase feelings of self-efficacy and competence. On the other hand, overestimating one's control capabilities, and maintaining an illusion of control can cause anger, loss of self-esteem, and guilt (Karuza et al., 1986).

Having control can also lead in certain circumstances to unrealistic expectations for personal autonomy. Heightened expectations to exert control can be harmful when things do not go according to plan. Under some circumstances provision of control opportunities can lead to long-term, negative effects when those opportunities are removed. Schulz (1976) showed that visits on demand or on a predictable schedule by college students to nursing home residents improved elderly residents' health and well-being in comparison to groups receiving random or no visits. Yet in a long-term follow-up a few years after the visitation intervention had ceased, residents who had previously been in the higher self-control conditions were in poorer health (Schulz & Hanusa, 1978).

Heightened expectations for control may also cause some individuals to misperceive the environment, selectively ignoring cues that control is unavailable or not adaptive in the particular situation. Finally, as noted by Rodin (1986) and Weisz and his colleagues (Weisz, Rothbaum, & Blackburn, 1984) exercise of personal control often takes effort that in some cases may prove futile or exact greater costs than the demand itself. Sometimes giving in or using some other less instrumentally oriented coping strategy than actively exerting control is more adaptive.

Attempts to accommodate to the environment may be beneficial for older adults who find themselves in situations that cannot be changed. Examples of such situations that are common for older adults include: (a) medical insurance bureaucracies; (b) institutional settings, such as hospitals; (c) chronic physical conditions such as arthritis and; (d) forced retirement. Additionally, accepting situations that previously were controllable and are currently not, could significantly decrease anxiety associated with the situation. Developing accommodative strategies for dealing with losses in memory or physical strength could significantly decrease frustration about being unable to do certain tasks. Intelligence would be reflected by having a well-developed set of active and accommodative control strategies plus knowing when and how to apply the correct strategy. The relationship between control and its utility in later years is complex. Although being able to control one's life and environment can facilitate adaption, increasing feelings of control, self-efficacy, and responsibility may not always be wise. In some situations more accommodative modes of control may be most useful. An important skill is being able to judge when control attempts are failing, and adjust behavior accordingly. Developing a repertoire of active and accommodative control strategies plus the ability to assess their utility are important intellectual functions.

THE ROLE OF ADAPTIVE PROCESSES
IN INTELLECTUAL FUNCTIONING

As noted by Berg, one avenue for gaining insight into intellectual functioning over the life span is to examine the adaptive tasks confronted by people as they age. In this section we describe some of the salient adaptive tasks and coping processes that accompany aging, speculating on what intellectual skills would enable the competent execution of those adaptive tasks.

Physical Health

Although individuals over 60 experience fewer total life events or daily hassles, a higher proportion of them are health-related (Folkman, Lazarus, Pimley, & Novacek, 1987; Lazarus & De Longis, 1983). Among some of the more demanding concomitants of change in physical health with age are declines in physical capacity, mobility, and energy; increased fatigue and pain; and more contact with medical institutions. Declines in physical capacity, mobility, and energy may in turn engender frustration and perhaps influence one's self-image. Frustration may occur as one realizes that they can no longer do some of the same things or do them as efficiently as they could before. Interaction with medical institutions is often stressful as well because of bureaucratic practices that lead to waiting, impersonal treatment, and in some cases unsatisfactory care.

Dealing with insurance, social security, previous employers, as well as with medical institutions requires flexibility in problem solving, sustained effort, and often the ability to move forward without taking slights and various delays personally. Patience and flexibility would also seem to be critical in dealing with changes in physical condition that render the individual less able. Along the same lines, creativity in learning how to perform tasks in alternative ways that are less physically demanding is an important skill that might facilitate more successful aging.

Thinking of oneself as having the same physical abilities and strength as in earlier years can lead to greater physical activity than is healthy. This can be especially important for older people recovering from illnesses, or whose stamina and strength have diminished. Knowing the limits of one's physical condition, and how to modify circumstances to accommodate change in physical ability can be an important intellectual ability.

Peck (1968) suggested that wisdom that comes with age is the "ability to make most effective choices among the alternatives which intellectual perception and imagination present for one's decision" (pp. 88–89). Older adults' wisdom may be linked to metacognition. Years of experience may lead to better self-knowledge about the thoughts and feelings that lead to unhealthy behavior or upsetting emotions. Because older people may have greater insight into the types of events that elicit certain behaviors and feelings, they can more easily avoid situations that cause distress. Additionally, they can seek out and utilize situations that enhance their well-being.

In addition to flexibility and patience, another intellectual skill that physical aging may demand is the ability to redefine one's self-image and, as a result alter personal goals and objectives. For example, adaptive functioning in old age can be accomplished in part by body transcendence where one redefines pleasure and comfort in broader terms than physical well-being and pleasure. Social relationships, mental activities, and other important endeavors can become more important objectives vis a vis physical comfort (Peck, 1968). Erikson (1950) noted the critical importance of generative activities during late adulthood including activities such as nurturing young persons, mentoring, or volunteer work to assist others in need.

A related intellectual function that may be important in dealing with the adaptive tasks called forth by changing physical health status is planning. The ability to anticipate and expect that certain normative changes will occur and recognize that they occur to most others of approximately the same age may make it easier to adapt to physical changes. Neugarten (1970), for example, found that for most women, menopause did not precipitate crises because it was part of what women expected to go through, and they had discussed it with similar aged friends.

Changing Role Demands and Altered Self-Image

Movement from middle age to older adulthood for many is accompanied by major shifts in role demands that in turn can have profound impacts on self-image. As one grows older competing role demands may occur. For example, schemas about parent and grandparent roles contain much overlapping information, but important divergent information as well. It takes insight to know when it is appropriate to act for example, as a grandmother and not a mother. Conflicts between family members arise when grandparents go beyond their appropriate role in dealing with grandchildren.

Not only are older adults evaluated by others based on new role demands, but as people grow older they are also viewed differently by others based on changes in physical appearance. Older adults may feel they are exactly the same person, but they are treated differently by others because they have begun to look older. Younger people, employers, and social service agencies may make misattributions leading to erroneous views about the feelings and behaviors of older adults. Awareness and understanding of how one is perceived by others, and ability to identify sources of error entail intellectual skill. Further, correcting faulty misattributions involves tact as well as courage. Letting faulty views go uncorrected has many implications for the functioning of older adults, including how they are perceived intellectually.

Most men and many women change their job status through retirement, shifting from an independent productive worker to an individual who no longer has a "job" and often is confronted with fewer external demands on his or her time. There are several potentially important adaptive tasks imposed by retirement.

First, one must learn how to cope with the shift in self-image from one who has been an independent, productive citizen who could provide not only for self but for home and family to a new role in which one is retired. Retirement poses a major challenge to redefine oneself in ways that are not viewed as nonproductive, or dependent. At work, especially if capping off a long career, many individuals correctly see themselves as an expert, highly competent in solving important problems and challenges posed by the workplace milieu. With retirement people move into a new situation in which they are essentially novices, unpracticed in dealing with many of the new demands they must face.

As older people experience the transition from work and parenting as major roles, the amount and quality of daily demands placed on the individual change as well. Many of the typical demands associated with work and with parenting are external in character arising from outside the individual. With retirement as well as the exiting of children from the home, there is a drop in external demands. If people become accustomed to a certain level of stimulation, marked downward shifts in stimulation can be stressful (Evans & Cohen, 1987). A different but related change is the shift for many from highly structured to largely unstructured demands. Fewer tasks must be completed at a specific time or in a particular place.

Peck (1968) suggested that flexibility in identifying oneself with multiple roles can enable the older adult to define him or herself in meaningful ways where competence can be achieved in domains other than work or parenting. As before, recognition and appreciation for the normative aspects of changing job status can facilitate this transition. Knowledge about other's career transitions and thought about other domains of existing or potential competence can help as well.

In addition to the changing self-image and social definitions caused by retirement and/or children leaving the home, these changes also create challenges related to increased leisure time and changing financial status. Leisure is typically defined in relation to work as a respite or break rather than as free time that needs to become filled and occupied with worthwhile activities. Thus, the ability to redefine the role of leisure in socially meaningful and personally fulfilling ways is an additional intellectual task related to shifts in job status. Problem solving related to leisure entails several components. First, finding ways to utilize one's skills and talents in an active way would seem one salient component of effectively dealing with leisure time. Second, deriving a new meaning of leisure apart from work, where leisure is not a break, but instead becomes a productive, engaging, and challenging set of one or more activities would seem essential. It is probably no coincidence that many men and women who no longer "work" in fact spend considerable amounts of time and energy engaging in activities that from the outside one would judge as work. A few typical examples might include the vast array of volunteer activities that older adults carry out; the increasing participation of older Americans in politics; and taking courses or even greater immersion in higher education.

Another major concomitant of retirement for many older Americans, at least, are important shifts in financial status. This can have at least two very salient implications. Most directly people may have to alter the lifestyle and possibly the residence they have been used to. Second, shifts in financial status, particularly if dramatic, may render some individuals dependent on either their children and/or society for their survival. One goes from being a provider to being a recipient. Dealing with new and increased financial demands requires creativity, risk-analysis skills, and good money management strategies.

Changing Social Networks

One of the more troubling aspects of aging is the loss of close confidants and alterations in one's social support network as a consequence of death and illness among friends. Changes in job status and relocation also influence the availability of support, and these changes in network composition can impact older adults' well-being. High levels of social support in older adults reduce the negative impact of stress on mental health and are positively linked to physical health status (Cutrona, Russell, & Rose, 1986). Prospective studies have also linked social contact as a negative predictor of mortality for older adults (Blazer, 1982).

For many people, one of the primary benefits of work is the source of friendships and social contacts afforded by the worksite. With retirement, workers are less likely to see associates from work on a regular basis and they are more removed from an important commonality they may have helped form and sustain the friendship bonds. Relocation, which is discussed in more detail later, often decreases physical proximity from friends both at work and where one used to live making it harder to sustain social bonds.

Changing social relationships that occur with aging may be related to problem solving. First, people who are better at seeking out and making new friends should cope better with problems related to the loss of social support. Related to this ability is flexibility in emotional investments in various people. One's range and ability to reinvest following loss are probably critical processes for coping with deteriorating social relationships (Peck, 1968). In the case of a loss of spouse, presumably people who have already established good socially supportive relationships outside the home should fare better than those who have depended solely on spousal support. Some research findings suggest this. The higher rates of morbidity and mortality in widowers in comparison to widows following the death of their spouse (cf. Sanders, 1988; Ward, 1976) has been attributed to the fact that men are more likely to depend solely on their spouse for social support, whereas women more often have multiple sources of support (Minkler, 1985; Stroebe, Stroebe, & Hansson, 1988).

One aspect of social support on the job that has largely been overlooked is group problem solving. For many individuals socially supportive relationships on the job grow out of group problem-solving experiences. With the loss of this source of support, opportunities for group interaction around common problems may markedly decline. Individuals who have come to depend heavily on this form of problem solving may be at greater risk for dealing with new demands in a manner that does not fit with their own coping style. This suggests that another important intellectual skill related to aging is the ability to locate and utilize pre-existing groups that enhance the fit between demands and coping. Organized community services, or using friends and family members are examples of groups that can facilitate this process.

There are several ways that the nature of support resources may change in one's later years independent of the composition of support networks. First, older adults may feel less inclined to seek support from others if they do not feel confident about being able to reciprocate at some future time. Studies examining reciprocity of support indicate that some exchanges of support are distinguished by reciprocity, and the degree of reciprocity may influence psychological well-being (Rook, 1987). With increasing age the resources one has to reciprocate with may decrease. Older adults may be unable to lend money to their adult children when needed, or they may be unable to help with physically demanding tasks such as taking care of grandchildren. Knowing when to choose sources of support that do not evoke the need to reciprocate may be an important intellectual function for some older adults.

Changes in family members' ability to provide support is a second manner in which support resources may change in later years. Family members serve as the primary support providers for older adults (Rook, in press). Increases in life expectancy may find more parents and adult children growing old together. Adult children may feel angry about the obligations of having to care for aging parents, and in some cases the quality of support may suffer. Further, as adult children age and experience decreases in their own physical and financial abilities they may be less able to provide support for their parents.

Under some circumstances support may undermine self-efficacy among older adults. Supportive acts and information that encourage competence and autonomous coping processes are likely to enhance self-efficacy. Other forms of support may constrain autonomy by doing too much for older adults and taking care of too many demands such that the exercise of coping skills are discouraged (Rowe & Kahn, 1987). A recent experimental study is interesting in light of the distinction between competence-enhancing and competence-diminishing social support. Avorn and Langer (1982) gave one group of elderly subjects encouragement while they practiced solving puzzles. A second group was given direct assistance and a third group was given no assistance or encouragement. Subjects given encouragement improved in both performance and speed comparing before and after training puzzle performance. Subjects in the no assistance or encouragement group did the same in performance, whereas those who had received direct assistance, declined in performance.

There are at least two direct implications for intellectual functioning and the distinction between control-enhancing and control-reducing forms of social support. First, older adults who can discern this difference, sorting out the former type of support from the latter, may benefit more from socially supportive relationships. Related to this first point, one must learn how to choose appropriate sources of support be they friends, family, or social institutions. Support in all its forms is probably not helpful—some people and some institutions may provide types of support that decrease self-efficacy and autonomy in coping with everyday demands.

Physical-Setting Changes

As people grow older, one of the more profound changes that occurs is in their physical surroundings. People leave or change jobs and often change their home residence. In addition to the potential impacts on social relationships, physical-setting changes place many additional demands on individuals. For some individuals, home and neighborhood are places of meaningful attachment that provide important psychological functions related to identity (Stokols & Shumaker 1982). People who are typically attached to such spaces rely also on them as familiar loci where they can act and function competently, know where things are, and how to achieve various goals and objectives associated with daily living.

Related to these functions are geographic knowledge and cognitive mapping. People develop reasonably accurate, functional cognitive maps of familiar environments that allow them to behave efficiently (Evans, 1980). One of the important functions of such cognitive representations of real-world spaces is to allow people to know where important services are. The use and access to services is strongly mediated by the cognitive representations people possess. This relationship has been empirically demonstrated in studies of elderly residents. Walsh, Krauss, and Regnier (1981) found that under utilization of services, some specifically designed for elderly clients, occurred in part because of poorly developed cognitive maps of the geographic areas where the services were located. Moreover, changes in the familiar urban landscape through renewal and other programs have a disproportionally negative impact on older urban residents' geographic knowledge (Evans, Brennan, Skorpanich, & Held, 1984).

Both the amount and type of stimulation may change with relocation as well. Shifts from a work environment to a home setting or changes in the home residence can significantly alter the variety and level of stimulation one is confronted with on a daily basis. Often relocation for the elderly occurs in part because of financial constraints, leading to a residential setting of diminished quality.

There is an increasingly voluminous literature on the effects of relocation on older adults. Although much of this research is not methodologically rigorous, there is a disturbing convergence suggesting declines in physical health accompanying moves, especially when involuntary (Lawton, 1980). Several factors may contribute to the harmful effects of relocation on the elderly. First, as reviewed by Rodin (1986), individual participation and sense of autonomy and control in the residential environment appear crucial for good health among older adults. Relocations that are involuntary as well as those that place individuals in new situations that discourage self-efficacious functioning are apt to be more harmful. Second, individual competence prior to the move is an important variable. Individuals with physical or psychological problems prior to the move are at greater risk for negative health outcomes following the move (Eisdorfer & Wilkie, 1977). Lastly, the environmental quality of the new space may be important. Environments with better amenities may enable a better, smoother transition to the new setting (Lawton, 1980; Schooler, 1982).

Schooler (1982) in an interesting study of voluntary moving, found that expectations can impact the outcomes of the relocation process. Individuals who anticipated a change in residence tended to perceive the move as threatening and worried about it more than those with little or no lead time. Those who expected to relocate had worse physical health outcomes subsequent to the move than those with little warning. This finding, coupled with some work indicating that preparation about the move (e.g., pre on-site visits, participation in design and planning) can facilitate adjustment to a new residence among the elderly (Krantz & Schulz, 1980), indicates that cognitive appraisals of the relocation process are probably very important for the health and well-being of older adults who are relocating.

Changes in physical settings place numerous adaptive demands on older adults. Social networks change, feelings of uprootedness may occur, knowledge about and access to services may decline, the variety and quantity of usual stimulation levels may shift, and anxiety about the change may occur. Several intellectual skills can ease the disruptive aspects of some of these demands. First, as noted earlier, the ability to meet new people and make friends easily probably facilitates relocation. People who are able to achieve a sense of place and connection in more abstract terms, apart from the actual ground where they live, may be better able to adjust to the disruptive effects of moving. Individuals with better cognitive mapping abilities and who learn how to orient more quickly presumably will function better when the physical setting changes. Prior experience in dealing with shifting stimulation levels as well as the ability to regulate one's own sources of stimulation may also be valuable intellectual skills. Various cognitive and behavioral strategies exist to both enhance and diminish stimulation. For example, meditation or a private room can both reduce the levels of external stimulation that one must contend with. Social events, exercise, hobbies, and other cultural activities are examples of mechanisms for augmenting stimulation. Finally, learning how to appraise change in more optimistic (e.g., challenge) or at least balanced ways (e.g., seeing the potential benefits and costs) are potentially valuable skills for problem solving as one ages.

As environmental opportunities change for older people, becoming adventuresome, assertive, and taking risks by trying out new environments and ways of coping with different environments become important. As people's skills evolve, finding ways to adapt to change is needed. Such adaptions can include beginning to utilize community services or even being more assertive with family members who expect more than an older person can do. Such skills serve to bring the personal, social and physical environment more in line with older adults' abilities, needs, and preferences.

SUMMARY AND CONCLUSION

In this chapter we have offered some criticisms of Berg's analysis of intellectual functioning across the life span, and suggested that a complementary strategy for understanding intelligence is to analyze the salient, adaptive tasks that are placed on individuals in concert with their personal resources for coping with those demands.

Although we have made several general proposals about adaptive processes and intellectual functioning among older adults, several caveats are in order. First, older adults are a heterogeneous groups of individuals who encounter different types of demands and possess different resources for coping with these demands. Consistent with a contextual perspective, one must take into account how adaptive processes influence intellectual functioning for different groups of older adults. It is most likely that there are great differences in resources among rich versus poor, urban versus rural, and healthy versus unhealthy older adults. Second, our analysis has not dealt with cultural differences in terms of adaptive processes and intellectual functioning. Differences in norms and practices among cultures shape what is intelligent behavior and how this relates to dealing with adaptive demands. Further, there may be cohort differences within and between cultures regarding the definition of intelligent behavior. Third, longitudinal research is needed to assess how the processes we have examined relate to intellectual functioning in late life. Fourth, we have not discussed how these adaptive demands influence the intellectual functioning and problem solving of family members of an older person. As people age, changes in their abilities and needs influence those around them. There are important intellectual functions required by others who interact closely with older adults. These intellectual skills could include recognizing older people's needs, possessing flexible problems-solving strategies, and possibly changing expectations about the abilities of older adults. Examination of the intellectual functioning of those surrounding older adults would complement a contextual perspective.

We have emphasized the importance of a contextual perspective in our analysis of the adaptive processes faced by older adults, and suggested that intelligence can be understood in part from a functional perspective. Cognitions and behaviors that help older adults to function competently in meeting the tasks imposed by everyday, adaptive demands are manifestations of intelligence. Intellectual skills and processes that enable competent functioning may be better recognized and understood by a more thorough examination of the transactions between older adults and the adaptive changes they face.

ACKNOWLEDGMENTS

We thank Penny Brennan and Karen Rook for critical feedback on an earlier draft.

REFERENCES

Avorn, J., & Langer, E. J. (1982). Induced disability in nursing home patients. *Journal of American Geriatric Society, 30,* 397–400.

Blazer, D. G. (1982). Social support and mortality in an elderly community population. *American Journal of Epidemiology, 115,* 604–694.

Brennan, P. L., Moos, R. H., & Lemke, S. (in press). Preferences of older adults and experts for policies and services in group living facilities. *Psychology and Aging.*

Cutrona, C. E., Russell, P., & Rose, J. (1986). Social support and adaption to stress by the elderly. *Psychology and Aging, 1,* 47–54.

Eisdorfer, C., & Wilkie, F. (1977). Stress, disease, aging and behavior. In J. E. Birren & K. W. Schaie (Eds.), *Handbook of the psychology of aging* (pp. 251–275). New York: Van Nostrand Reinhold.

Erikson, E. (1950). *Childhood and society.* New York: Norton.

Evans, G. W. (1980). Environmental cognition. *Psychological Bulletin, 88,* 259–287.

Evans, G. W., Brennan, P., Skorpanich, M. A., & Held, D. (1984). Cognitive mapping and elderly adults: Verbal and location memory for urban landmarks. *Journal of Gerontology, 39,* 452–457.

Evans, G. W., & Cohen, S. (1987). Environmental stress. In D. Stokols & I. Altman (Eds.), *Handbook of environmental psychology* (pp. 571–610). New York: Wiley.

Folkman, S., Lazarus, R. S., Pimley, S., & Novacek, J. (1987). Age differences in stress and coping processes. *Psychology and Aging, 2,* 171–184.

Karuza, J., Rabinowitz, U. C., & Zevon, M. A. (1986). Implications of control and responsibility on helping the aged. In M. M. Baltes & P. B. Baltes (Eds.). *The psychology of control and aging* (pp. 373–396). Hillsdale, NJ: Lawrence Erlbaum Associates.

Krantz, D. S., & Schulz, R. (1980). A model of life crisis, control, and health outcomes: Cardiac rehabilitation and relocation of the elderly. In A. Baum & J. E. Singer (Eds.), *Advances in environmental psychology* (Vol. 2, pp. 25–59). Hillsdale, NJ: Lawrence Erlbaum Associates.

Lawton, M. P. (1980). *Environment and aging.* Monterey, CA: Brooks-Cole.

Lawton, M. P. (1982). Competence, environmental press, and the adaptation of older people. In M. P. Lawton, P. G. Windley, & T. O. Byerts (Eds.), *Aging and the environment* (pp. 33–59). New York: Springer.

Lazarus, R. S., & De Longis, A. (1983). Psychological stress and coping in aging. *American Psychologist, 38,* 245–254.

Minkler, M. (1985). Social support and health of the elderly. In S. Cohen & L. Syme (Eds.), *Social support and health* (pp. 199–218). New York: Academic Press.

Neugarten, B. L. (1970). Dynamics of transition of middle age to old age. *Journal of Geriatric Psychiatry, 4,* 71–87.

Peck, R. C. (1968). Psychological developments in the second half of life. In B. L. Neugarten (Ed.), *Middle age and aging* (pp. 88–92). Chicago: University of Chicago Press.

Rodin, J. (1986). Aging and health: The effects of sense of control. *Science, 233,* 1271–1275.

Rodin, J., & Langer, E. (1980). Aging labels: The decline of control and the fall of self-esteem. *Journal of Social Issues, 36,* 12–29.

Rook, K. S. (1987). Reciprocity of social exchange and social satisfaction among older women. *Journal of Personality and Social Psychology, 46,* 1097–1108.

Rook, K. S. (in press). Social relationships as a source of companionship: Implications for older adults' psychological well-being. In I. G. Sarason, B. R. Sarason, & O. R. Pierce (Eds.), *Social support: An interactional view: Issues on social support research.* New York: Wiley.

Rowe, J. W., & Kahn, R. L. (1987). Human aging: Usual and successful. *Science, 237,* 143–149.

Sanders, C. M. (1988). Risk factors in bereavement outcome. *Journal of Social Issues, 44,* 97–112.

Schooler, K. K. (1982). Response of the elderly to environment: A stress-theoretical perspective. In M. P. Lawton, P. G. Windley, & T. O. Byerts (Eds.), *Aging and the environment* (pp. 80–96). New York: Springer.

Schulz, R. (1976). Effects of control and predictability on the physical and psychological well being of the institutionalized aged. *Journal of Personality and Social Psychology, 33,* 563–573.

Schulz, R., & Hanusa, B. H. (1978). Long-term effects of control and predictability-enhancing interventions: Findings and ethical issues. *Journal of Personality and Social Psychology, 36,* 1194–1201.

Stokols, D., & Shumaker, S. A. (1982). The psychological context of residential mobility and well being. *Journal of Social Issues, 38,* 149–172.

Stroebe, M., Stroebe, W., & Hansson, R. O. (1988). Bereavement research: An historical introduction. *Journal of Social Issues, 44,* 1–18.

Taylor, S. E. (1983). Adjustment to threatening events: A theory of cognitive adaption. *American Psychologist, 38,* 1161–1173.

Walsh, D. A., Krauss, I. K., & Regnier, V. A. (1981). Spatial ability, environmental knowledge, and environmental use: The elderly. In L. S. Liben, A. H. Patterson, & N. Newcombe (Eds.), *Spatial representation and behavior across the life span* (pp. 321–360). New York: Academic Press.

Ward, A. M. (1976). Mortality of bereavement. *British Medical Journal, 1,* 700–702.

Weisz, J. R., Rothbaum, F. M., & Blackburn, T. C. (1984). Standing out and standing in: The psychology of control in America and Japan. *American Psychologist, 39,* 955–969.

Self-Perceptions of
Memory Performance

Douglas J. Herrmann
National Institute of Mental Health

The field of human memory first entertained constructs like self-efficacy, self-directedness, agency, and control in the mid-1970s. Independently and almost simultaneously, a number of memory researchers in the United States and in England developed "memory" questionnaires that asked people about their memory performance in everyday life (e.g., Bennett-Levy & Powell, 1980; Broadbent, Cooper, Fitzgerald, & Parks, 1982; Herrmann & Neisser, 1978; Sehulster, 1981a, 1981b, 1982). To date, more than 30 different questionnaires have been developed and reported in the literature (see Gilewski & Zelinski, 1986; Herrmann, 1982, 1984).

The impetus for the development of these memory questionnaires came from a widespread dissatisfaction with the traditional laboratory approach to memory investigation. The laboratory approach had come to be seen as espousing methods and theories that were largely useless in dealing with memory phenomena in everyday life (Baddeley, 1981; Neisser, 1978). Memory questionnaires asked about memory experiences in everyday life and, therefore, held the promise of helping researchers deal with phenomena that were outside of the scope of the traditional approach.

Initial theoretical understanding of memory questionnaires was simple. Self-perceptions of memory performance, as reported on memory questionnaires, were assumed to represent a person's actual memory performance (Herrmann & Neisser, 1978). Self-perceptions were expected to be accurate because they were surmised from supposedly accurate metamemory records of past uses of memory. Moreover, because

199

people are presumed competent to report about many kinds of behavior other than memory (e.g., how well one plays a certain sport, how well one can cook), they were expected to report accurately about memory as well. Memory self-perceptions were expected to guide performance (about what tasks to attempt and how much effort is needed to success-fully perform them), but because these perceptions were assumed to be largely correct, the guidance issue was not seen as deserving investigation.

Some researchers dreamed—perhaps half seriously—that memory questionnaires would render traditional memory research, and its exten-sive observation and testing of subjects, obsolete. To ascertain the bases of a memory phenomenon and further develop memory theory, future researchers would merely have to ask subjects how their memory per-formed when certain independent variables were present. Thus, initial questionnaire research held that perceptions of memory self-efficacy might reflect a person's actual memory efficacy.

However, subsequent findings required researchers to reconceptualize what memory questionnaires were measuring and what self-perceptions of memory performance were all about. In this discussion, I briefly review research with memory questionnaires. Like Berg's chapter on the self-perception of intelligence, the review illustrates how questionnaires may be used to investigate self-perceptions in general. Additionally, the review addresses the nature of memory self-perceptions, the role that memory self-perceptions plays in memory performance, and how memory self-perceptions may be altered to enhance memory performance.

THE NATURE OF MEMORY SELF-PERCEPTIONS

Reliability.   It was discovered early on that people make reports about their memory performance readily and with high confidence. Reliability coefficients of these questionnaires are typically .8 or higher (Herrmann, 1982). When confidence ratings have been made regarding memory self-reports, they also have been high (about a 6 on a 7-point scale ranging from "no confidence" to "certain"; Shlechter & Herrmann, 1981).

Performance Validity.   Although memory self-perceptions are very reliable, research also revealed that these self-perceptions are not very accurate. Typically, validity coefficients ranged from about 0 to .5. Often the correspondence between perceptions of memory performance and actual performance has been as low as zero, even when the validity tests were ecologically sound. For example, in several studies, self-reports of one's ability to remember faces were correlated poorly ($r = .3$) or not at all in face recognition tested after staged incidents (Deffenbacher, cited in Herrmann, 1982). Since the initial investigations in the late 1970s and early 1980s, many more studies have replicated the initial low-validity coefficients and extended the findings of low validity to more memory questionnaires and more memory tasks (Abson & Rabbitt, 1988; Bennett-Levy & Powell, 1980; Cavanaugh & Murphy, 1986; Cavanaugh & Poon, in press; Devolder, 1988; Dixon, Hertzog, & Hultsch, 1986; Dixon & Hultsch, 1983; Shlechter, Herrmann, Stronach, Rubenfeld, & Zenker, 1982; Sunderland, Harris, & Baddeley, 1983; Zelinski, Gilewski, & Thompson, 1980; for partial reviews of validity research see Gilewski & Zelinski, 1986; Herrmann, 1982, 1984).

Although validity coefficients have generally been low, it should be noted that self-perceptions for some memory tasks are accurate (i.e., have higher validity coefficients) than for other tasks. For example, self-perceptions of ability to recall specific domains of knowledge (e.g., about soccer) sometimes are correlated highly ($r = .8$) with subsequent tests of such knowledge (e.g., Morris, Grunesberg, Sykes, & Merrick, 1981). Self-perceptions of remembering a phone number after having read it in a phone book are moderately accurate ($r = .5$; Bennett-Levy & Powell, 1980; Herrmann, 1979).

Construct Validity Pertaining to Memory and Aging.   It was initially expected that older adults would perceive their efficacy at memory tasks to be less than that of younger adults. This result was obtained in some studies. However, in other studies older adults perceived their memory as just as capable as the memory of young adults and in other studies yet, older adults perceived their memory as more capable than the memory of young adults. The differences in self-perceptions of memory with age have yet to be fully understood (Bennett-Levy & Powell, 1980; Cavanaugh & Poon, in press; Chaffin & Herrmann, 1983; Devolder & Pressley, in press; Dixon & Hertzog, 1988; Dixon, Hertzog, & Hultsch, 1986; Hultsch, Hertzog, & Dixon, 1987; Hultsch, Hertzog, Dixon, & Davidson, 1988; Martin, 1986; Perlmuter, 1978; Sunderland, Watts, Baddeley, & Harris, 1986; West, Boatwright, & Schlesser, 1984; Zelinski, Gilewski, & Thompson, 1980; for partial reviews of this research see Dixon, in press; Gilewski & Zelinski, 1986).

There are several possible reasons for the inconsistencies among the findings concerning memory self-perceptions and aging. Different self-report instruments have been used in different studies. Subject samples within and between studies (including those representing the same cohort) have differed according to several individual characteristics, e.g., educational history, state of health (see Cutler & Grams, 1988) and context (see Berg, this volume). Also, research has not taken into account how much effort subjects of different ages invest into memory tasks.

Intercorrelations of Memory Self-Perceptions. Although memory self-perceptions were found to possess low validity, the intercorrelations of these self-perceptions were initially thought, nevertheless, to suggest some of the structural properties of the memory system. Intercorrelations, based on the self-perceptions of many subjects, were assumed to reflect relationships of actual memory performance despite the low validity of these self-perceptions. However, factor analyses of memory-questionnaire responses indicated that it would be unwise to draw inferences about actual memory performance from the intercorrelations of memory self-perceptions.

First, factor analyses of memory questionnaires were often found to be less replicable than one would like (Cordoni, 1981; Johnson & Anderson, 1988). Second, although some memory questionnaires appear to agree closely in reflecting overall general beliefs about memory competence (Cavanaugh & Poon, in press; Hertzog, Hultsch, & Dixon, 1988), other scales presumed to be measuring the same or similar aspects of memory performance, correlated as little as .6 (Broadbent et al., 1982). Third, when different questionnaires have produced different factors, it has been unclear whether the questionnaires tapped genuinely different factors or different content (Herrmann, 1984; Johnson & Anderson, 1988). Fourth, careful inspection of the nature of intercorrelations on memory questionnaires further suggested that self-perceptions are not to be taken as providing a literal account of subjects' memory performance (Hertzog, Dixon, Schulenberg, & Hultsch, 1987). For example, Herrmann and Neisser (1978) found that subjects' self-reports ignored certain obvious disjunctures in memory phenomena (such as short-term/long-term memory; learning/remembering) in favor of everyday themes (remembering names, appointments, rote information).

Correlates of Self-Perceptions of Memory Performance. Although self-perceptions of memory performance and their intercorrelations are not very valid, their high reliability suggested to researchers that memory self-perceptions were psychologically significant. Accordingly, several researchers set about to examine whether measures of other psychological processes correlate with memory questionnaire reports.

First, memory self-reports were linked with vulnerability to stress. Broadbent et al. (1982) found that self-perceptions of cognitive failures (at memory and other tasks) were correlated with the susceptibility of nurses to stress on intensive care wards (see also Martin & Jones, 1984). Reason (1988) found that women who are about to undergo a mastectomy report a greater occurrence of absentminded behaviors in the period just before the operation. Additionally, Zarit (1982) found that depressed people complain about memory problems so frequently that memory complaints may be a symptom of depression in patients who seek treatment but do not say they are depressed.

Second, memory self-perceptions are influenced by stereotypical prejudices. For example, males and females tend to expect other males to excel at remembering directions and females to excel at remembering shopping lists (Crawford, Herrmann, Holdsworth, Randal, & Robbins, in press). Also wives know more about their husband's self-perceptions of memory performance than husbands know about their wives' memory self-perceptions (Broadbent et al., 1982; Chaffin, Crawford, Herrmann, & Deffenbacher, 1985).

Third, memory self-perceptions are influenced by some aspects of personality. Self-perceptions of memory strategy use and of change in memory over time appear to be correlated with attributions of internality (Cavanaugh & Morton, 1988; Lachman, 1986; Shlechter et al., 1982) and introversion–extraversion (Sehulster, 1982).

Reasons Why Memory Self-Perceptions are Inaccurate. The poor validity of memory self-perceptions indicates that people acquire misinformation, or fail to acquire good information, about how they perform memory tasks. Presumably, people come to develop memory self-perceptions *firsthand* through observation of their performance of memory tasks or *secondhand* from what others say to them about their memory performance (Herrmann, 1982; Morris, 1984; Ross, in press; Sehulster, 1988). Neither source, first- or secondhand, is guaranteed to provide accurate information about memory performance.

Firsthand reports are often inaccurate because we usually do not observe ourselves while performing a memory task (Brock, 1986; Herrmann, Grubs, Sigmundi, & Grueneich, 1986; Pressley, Levin, & Ghatala, 1984; Shlechter & Herrmann, 1981). Firsthand observations may also be inaccurate because of inferior memory ability. People with low memory ability will typically remember less well their memory failures than people with superior memory ability (a relationship between memory ability and accuracy of memory self-perceptions that has been referred to as the *memory introspection paradox*; Herrmann, 1979).

Secondhand reports are often inaccurate because others may choose to misrepresent a person's memory performance in order to influence a social interaction (Herrmann & Gentry, 1985). For example, statements that a person has a "good" memory or a "bad" memory may be uttered to flatter or intimidate (respectively).

Conclusions About the Nature of Memory Self-Perceptions. The low-validity coefficients of memory self-perceptions, inconsistencies in their intercorrelations (and factor analyses), discrepancies in the question-naire's construct validity pertaining to age, and the correlations between memory self-perceptions and measures of nonmemory processes (e.g., stress) made it very clear that memory self-perceptions could not be used as measures of actual memory performance. Memory self-perceptions reflect at best a mix of memory for past experiences and beliefs about such experiences, and frequently these perceptions may be based solely on unfounded beliefs (Herrmann, 1982, 1984; Morris, 1984).

THE ROLE OF MEMORY SELF-PERCEPTIONS
IN MEMORY PERFORMANCE

The recognition that self-perceptions are often inaccurate made it possible for researchers to better appreciate the importance of these percep-tions. It had been known for some time that children have a naive view of their memory abilities (Brown, 1978; Flavell, 1977; Flavell & Wellman, 1977) but it had not been recognized that adults also operate on the basis of mistaken self-perceptions of memory. Had the memory self-perceptions of adults been found highly accurate, these perceptions would probably have not been investigated further because they could have been counted on to guide people in their use of memory. However, because these perceptions were often found to be inaccurate, they offered a possible key to the misuse of memory.

Inaccurate self-perceptions can mislead a person about what tasks to perform and how hard to try at the tasks attempted (see Ables, this volume; Klatzky, 1984). An exaggerated sense of memory superiority might lead some people to attempt a memory task for which they are unfit or to not try hard enough at those tasks attempted. Alternatively, an exaggerated sense of memory inferiority might lead some people to avoid a memory task for which they are fit or to not try hard enough at those tasks attempted. Memory self-perceptions are not the only factor affecting how people approach memory tasks. Other factors such as task incentives and need achievement will obviously influence one's approach to a memory task as well.

The recognition that memory self-perceptions may play a role in guiding memory performance inspired researchers to determine how memory self-perceptions affect memory performance. Subsequently, several memory-questionnaire studies demonstrated that memory self-perceptions do indeed affect memory performance. People with poorer impressions of their memory ability also report using both external aids (such as notepads) and internal aids (such as rehearsal strategies) more so than people who have a good impression of their memory ability (Cavanaugh, Grady, & Perlmutter, 1983; Jackson, Bogers, & Kerstholt, 1988; Perlmuter, 1978; Zelinski et al., 1980).

The effect of memory self-perceptions on the likelihood of attempting a memory task was shown very nicely in a study by Sehulster (1981a). Subjects completed a memory questionnaire that asked, among other things, how good was their memory for trivia. Subsequently, subjects were told they would have an opportunity to play a trivia recall game. They were further instructed that before attempting each trivia question, they would be informed about the category of information from which a question would come and that they would have an opportunity to make a wager concerning whether they would be able to successfully answer the question. Factor scores, based on responses to the trivia questions on the memory questionnaire, were found to be correlated ($r = .326$) with the size of wagers made on the trivia task (the correspondence between the trivia factor and success on the trivia recall task was low, $r = .161$, consistent with validity data reviewed earlier).

Finally, the influence of memory self-perceptions on the attempting of memory tasks has long been recognized in clinical experience with amnesics. Amnesics who have insight into their condition (i.e., they have an accurate self-perception about their lack of memory ability) take care not to attempt memory tasks they cannot perform. Amnesics who lack insight are well known to get into difficulties because they do not recognize when they need to use memory (e.g., they will wander away from their home or clinic without realizing that they should not do so because they are unable to remember their way).

IMPROVING MEMORY PERFORMANCE BY ALTERING MEMORY SELF-PERCEPTIONS

Altering Memory Self-Perceptions. A person's memory perceptions may be altered by providing either feedback, relevant experience, or a combination of feedback and relevant experience. For example, a series of experiments have examined the influence of relevant experience on the nature of a memory self-perception. Subjects were asked to make self-reports (SR1) on memory questionnaires, perform (P) memory tasks without providing feedback on the accuracy of responses, then to make self reports (SR2) once again (i.e., SR1−P−SR2). Where the initial validity of self-reports was low (SR1−P, $r = .2$), the validity of the post-performance reports was substantial (e.g., SR2−P, r = .6; Herrmann, Grubs, Sigmundi, & Grueneich, 1986; Shlechter & Herrmann, 1981; see also McEvoy & Moon, 1988; Pressley et al., 1984). Memory self-perceptions that have been altered in this manner appear to remain altered (one study assessed perceptions after 2 months and did not find any noticeable change, Brock, 1986). The process of comparing perceptions with actual experience appears to be able to improve the accuracy of self-perceptions even in amnesics, a group often regarded to be incapable of improving insight into their memory abilities (Gervasio & Blusewicz, 1988).

Altering Memory Performance With Feedback.   Educators have long recognized the importance of providing students with feedback on their learning over a series of attempts to learn. Research has demonstrated that the degree of feedback given to learners is directly related to their memory performance. Feedback works because it enables the learner to develop an accurate self-perception of memory performance that can be used to guide performance (Palmer & Goetz, 1988; Pressley, Borkowski, & Schneider, 1987).

Conversely, false feedback that lowers self-regard for memory ability has been known to impair memory performance (Rapaport, 1942). For example, Sullivan (1927) investigated the influence of positive and negative feedback on the learning of nonsense syllables. She used this learning task because subjects could be expected to have little intuition into their typical performance on this task and, hence, would be more disposed to accept the feedback given them. After initial learning trials, the subjects were divided into two subgroups that were matched for their level of learning nonsense syllables. Each group was then given false feedback about their efficacy at the nonsense-syllable task. One group was told that they possessed superior ability for learning nonsense syllables, whereas the other group was told that their ability at this kind of learning was inferior. Recall on a subsequent nonsense-syllable learning task increased for those subjects given a false belief of superior learning ability and decreased for those subjects given a false belief of inferior learning ability.

Altering Memory Performance With Antistereotype Training.   Memory performance has been improved by instructions designed to rectify false self-perceptions foisted on people by stereotypes. Hamlett, Best, and Davis (1979) instructed a group of older adults about the stereotypical myths and truths of changes in memory and cognition that attend aging. Three additional groups of older adults participated as well: One group was given training in mnemonic strategies; one group was given lectures in art appreciation; and one group was given no training. All four groups performed a series of memory tasks after instruction and 1 month later.

On the immediate test, the group that was given information about cognition and aging and the group that was given mnemonic training performed at a comparable level that was substantially higher than the other two control groups. After 1 month, the mnemonics group maintained its superiority, whereas the cognition and aging group performed at the same levels as controls. Although the result after the delay indicates that the change in stereotypical attitudes was not permanent, the result obtained just after training suggests that stereotypical self-perceptions may be altered at least temporarily.

DISCUSSION

Research on memory self-perceptions has much in common with research on self-efficacy, self-directedness, agency, and control in other research areas (Bandura, 1984; Kohn & Schooler, 1983). As has been discussed here, memory-questionnaire researchers distinguish between global and specific self-perceptions. Global memory perceptions appear to be similar to self-efficacy (Cavanaugh & Morton, 1988; Dixon, Hertzog, & Hultsch, 1986; Lachman, 1986) and to self-directedness (Miller, Kohn, & Schooler, 1986). Additionally, the notion of agency has been very important to research on memory self-perceptions. The field of memory has recognized for many years that some memory processes are under a person's cognitive control, whereas others are beyond such control (Atkinson & Shiffrin, 1968; Flavell, 1977).

However, research on memory self-perceptions has emphasized one issue more than other kinds of research on self-efficacy, self-directedness, agency, and control (Bandura, 1984; Kohn & Schooler, 1983). Memory research has been preoccupied with the validity of memory self-perceptions and the factors that underlie this validity (the perceived level of memory proficiency and the task specificity of the perception). In so doing, memory research has shown that performance depends not only on the degree of self-regard or self-directedness but also on the accuracy of such perceptions. It remains for memory researchers, as well as researchers in other areas, to determine when performance is influenced solely by the degree of self-efficacy or self-directedness and when performance is also influenced by the accuracy of such self-perceptions.

ACKNOWLEDGMENTS

I thank Cynthia Berg, Dick Neisser, Jonathan Schooler, and Tonya Engstler-Schooler for advice on many of the issues discussed here.

REFERENCES

Abson, V., & Rabbitt, P. (1988). What do self rating questionnaires tell us about changes in competence in old age? In M. M. Gruneberg, P. E. Morris, & R. N. Sykes (Eds.), *Practical aspects of memory: Current research and issues* (Vol. 2, pp. 186–191). New York: Wiley.

Atkinson, R. C., & Shiffrin, R. M. (1968). Human memory: A proposed system and its control processes. In K. W. Spence & J. T. Spence (Eds.), *The psychology of learning and motivation* (Vol. 2, pp. 89–196). New York: Academic Press.

Baddeley, A. D. (1981). The cognitive psychology of everyday life. *British Journal of Psychology, 72*, 257–269.

Bandura, A. (1984). Recycling misconceptions of perceived self-efficacy. *Cognitive Therapy and Research, 8*, 231–255.

Bennett-Levy, J., & Powell, G. E. (1980). The subjective memory questionnaire (SMQ): An investigation into the self-reporting of "real-life" memory skills. *British Journal of Social and Clinical Psychology, 19*, 177–188.

Broadbent, D. E., Cooper, P. E., Fitzgerald, P., & Parkes, K. R. (1982). Cognitive Failures Questionnaire (CFQ) and its correlates. *British Journal of Clinical Psychology, 21*, 1–16.

Brock, A. C. (1986). *The accuracy of subjective reports on memory performance: Intentional and incidental self-monitoring compared.* Unpublished Honor's thesis, Manchester Polytechnic, Manchester, England.

Brown, A. L. (1978). Knowing when, where, and how to remember: A problem of metacognition. In A. R. Glaser (Ed.) *Advances in instructional psychology* (pp. 77–165). Hillsdale, NJ: Lawrence Erlbaum Associates.

Cavanaugh, J., Grady, J. C., & Perlmutter, M. (1983). Forgetting and the use of memory aids in 20 to 70 year olds in everyday life. *International Journal of Aging and Human Development, 17*, 113–122.

Cavanaugh, J., & Morton, K. R. (1988). Older adults' attributions about everyday memory. In M. M. Gruneberg, P. E. Morris, & R. N. Sykes (Eds.), *Practical aspects of memory: Current research and issues* (pp. 209–214). New York: Wiley.

Cavanaugh, J. C., & Murphy, N. Z. (1986). Personality and metamemory correlates of memory performance in younger and older adults. *Educational Gerontology, 12*, 385–394.

Cavanaugh, J. C., & Poon, L. W. (in press). Metamemorial predictors of memory performance in young and old adults. *Journal of Psychology and Aging.*

Chaffin, R., Crawford, M., Herrmann, D. J., & Deffenbacher, K. A. (1985). Gender differences in the perception of memory abilities in others. *Human Learning, 4*, 233–241.

Chaffin, R., & Herrmann, D. J. (1983). Self reports of memory abilities by old and young adults. *Human Learning, 2*, 17–28.

Cordoni, C. N. (1981). *Subjective perceptions of everyday memory failure.* Unpublished doctoral dissertation, Duke University Chapel Hill, NC.

Crawford, M., Herrmann, D. J., Holdsworth, M., Randal, E., & Robbins, D. (in press). Gender and beliefs about memory. *British Journal of Psychology.*

Cutler, S. J., & Grams, A. E. (1988). Correlates of self-reported everyday memory problems. *Journal of Gerontology, 43*, 582–590.

Devolder, P. A., & Pressley, M. (in press). Memory complaints in younger and older adults. *Applied Cognitive Psychology.*

Dixon, R. A. (in press). Questionnaire research on metamemory and aging: Issues of structure and function. In L. W. Poon, D. C. Rubin, & B. A. Wison (Eds.), *Everyday cognition in adulthood and old age.* New York: Cambridge University Press.

Dixon, R. A., & Hertzog, C. (1988). A functional approach to memory and metamemory development in adulthood. In F. E. Weinert & M. Perlmutter (Eds.), *Memory development across the life-span: Universal changes and individual differences* (pp. 293–330). Hillsdale, NJ: Lawrence Erlbaum Associates.

Dixon, R. A., Hertzog, C., & Hultsch, D. F. (1986). The multiple relationships among metamemory in adulthood (MIA) scales and cognitive abilities in adulthood. *Human Learning, 5,* 165–177.

Dixon, R. A., & Hultsch, D. F. (1983). Metamemory and memory for text relationships in adulthood: A cross validation study. *Journal of Gerontology, 38,* 689–694.

Flavell, J. H. (1977). *Cognitive development.* Englewood Cliffs, NJ: Prentice-Hall.

Flavell, J. H., & Wellman, H. M. (1977). Metamemory. In R. V. Kail & J. W. Hagan (Eds.), *Perspectives on the development of memory and cognition* (pp. 3–33). Hillsdale, NJ: Lawrence Erlbaum Associates.

Gervasio, A. H., & Blusewicz, M. J. (1988). Prediction and evaluation of everyday memory in neurological patients. *Bulletin of the Psychonomic Society, 26,* 339–342.

Gilewski, M. J., & Zelinski, E. M. (1986). Questionnaire assessment of memory complaints. In L. W. Poon (Ed.), *Clinical memory assessment of older adults* (pp. 93–107). Washington, DC: American Psychological Association.

Hamlett, K. W., Best, D. L., & Davis, S. W. (1979). *Modification of memory complaint and memory performance in elderly adults.* Unpublished manuscript, Catholic University, Washington, DC.

Herrmann, D. J. (1979). The validity of memory questionnaires as related to a theory of memory introspection. *Bulletin of the British Psychological Society, 33,* 26.

Herrmann, D. J. (1982). Know thy memory: The use of questionnaires to study and assess memory. *Psychological Bulletin, 92,* 434–452.

Herrmann, D. J. (1984). Questionnaires about memory. In J. Harris & P. Morris (Eds.), *Everyday memory, actions, and absentmindedness* (pp. 133–152). London: Academic Press.

Herrmann, D. J., & Gentry, M. (1985). *Memory contrivances in everyday life.* London: British Psychological Society.

Herrmann, D. J., Grubs, L., Sigmundi, R., & Grueneich, R. (1986). Awareness of memory ability before and after relevant memory experience. *Human Memory, 5,* 91–108.

Herrmann, D. J., & Neisser, U. (1978). An inventory of everyday memory experiences. In M. M. Gruneberg, P. E. Morris, & R. N. Sykes (Eds.), *Practical aspects of memory* (pp. 35–51). London: Academic Press.

Hertzog, C., Dixon, R. A., Schulenberg, J. E., & Hultsch, D. F. (1987). On the differentiation of memory beliefs from memory knowledge: The factor structure of the Metamemory in Adulthood scale. *Experimental Aging Research, 13,* 101–107.

Hertzog, C., Hultsch, D. F., & Dixon, R. A. (1988). *Evidence for the convergent validity of two self-report metamemory questionnaires.* Unpublished manuscript.

Hultsch, D. F., Hertzog, C., & Dixon, R. A. (1987). Age differences in metamemory: Resolving the inconsistencies. *Canadian Journal of Psychology, 41,* 193–208.

Hultsch, D. F., Hertzog, C., Dixon, R. A., & Davidson, H. (1988). Memory self-knowledge and self-efficacy in the aged. In M. I. Howe & C. J. Brainerd (Eds.), *Cognitive development in adulthood: Progress in cognitive development research* (pp. 65–92). New York: Springer-Verlag.

Jackson, J. L., Bogers, H., & Kerstholt, J. (1988). Do memory aids aid the elderly in their day to day remembering? In M. M. Gruneberg, P. E. Morris, & R. N. Sykes (Eds.), *Practical aspects of memory: Current research and issues* (Vol. 2, pp. 137–142). New York: Wiley.

Johnson, J. W., & Anderson, N. S. (1988). A comparison of four metamemory scales. In M. M. Gruneberg, P. E. Morris, & R. N. Sykes (Eds.), *Practical aspects of memory: Current research and issues* (pp. 543–548). New York: Wiley.

Klatzky, R. L. (1984). *Memory and awareness.* New York: Freeman.

Kohn, M. L., & Schooler, C. (1983). *Work and personality: An inquiry into the impact of social stratification.* Norwood, NJ: Ablex.

Lachman, M. E. (1986). Locus of control in aging research: A case for multidimensional and domain-specific assessment. *Psychology and Aging, 1,* 34–40.

Martin, M. (1986). Aging and patterns of change in everyday memory and cognition. *Human Learning, 5,* 63–74.

Martin, M., & Jones, G. V. (1984). Cognitive failures in everyday life. In J. Harris & P. Morris (Eds.), *Everyday memory, actions, and absentmindedness* (pp. 173–190). London: Academic Press.

McEvoy, C. L., & Moon, J. R. (1988). Assessment and treatment of everyday memory problems in the elderly. In M. M. Gruneberg, P. E. Morris, & R. N. Sykes (Eds.), *Practical aspects of memory: Current research and issues* (Vol. 2, pp. 155–160). New York: Wiley.

Miller, K. A., Kohn, M. L., & Schooler, C. (1986). Educational self-direction and the cognitive functioning of students. *Social Forces, 63,* 923–944.

Morris, P. E. (1984). The validity of subjective reports on memory. In J. Harris & P. Morris (Eds.), *Everyday memory, actions, and absentmindedness* (pp. 153–172). London: Academic Press.

Morris, P. E., Gruneberg, M. M., Sykes, R. N., & Merrick, A. (1981). Football knowledge and the acquisition of new results. *British Journal of Psychology, 72,* 479–484.

Neisser, U. (1978). Memory: What are the important questions? In M. M. Gruneberg, P. E. Morris, & R. N. Sykes (Eds.), *Practical aspects of memory* (pp. 3–24). New York: Academic Press.

Palmer, D. J., & Goetz, E. T. (1988). Selection and use of study strategies: The role of the studier's beliefs about self and strategies. In C. E. Weinstein, E. T. Goetz, & P. A. Alexander (Eds.), *Learning and study strategies* (pp. 41–61). San Diego: Academic Press.

Perlmutter, M. (1978). What is memory the aging of? *Developmental Psychology, 14,* 330–345.

Pressley, M., Borkowski, J. G., & Schneider, W. (1987). Cognitive strategies: Good strategy users co-ordinate metacognition and knowledge. In R. Vasta & G. Whitehurst (Eds.), *Annals of child development* (Vol. 4, pp. 89–129). Greenwich, CT: JAI Press.

Pressley, M., Levin, J. A., & Ghatala, E. S. (1984). Memory strategy monitoring in adults and children. *Journal of Verbal Learning and Verbal Behavior, 23,* 270–439.

Rapaport, D. (1942). *Emotions and memory.* Baltimore: Williams & Wilkins.

Reason, J. T. (1988). Stress and cognitive failure. In S. Fisher & J. T. Reason (Eds.), *Handbook of life stress, cognition and health* (pp. 405–419). New York: Wiley.

Ross, M. (in press). The relation of implicit theories to the construction of personal histories. *Psychological Review.*

Sehulster, J. R. (1981a). Structure and pragmatics of a self theory of memory. *Memory and Cognition, 9,* 263–276.

Sehulster, J. R. (1981b). Phenomenological correlates of a self theory of memory. *American Journal of Psychology, 94,* 527–537.

Sehulster, J. R. (1982). Phenomenological correlates of a self theory of memory: II. Dimensions. *American Journal of Psychology, 95,* 441–454.

Sehulster, J. R. (1988). Broader perspectives on everyday memory. In M. M. Gruneberg, P. E. Morris, & R. N. Sykes (Eds.), *Practical aspects of memory: Current research and issues* (Vol. 1, pp. 323–328). New York: Wiley.

Shlechter, T. M., & Herrmann, D. J. (1981). *A multi-method approach for investigating everyday memory.* New York: Eastern Psychological Association.

Shlechter, T. M., Herrmann, D. J., Stronach, P., Rubenfeld, L., & Zenker, S. (1982). *An investigation of people's knowledge of their everyday memory abilities.* New York: American Education Research Association.

Sullivan, E. B. (1927). Attitude in relation to learning. *Psychological Monographs, 36*, 1–149.

Sunderland, A., Harris, J. E., & Baddeley, A. D. (1983). Do laboratory tests predict everyday memory? A neuropsychological study. *Journal of Verbal Learning and Verbal Behavior, 22*, 341–357.

Sunderland, A., Watts, K., Baddeley, A. D., & Harris, J. E. (1986). Subjective memory assessment and test performance in elderly adults. *Journal of Gerontology, 41*, 376–384.

West, R. L., Boatwright, L. K., & Schlesser, R. (1984). The link between memory performance, self assessment, and affective status. *Experimental Aging Research, 10*, 197–200.

Zarit, S. H. (1982). Affective correlates of self reports about memory of older people. *International Journal of Behavioral Geriatrics, 1*, 25–34.

Zelinski, E. M., Gilewski, M. J., & Thompson, L. W. (1980). Do laboratory tests relate to self-assessments of memory ability in the young and old? In L. W. Poon, J. L. Fozard, L. S. Cermak, D. Arenberg, & L. W. Thompson (Eds.), *New directions in memory and aging: Proceedings of the George A. Talland Memorial Conference* (pp. 519–544). Hillsdale, NJ: Lawrence Erlbaum Associates.

Control and Health: An Epidemiological Perspective

S. Leonard Syme
University of California at Berkeley

STATEMENT OF THE PROBLEM

There was a time, many years ago, when I was a sociologist. In those days, I was interested in the study of a variety of psychosocial concepts, and I used to study disease as one convenient way of learning more about those concepts. Later, I became interested in epidemiology. From this perspective, my major interest was in the study of disease. Although I examined the same psychosocial concepts as before, I did it with the hope that my studies would help me understand more about the causes of disease.

I raise this issue to emphasize one particular point. I come to the study of concepts such as control and self-directedness not because I am interested in them per se but because I have been driven to them in order to explain disease patterns that are otherwise to me inexplicable. That I approach these concepts via this route has two consequences. One is that I come to the study of control in innocence. I come with very little previous knowledge and with a degree of naivete that is, as becomes clear here, distressing. On the other hand, my research on these concepts has been developed with a minimum of preconceptions. That I have been reluctantly driven by the data to the idea of control is in some measure a stronger argument for its importance than if I already was a believer.

The problem that first brought me to the concept of control involved a research project on socioeconomic status (SES). I had for several years been interested in the fact that disease rates varied by SES: The lower the

SES position, the higher the rate of virtually every disease and condition known to researchers (Antonovsky, 1967; Kitagawa & Hauser, 1973; Syme & Berkman, 1976). Most of the efforts to explain this well-known phenomenon had focused on such factors as inadequate medical care, unemployment, low income, racial factors, poor nutrition, poor housing, and poor education. The difficulty with this approach was that these factors could not account for the existence of a gradient of disease rates by SES. It is not simply that people at the bottom of the SES hierarchy have higher rates of disease but that rates of disease increase progressively as one moves down from the top of the SES hierarchy to the bottom.

For example, in the work of Marmot, Rose, Shipley, and Hamilton (1978), British civil servants in the highest social class (administrators) have the lowest rate of coronary heart disease, whereas those in the lowest class have rates 4 times as high. Interestingly, however, is the fact that civil servants in the professional and executive class and in the clerical class have rates 2 times and 3.2 times as high as administrators, respectively. After account had been taken of such coronary heart disease risk factors as serum cholesterol, cigarette smoking, blood pressure, physical activity, obesity, and glucose tolerance, this gradient of disease rates remained unchanged. Although it might be possible to explain the high rates of coronary heart disease among less-skilled manual workers in the British civil service in terms of such factors as income, education, housing, and nutrition, these factors are unlikely to explain the difference in rates between administrators and professionals/executives, or clerical workers.

This gradient is not unique to British civil servants. It has been observed in a wide variety of populations in many different countries and it is not confined to a single disease entity or age group. The gradient has been observed for many body systems including the digestive, genitourinary, respiratory, circulatory, nervous, blood, and endocrine systems. It has been observed also for most malignancies, congenital anomalies, infections and parasitic diseases, accidents, poisoning and violence, perinatal mortality, diabetes, and musculo-skeletal impairments (Susser, Watson, & Hooper, 1985). It is very difficult to explain these gradients and, especially, to account for differences between those at the top of the hierarchy and those just one or two steps down.

One hypothesis consistent with these data involves the concept of control. It could be postulated that the lower down one is in the SES hierarchy, the less control one has over the factors that affect life and living circumstances. Of course, this hypothesis is very general and it does not specify whether control involves money, power, information, prestige, experience, or something else. Although not precise, the hypothesis does at least direct attention to a general range of issues. In this way, the concept of control can be seen as a "sensitizing concept" that deserves further research and examination.

THE CONCEPT OF CONTROL

Whatever the merits of this hypothesis, it does fit the data regarding SES, whereas most other hypotheses do not and, furthermore, it is the only hypothesis that seems to easily fit the facts. The plausibility of the control hypothesis is strengthened by the fact that it is consistent also with many other research findings that have little or nothing specifically to do with SES.

It is important to recognize the dangers inherent in such a search of the literature to find support for a favored hypothesis. This activity is dangerous because it is virtually certain that such support will be found. Searches of this kind tend to give more weight to findings that are consistent with the hypothesis and less weight to those that are not. In spite of this, the existence of such supportive evidence does tend to increase the plausibility of the hypothesis and, as long as appropriate skepticism and caution is exercised, such searches can be worthwhile.

One body of supportive evidence involved the work on job stress that had been carried out by Karasek, Baker, Marxer, Ahlbom, and Theorell (1981), Alfredsson, Karasek, and Theorell (1982), and Theorell et al. (1984) in Sweden and the United States. These investigators had shown that rates of coronary heart disease were higher among workers who experienced not only high job demand but low discretion and latitude for dealing with those demands. The work of these researchers is especially impressive because previous studies of job stress had for decades failed to establish a link between job pressures and health even though this issue had been examined intensively. When the concepts of control and discretion were included in the research, important findings at last emerged and in fact are now being replicated by others (Haan & Aro, 1988; House, Strecher, Metzner, & Robbins, 1986). In our work on hypertension among San Francisco bus drivers, and in our studies of British civil servants, we also are using this concept, and it is proving to be a very useful tool.

As pleasing as it was to find support for the concept of control in the job-stress literature, it was somewhat unsettling to learn that it had already been studied very successfully for years by many psychologists and sociologists in the study of health and illness. The naivete associated with this discovery is embarrassing: A great truth had been identified that in fact had been worked on by literally dozens of scholars for many years.

A partial listing of such usage illustrates this point. Pearlin, Menaghan, Leiberman, and Mullan (1981) have studied the concept of mastery; Bandura (1982) and O'Leary (1985) among others have studied self-efficacy; Rotter (1975) and Wallston and Wallston (1982) have studied locus of control; Seligman (1975), learned helplessness; Glass and Singer (1972) and Sherrod (1974), controllability; Cohen (1980), predictability; Burger (1985), desire for control; Langer (1983), Rodin (1986), and Schulz (1976), sense of control; Bauman and Udry (1972), powerlessness; Kobasa (1982), hardiness; Libassi and Maluccio (1986), competence; and so on. In addition, other scholars have used concepts that easily can be seen as related to the notion of control. For example, James, Hartnett and Kalsbeek (1983) have suggested the importance of "John Henryism" in accounting for the high rates of hypertension among poor Blacks in the United States; by this term, James is referring to Blacks who enthusiastically have accepted American middle-class goals relating to success and achievement but who by reason of poor education are not likely to reach these goals.

CONTROL AS AN INTEGRATIVE CONCEPT

It is important not to overinterpret the fact that so many investigators have suggested the importance of control for health and well-being. In fact, few of these people are using the same term in exactly the same way; each use tends to have a special focus and each has been found of value in explaining different disease outcomes. For this reason, it is an exaggeration to claim that they are variations on one theme. On the other hand, it is intriguing that so many different scholars, from different backgrounds and with different research objectives, should come up with ideas that are so similar to one another.

There is more. The idea of control is not inconsistent with other major findings in social epidemiology. Everyone has a different list of major findings but my listing includes mobility, social support, Type A behavior, and stressful life events (Syme, 1986). The evidence on these factors suggests that each is associated with the higher incidence and prevalence of disease independently of other known risk factors. Although these associations are fairly clear, the reasons for them are not. Each of these factors has been studied relatively independently of the others and, to my knowledge, no one has seriously attempted a search for commonalities. Seen from the perspective of control, however, it is possible to suggest that all of these factors are simply different facets or manifestations of control or of its absence.

With the caution appropriate for such ad hoc reasoning, we can suggest that social support is useful in helping to influence the events that affect our lives. This idea, of course, is an old one, but its first and most elegant expression in modern writings comes from the work of John Cassel (1974). More recently, Pearlin et al. (1981) reported that people with confidants exhibited higher levels of self-esteem and personal control. Seeman and Syme (1987) have found also that people with high levels of social support are in a better position to control the events that impinge upon them. In our study of people undergoing coronary angiography, a comparison was made of the various components that are included in the concept of social support. We studied number of friends, number of close friends, frequency of seeing people, satisfaction with the quantity and quality of relationships, what one did for people, what people did for one, and so on. Comparing the predictive power of these various approaches, the most powerful was the instrumental view of support. Compared to other definitions of social support, less coronary atherosclerosis was seen among people who could count on specific people to help them when they needed specific kinds of help (e.g., to borrow money, help with household repairs, advice with problems).

If social support is important as an aid in dealing with events that affect life, it is not difficult to see that mobility and stressful life events disturb control by interrupting social relationships. Mobility involving changes in jobs and places of residence inevitably affects social ties, as do most other important life events such as marriage, divorce, or death of a loved one. However, if people can participate in controlling issues related to the disruption, the likelihood of disease consequences may be lessened. For example, when elderly persons are geographically relocated, the morbidity and mortality results usually seen are much less pronounced if these people are given a choice about when and where to move or about various aspects of their new living arrangements (Krantz & Schulz, 1980). In the same spirit of ad hoc reasoning, it is possible to suggest that those exhibiting Type A behavior have higher rates of coronary heart disease because of their continual, but unsuccessful, efforts to control events in their lives (Glass, 1977).

It is unnecessary to go on in this vein. Obviously, with some ingenuity and motivation, it is not difficult to weave a consistent story regarding control from almost any set of data. Enough perhaps has already been said to suggest that the concept does provide for the integration of a wide variety of apparently unconnected and independent observations. It is difficult to think of other concepts that do this as easily or simply. This is attractive because, as we know, it is the aim of science to present facts in the simplest and most economical conceptual formulation.

THE INTERDISCIPLINARY SEARCH FOR CAUSES OF DISEASE

Another attractive feature of the concept of control, in addition to its attractiveness as an integrating concept, is that it may help us in our search for the causes of disease—the major goal of epidemiology. It is obvious that discovering the causes of a disease requires the collaboration of researchers from many disciplines. However, those who have actually tried to engage in interdisciplinary research know how difficult and frustrating this experience can be. Researchers from different disciplines often use different methods and techniques, define terms differently, and have different research priorities and objectives. As a consequence, many investigators simply give up on interdisciplinary collaboration and opt instead for working with people who share their own research approach. Although understandable, this withdrawal is unfortunate because it makes the search for the causes of disease more difficult.

The search for the causes of disease can be seen as taking place at several levels. At one level, we ask how specific disease agents act alone or together to produce disease in one individual. At another level, we ask why one person gets sick instead of another. At yet another level, we ask why rates of disease are higher in one group than in another.

One would think that the answer to a question at any one of these levels of inquiry would be useful in answering the questions posed at the other levels. Unfortunately, this often is not the case. For example, we have a very solid body of research information regarding the biologic consequences that follow infection of the body by the cholera vibrio. This information is only of limited value in understanding why one person develops cholera, whereas another does not. It is of even less use in shedding light on reasons for the distribution of cholera throughout the world.

The problem is not that there exists different levels of analysis in the search for the causes of disease. The problem is that researchers tend to focus their efforts at only one level so that, over time, scientific disciplines develop different techniques, methods, and concepts that are particularly suitable to study at that level. This specialization tends to make difficult interdisciplinary communication and collaboration. This problem is not amenable to simple solution and it certainly cannot be resolved by well-meaning conferences in which researchers from different disciplines are urged to try hard to be cooperative and sharing.

Interdisciplinary cooperation might be enhanced if we could identify concepts that transcended various levels of research strategy. Control may be one of these concepts. If it were agreed that the concept of control is important, it might be easier to begin to specify and to more clearly visualize these differences in approach. This does not solve the problem but it narrows the range of disagreement and permits a specification of differences so that communication can proceed. In recent years, the concept of *control* has appeared more and more frequently to help explain variations in biologic functioning in laboratory, clinical, and population research. In this research, the term has of course been defined and measured differently, but enough common content seems included in this usage to suggest that a transcendent core may exist.

DEFINING CONTROL

And now, we come to a key problem: It is perhaps not surprising that a concept as general and ill-defined as control should provide for integration among different research findings as well as across disciplinary boundaries. Indeed, this vagueness may be the reason that the concept can encompass such a wide variety of heterogeneous ideas. Loss of control has been defined in terms of constraints on coping ability, diminished authority over decisions, threats to status and self-esteem, lessened opportunity to learn new skills, and inappropriateness of coping. The question has been raised in the literature as to whether the concept refers to perceived control or to actual control (see Rodin, this volume). Some view controllability in terms of predictability, whereas others see it in terms of a sense of coherence or a sense of permanence. Control can be assessed as a property of individuals or of situations; it can reflect a quality of individuals as well as be a function of training and opportunities or of social and cultural circumstances. Control can be a positive or negative force depending on personality, cultural milieu, and previous experiences. It can involve specific situations or all situations. People can be seen to desire, need, or abhor control. The idea can refer to control over big, little, or all things. Some think of control as a personal "state of being" (of *being* in control), whereas others see it as a "condition" (where *things* are under control).

In this circumstance, the temptation to move toward one common definition is strong. If we could agree on such a definition, we then could develop appropriate assessment methods and hopefully a coherent and comparable body of research evidence. Although this is reasonable, there are some serious hazards in such an approach. In the first place, it is difficult to accomplish, given our present state of knowledge. Each of the various conceptions of control currently in use have merit and it is not easy to see how one would choose the "right" one. As noted earlier, with some ingenuity, substantial research evidence can be arranged to support any one of these approaches. In the end of course, the selection of the "best" definition will depend on its usefulness in accounting for research observations.

In the second place, there is a hazard in prematurely moving toward one commonly agreed-upon definition of such concepts. One need only review the recent history of research on Type A behavior to see the damage that can follow from the decision to prematurely define terms and agree on measurement methods. Rosenman et al. (1975) had shown that, at least in their hands, a behavior type could be identified and measured so that it predicted coronary heart disease. Based on their one prospective study, investigators around the world tacitly accepted their definition of Type A behavior and attempted to measure it by use of the structured interview and by questionnaires such as the Jenkins Activity Scale, the Bortner Scale, or the Framingham Scale.

The results of this outpouring of research are so varied as to be uninterpretable. Many studies found a relationship between the behavior pattern but an approximately equal number have failed to do so. Several major conferences and workshops have been convened aimed at developing some consensus regarding these varied results, but these meetings have not achieved agreement (Ostfeld & Eaker, 1985). It is only in the last few years that new work by Williams, Barefoot, and Shekelle (1985); Scherwitz, McKelvain, Laman, Patterson, and Dutton (1983); Kobasa (1982), and others (Matthews & Haynes, 1986) is now providing some clarification in this area. This new work suggests that the concept of Type A behavior was probably too vague a concept in the first place and that it was premature to try to capture it using one or another questionnaire or scale. The research now going on in this field is suggesting that the important element in Type A behavior may really be a particular subcomponent that the global concept was reflecting but that now should be measured directly. Of course, these investigators have their own view of what that subcomponent is, and few of them agree with one another about what it is. For example, one or another of these investigators has suggested that the important dimension of Type A behavior is hostility, others that it is need for control, others that it is self-reference behavior, yet others that it is hardiness, and so on.

Although we are still far from having a clear view of the meaning and importance of Type A behavior, it is refreshing to see that research now under way is directed toward achieving an understanding of the concept rather than a more or less mindless and repetitive effort to replicate findings that emerged from one early study. This phenomenon is not limited to Type A behavior. A more or less similar scenario can now be seen with reference to such other popular concepts as social support and stressful life events.

There are at least two alternatives to the "consensus" movement. One, suggested by Cohen (personal communication, 1988), is to bring together in one place all of the various approaches and definitions of control so that a typology can be developed. This typology would help us to see what various definitions have in common and, at the same time, to see how they differ from one another. An important contribution of this approach would be to help in discerning underlying issues, themes, and processes. A somewhat different approach is to think of control as a "sensitizing" concept—a concept that raises consciousness about an issue and that directs thinking along certain lines but that does not provide specific guidance about definitions or assessment methods. This approach suffers from lack of rigor but it does encourage a very wide range of research perspectives so that the relative power of each can more easily be appreciated.

In either case, the issue of definitions is an empirical one, better settled by research than by argument and debate. As such, a major priority in this area of work is the initiation of research that specifically and systematically compares the usefulness of various definitions and approaches.

THE PREVENTION OF DISEASE

To this point, we have discussed the potential value of control as an integrating concept and as a concept that would be helpful in facilitating interdisciplinary research—an activity necessary in the search for the causes of disease. A third usefulness of the concept is its value in efforts to prevent disease. In the health field, the usefulness of a concept obviously is enhanced if it can be used to help prevent disease. The special and exciting potential of the concept of control, however, is that it is amenable to intervention and application not only at the individual level but also at the community and environmental level. This usefulness at the environmental level is noteworthy because we have had great difficulty in helping individuals to make changes in many behaviors that affect health. Many people who try to quit smoking fail (Syme & Alcalay, 1982). We have little success in getting people to lower the fat and salt content of their diet (Kirscht & Rosenstock, 1979), and the majority of people who try to lose weight and maintain losses do not succeed. Even in a specially designed program like the Multiple Risk Factor Intervention Trial (MR-FIT; 1981, 1982), where optimal conditions existed for behavior change, many people were unable to follow recommendations for dietary change and smoking cessation. This occurred in spite of the fact that MRFIT included an informed and highly motivated group of participants, a superb behavioral intervention plan, excellent and numerous staff, and enough time to work with each participant over a 6-year period.

One major limitation of almost all intervention programs is that we have viewed high-risk behaviors almost exclusively as problems of the individual. When intervention programs focus exclusively on the individual and his or her behavior, they ignore the fact that these behaviors occur in a social and cultural context. By focusing on the individual's motivations and perceptions, we may be neglecting some of the most important influences on behavior such as social values, fashions, and priorities (Leventhal & Cleary, 1980).

Even if we could induce people to change their behavior in one-to-one programs, the impact of such changes in the population would be modest. The reason for this is that new people continue to enter the "at-risk" population even as high-risk people leave it because individually oriented programs do nothing to deal with the environmental factors that initiated the problem. In this circumstance, an environmental approach may be more useful than an individual one.

Although control is a characteristic of individuals, it is also a product of the environment. Interventions to enhance control therefore can be directed both to the individual and to the environment. The work of Langer and Rodin (1976) and Rodin and Langer (1977) provides a classic example of the way in which control can be dealt with at the environmental level. These investigators provided arrangements whereby a group of elderly convalescent home residents could make more choices about their living circumstance and have more control of day-to-day events. After 18 months of follow-up, these residents showed a significantly greater improvement in health than a comparable group of residents who were "looked after" by the staff. Compared to a 25% mortality rate in the nursing home in the 18 months before intervention, only 15% of the subjects in the intervention group died. In the same time period, 30% in the control group died. Several other important interventions among elderly persons have yielded positive results (Rodin, 1986), as have interventions in other organizational contexts such as hospitals (Langer, Janis, & Wolfer, 1975; Taylor, 1979).

Another illustration of the power of environmental manipulations of control comes from the other end of the age spectrum. In this case, children 3 to 4 years of age from disadvantaged backgrounds during the 1960s in the United States were offered 1 or 2 years of special education prior to their enrollment in regular school. Especially interesting are the results reported from a 22-year follow-up of low-income children from Ypsilanti, Michigan. These children had been randomly assigned either to an early education program or to no program (Berrueta-Clement, Schweinhart, Barrett, Epstein, & Weikart, 1984; Richmond & Beardslee, 1988). At age 19, those who had had 1 or 2 years of early education were more likely than those in the control group to have completed high school (67% vs. 49%) and to be employed (59% vs. 32%) and were less likely to have been arrested (31% vs. 51%) or to have been on public assistance (18% vs. 32%), and for girls, were 50% less likely to have had a teenage pregnancy. Because these children were assigned at random to the program, these reported differences are probably attributable to the program itself and not to such other factors as motivated parents or differences in baseline intellectual level.

Although these results come from only one study, other long-term follow-up studies have been done on children, and it would be useful to collect and critically review data obtained in those studies. A new series of similar programs is now underway in England. If subsequent analyses support the findings from the Ypsilanti study, it is important to explain how 1 or 2 years of early education could have such a profound impact on the quality of life many years later. Indeed, this type of analysis might be most useful in helping to identify crucial components of control.

Another illustration of interventions to enhance control comes from our work with San Francisco bus drivers. Several previous studies have noted that bus drivers, compared with workers in other occupations, have a higher prevalence of hypertension as well as diseases of the gastrointestinal tract and of the musculoskeletal and respiratory systems. These results have been obtained from studies in different transit systems, under different conditions, and in several countries (Berlinguer, 1962; Garbe, 1980; Morris, Kagan, Pattison, Gardner, & Raffle, Netterstrom & Laursen, 1981; Winkleby, Ragland, Fisher, & Syme, 1988). Based on these findings, it has been suggested that certain aspects of the bus-driving occupation may create an increased risk for disease among these workers.

In our study of drivers, we are monitoring such environmental factors as exposure to noise, vibration, and carbon monoxide fumes, but we are paying particular attention to the drivers' social environment (Ragland et al., 1987; Winkleby, Ragland, & Syme, 1988). One of the most important aspects of that environment is that drivers must keep to a specific schedule that is arranged without realistic reference to actual road conditions and, in fact, cannot be met. From the instant drivers sit in the bus, they are behind schedule and are continually reprimanded for this.

In this circumstance, intervention to improve the work situation of drivers can be introduced not merely among bus drivers but directly on the schedule itself. For example, it may be that by changing the way in which schedules are arranged, the bus company will be able to earn more money than it loses because of reduced rates of absenteeism among drivers as well as lower rates of sickness, accidents, and in particular, turnover. It is possible that drivers could be invited to share in the schedule-making process: They probably have useful information to provide regarding important elements of the schedule. Even if the schedule itself is not changed much, however, drivers will at least have had a hand in creating it. It often is true that we can better tolerate bad situations if at least they are of our own choosing rather than imposed by others.

These examples illustrate the possibility of aiming interventions to enhance control not just at individuals but at the social environment. The modification of living arrangements in a nursing home is an institutional and organizational matter; the provision of early enrichment programs for children is a community issue; the opportunity for workers to participate in determining the factors that affect their working lives is a company issue. Without the availability of these structural resources, it is difficult for people, on their own, to enhance control over their lives. Clearly, we need both environmental support and individual initiatives. The concept of control is especially attractive because it is amenable to intervention at both levels.

CONCLUSION

It has been suggested in this chapter that the concept of control is of importance because it provides a parsimonious integration of many seemingly unrelated concepts, because it may help us in the interdisciplinary research, and because it clearly is an issue amenable to intervention.

However defined, viewing control as an integrating concept permits me to better understand why higher rates of disease are found among people who have poor social support, who have been mobile, who have had stressful life events, who are in jobs with little latitude and little room for discretion, who are in lower socioeconomic positions, and who exhibit Type A behavior. So far, no findings in my field of knowledge have been found that are inconsistent with the control hypothesis.

There are at least four reasons for this phenomenon. The first is that all of the findings available have not been discovered, and, if a more rigorous search were initiated, contradictory evidence would surely be unearthed. The second is that with sufficient ingenuity, almost anything can be fit into pre-set schema. The third is that the concept is so vaguely and ambiguously defined that it can encompass virtually any idea simply because of that vagueness. The fourth is that it may really be a useful and parsimonious concept and that what we see is an accurate reflection of reality.

There probably is some validity to each of these possibilities and it should be a priority to see which have more weight. In reviewing the evidence available, it seems more useful to look not for confirmation of personal beliefs but for contradictions and negative evidence. Confirmatory evidence is reassuring but it does not help to clarify ideas. Negative evidence forces us to confront the inadequacy of our thinking and requires that we sharpen our concepts and assessment methods. Of course, all of us to some extent are reluctant or uneasy about seeking out such negative evidence and we perhaps have difficulties in recognizing such negative evidence when we see it. We tend to rationalize away such contradictory evidence with alarming ease so that the problems set before us rarely penetrate conscious thought. This is one of the special advantages of inviting to a conference researchers from different fields with different perspectives and commitments in order to examine together one idea. In a conference setting, we still are able to talk past each other and avoid confronting unpleasant and contradictory data, but it is not as easy.

Given the fact that control is of value, the question arises as to whether we can move toward a more precise definition of what is meant by the term *control* so that we can measure it reliably and validly. From an epidemiological perspective, this issue is reasonably clear cut. Which of the various approaches to control and self-directedness is most useful in explaining the occurrence of disease? Which is most useful in intervening to control or prevent disease? One of the special advantages of this epidemiologic perspective is that it provides a hard, quantifiable outcome variable (i.e., disease) against which more subjective and ambiguous predictor variables can be compared and evaluated. This admittedly is a narrow focus, but it is a meaningful and important one, and it may be of value in helping to sort through the various approaches to the issue of control and self-directedness.

So, where to from here? My answer is the time-honored one: More research is needed. The question remains "what kind of research?" If the foregoing arguments make sense, we need a variety of research approaches among animals and humans, and in laboratory, clinic, and population settings, aimed at answering questions such as why a person becomes ill, why one person becomes ill and not another, and why rates of illness are higher in one group than in another. But we can go further than this. One of the fascinating results from research on control is the diversity of outcomes that have been observed ranging from physiologic abnormalities to psychological distress to disease and death. In this work, a wide variety of organ systems and biologic processes are seen to be affected by control or its absence.

That this one factor, control, is associated with higher rates of so many different diseases and conditions may at first glance seem biologically implausible. Two models come to mind that might account for this phenomenon. One model postulates that the concept of control includes so many diverse elements that each element separately influences the likelihood of different diseases and conditions. This often is the explanation offered to account for the higher rate of so many diseases and conditions associated with cigarette smoking. The second model suggests that stressors associated with the breakdown of control (however defined) act to depress the body's defense systems so that people affected are more vulnerable to a wide range of disease agents (Laudenslager et al., 1983; Sklar & Anisman, 1979; Visintainer et al., 1982). In this model, the presence of such specific disease agents as viruses, bacteria, air pollutants, or high blood pressure would not result in diseases unless the person was vulnerable to them. For this reason, the presence of breakdowns in control would predict the likelihood of people getting sick, but not what disease they got. This model is attractive because it would account for the fact that (a) the concept of control is related to many different diseases involving many organ systems and (b) most well-recognized disease-specific risk factors only sometimes result in disease.

If the second model seems reasonable, research on control should focus not only on specific diseases and conditions but also on compromised defense systems in general. In this way, the study of control (a concept that parsimoniously integrates a variety of seemingly unrelated *psychosocial* concepts) can lead to studies of physiologic function—an approach that might parsimoniously integrate a variety of seemingly unrelated *disease* outcomes.

I think you can see from these remarks why I feel that the concept of control is of value for epidemiologic research. Although I agree that we should be guarded about the introduction of trendy new ideas or of new words that merely provide a fresh package for old ideas, in the case of the concept of control, we may really be on to something important. As I noted earlier, I come to this conclusion grudgingly and reluctantly; in my research, I have run out of better alternatives. I think research on control and self-directedness may really be worth our best effort.

REFERENCES

Alfredsson, L., Karasek, R., & Theorell, T. (1982). Myocardial infarction risk and psychosocial work environment: An analysis of the male Swedish working force. *Social Science and Medicine, 16*, 463–467.

Antonovsky, A. (1967). Social science, life expectancy and overall mortality. *Milbank Memorial Fund Quarterly, 45*, 31–73.

Bandura, A. (1982). Self-efficacy mechanisms in human agency. *American Psychologist, 37*, 122–147.

Bauman, K. E., & Udry, J. R. (1972). Powerlessness and regularity of contraception in an urban Negro male sample: A research note. *Journal of Marriage and the Family, 34*, 112–114.

Berlinguer, G. (1962). *Maladies and industrial health of public transportation workers*. Washington, DC: U.S. Department of Transportation.

Berrueta-Clement, J.R., Schweinhart, L. J., Barnett, W. S., Epstein A. S., & Weikart, D. P. (1984). *Changed lives: The effects of the Perry Preschool Program on youths through age 19*. Ypsilanti, MI: High/Scope Press.

Burger, J. (1985). Desire for control and achievement-related behaviors. *Journal of Personality and Social Psychology, 48*, 1520–1533.

Cassel, J. (1974). Psychosocial processes and "stress": Theoretical formulations. *International Journal of Health Services, 4*, 471–482.

Cohen, S. (1980). Aftereffects of stress on human performance and social behavior. *Psychological Bulletin, 88*, 82–108.

Garbe, C. (1980). *Health and health risks among city bus drivers in West Berlin*. Washington, DC: U.S. Department of Transportation.

Glass, D. C. (1977). *Behavior patterns, stress, and coronary disease*. Hillsdale, NJ: Lawrence Erlbaum Associates.

Glass, D. C., & Singer, J. E. (9172). *Urban stress: Experiments on noise and social stressors*. New York: Academic Press.

Haan, M. N., & Aro, S. (1988). Job strain and ischemic heart disease: An epidemiologic study of metal workers. *Annals of Clinical Research, 20*, 143–146.

House, J. S., Strecher, V., Metzner, H. L., & Robbins, C. A. (1986). Occupational stress and health among men and women in the Tecumseh Community Health Study. *Journal of Health and Social Behavior, 27*, 62–77.

James, S. A., Hartnett, S. A., & Kalsbeek, W. D. (1983). John Henryism and blood pressure differences among black men. *Journal of Behavioral Medicine, 6*, 259–278.

Karasek, R., Baker, D., Marxer, F., Ahlbom, A., & Theorell, T. (1981). Job decision latitude, job demands, and cardiovascular disease: A prospective study of Swedish men. *American Journal of Public Health, 71*, 694–705.

Kirscht, J. P., & Rosenstock, I. M. (1979). Patients' problems in following recommendations of health experts. In G. C. Stone, F. Cohen, & N. E. Adler (Eds.), *Health psychology: A handbook* (pp. 189–215). San Francisco, CA: Jossey-Bass.

Kitagawa, E. M., & Hauser, P. M. (1973). *Differential mortality in the United States*. Cambridge, MA: Harvard University Press.

Kobasa, S. C. (1982). The hardy personality: Toward a social psychology of stress and health. In G. S. Sanders & J. Suls (Eds.), *Social psychology of health and illness* (pp. 3–32). Hillsdale, NJ: Lawrence Erlbaum Associates.

Krantz, D., & Schulz, R. (1980). A model life crisis control and health outcomes: Cardiac rehabilitation and relocation of the elderly. In A. Baum & J. E. Singer (Eds.), *Advances in environmental psychology: Vol. 2. Cardiovascular disorders and behavior* (pp. 23–57). Hillsdale, NJ: Lawrence Erlbaum Associates.

Langer, E. J. (1983). *The psychology of control.* Beverly Hills, CA: Sage.

Langer, E. J., Janis, I. L., & Wolfer, J. A. (1975). Reduction of psychological stress in surgical patients. *Journal of Experimental and Social Psychology, 11,* 155–165.

Langer, E. J., & Rodin, J. (1976). The effects of choice and enhanced personal responsibility for the aged: A field experiment in an institutional setting. *Journal of Personality and Social Psychology, 34,* 191.

Laudenslager, M. L., Ryan, S. M., Drugan, R. C., Hyson, R. L., & Maier, S. F. (1983). Coping and immunosuppression: Inescapable but not escapable shock suppresses lymphocyte proliferation. *Science, 221,* 568–571.

Leventhal, H., & Cleary, P. D. (1980). The smoking problem: A review of the research and theory in behavioral risk modification. *Psychological Bulletin, 88,* 370–405.

Libassi, M. F., & Maluccio, A. (1986). Competence-centered social work: Prevention in action. *Journal of Primary Prevention, 6,* 168–180.

Marmot, M. G., Rose, G., Shipley, M., & Hamilton, P. J. S. (1978). Employment grade and coronary heart disease in British civil servants. *Journal of Epidemiology and Community Health, 3,* 244–249.

Matthews, K. A., & Haynes, S. G. (1986). Type A behavior pattern and coronary disease risk. *American Journal of Epidemiology, 123,* 923–961.

Morris, J. N., Kagan, A., Pattison, D. C., Gardner, M. J., & Raffle, P. A. B. (1966). Incidence and prediction of ischemic heart disease in London busmen. *Lancet, 1,* 533–559.

Multiple Risk Factor Intervention Trial Research Group. (1981). The Multiple Risk Factor Intervention Trial. *Preventive Medicine, 10,* 387–553.

Multiple Risk Factor Intervention Trial Research Group. (1982). The Multiple Risk Factor Intervention Trial—Risk factor changes and mortality results. *Journal of the American Medical Association, 248,* 1465–1476.

Netterstrom, B., & Laursen, P. (1981). Incidence and prevalence of ischemic heart disease among urban bus drivers in Copenhagen. *Scandinavian Journal of Social Medicine, 2,* 75–79.

O'Leary, A. (1985). Self-efficacy and health. *Behavior Research and Therapy, 23,* 437–451.

Ostfeld, A. M., & Eaker, E. D. (Eds.). (1985). *Measuring psychosocial variables in epidemiologic studies of cardiovascular disease: Proceedings of a workshop.* Bethesda, MD: National Institutes of Health Publication No. 85-2270.

Pearlin, L. I., Menaghan, E. G., Lieberman, M. A., & Mullan, J. T. (1981). The stress process. *Journal of Health and Social Behavior, 22,* 337–356.

Ragland, D. R., Winkleby, M. A., Schwalbe, J., Holman, B. L., Morse, L., Syme, S. L., & Fisher, J. M. (1987). Prevalence of hypertension in bus drivers. *International Journal of Epidemiology, 16,* 208–213.

Richmond, J. B., & Beardslee, W. R. (1988). Resiliency: Research and practical implications for pediatricians. *Developmental and Behavioral Pediatrics, 9,* 157–163.

Rodin, J. (1986). Aging and health: Effects of the sense of control. *Science, 233,* 1271–1276.

Rodin, J., & Langer, E. J. (1977). Long-term effects of a control-relevant intervention with the institutionalized aged. *Journal of Personality and Social Psychology, 35,* 897–902.

Rosenman, R. H., Brand, R. J., Jenkins, C. D., Friedman, M., Straus, R., & Wurm, M. (1975). Coronary heart disease in the Western Collaborative Group Study: Final follow-up experience of 8½ years. *Journal of the American Medical Association, 233,* 872–877.

Rotter, J. B. (1975). Some problems and misconceptions related to the construct of internal versus external reinforcement. *Journal of Consulting and Clinical Psychology, 43,* 56–67.

Scherwitz, L., McKelvain, R., Laman, C., Patterson, J., & Dutton, L. (1983). Type A behavior, self-involvement, and coronary atherosclerosis. *Psychosomatic Medicine, 45,* 47–57.

Schulz, R. (1976). Effects of control and predictability on the physical and psychological well-being of the institutionalized aged. *Journal of Personality and Social Psychology, 33,* 563–573.

Seeman, T. E., & Syme, S. L. (1987). Social networks and coronary artery disease: A comparison of the structure and function of social relations as predictors of disease. *Psychosomatic Medicine, 49,* 341–354.

Seligman, M. E. P. (1975). *Helplessness: On depression, development, and death.* San Francisco: Freeman.

Sherrod, D. R. (1974). Crowding, perceived control, and behavioral aftereffects. *Journal of Applied Social Psychology, 4,* 171–186.

Sklar, L. S., & Anisman, H. (1979). Stress and coping factors influence tumor growth. *Science, 205,* 513–515.

Susser, M. W., Watson, W., & Hopper, K. (1985). *Sociology in medicine.* New York: Oxford University Press.

Syme, S. L. (1986). Social determinants of health and disease. In J. M. Last (Ed.), *Public health and preventive medicine* (12th ed., pp. 953–970). Norwalk, CT: Appleton-Century-Crofts.

Syme, S. L., & Alcalay, R. (1982). Control of cigarette smoking from a social perspective. *Annual Review of Public Health, 3,* 179–199.

Syme, S. L., & Berkman, L. F. (1976). Social class, susceptibility and sickness. *American Journal of Epidemiology, 104,* 1–8.

Taylor, S. E. (1979). Hospital patient behavior: Reactance, helplessness or control? *Journal of Social Issues, 35,* 156–184.

Theorell, T., Alfredsson, L., Knox, S., Persk, A., Svensson, J., & Waller, D. (1984). On the interplay between socioeconomic factors, personality and work environment in the pathogenesis of cardiovascular disease. *Scandinavian Journal of Work and Environmental Health, 10,* 373–380.

Visintainer, M. A., Volpicelli, J. R., & Seligman, M. E. P. (1982). Tumor rejection in rats after inescapable shock. *Science, 216,* 437–439.

Wallston, K. A., & Wallston, B. S. (1982). Who is responsible for your health? The construct of health locus of control. In G. S. Sanders & J. Suls (Eds.), *Social psychology of health and illness* (pp. 65–95). Hillsdale, NJ: Lawrence Erlbaum Associates.

Williams, R. B., Barefoot, J. C., & Shekelle, R. B. (1985). The health consequences of hostility. In M. Chesney & R. Rosenman (Eds.), *Anger and hostility in cardiovascular and behavioral disorders* (pp. 173–185). Washington, DC: Hemisphere.

Winkleby, M. A., Ragland, D. R., Fisher, J. M., & Syme, S. L. (1988). Excess risk of sickness and disease in bus drivers: A review and synthesis of epidemiologic studies. *International Journal of Epidemiology, 17,* 101–108.

Winkleby, M. A., Ragland, D. R., & Syme, S. L. (1988). Self-reported stressors and hypertension: Evidence of an inverse relationship. *American Journal of Epidemiology, 27,* 124–134.

Control and the Epidemiology of Physical Health: Where Do We Go From Here?

Sheldon Cohen
Carnegie Mellon University

Syme (this volume) has eloquently argued for the potential importance of the control concept in the epidemiology of disease. He presents data from psychology, epidemiology, and sociology that support the role of control in the maintenance of health. Moreover, he convincingly argues that the control concept may provide explanations for the influence of other psychosocial risk factors such as Type A Behavior pattern, social class, and social support. I agree with Dr. Syme's basic premise. The existing evidence is provocative and indicates a need for further research to clarify the role of control in disease onset and progression. Where we disagree is on how to proceed from here. Syme proposes a generalist perspective. Specifically, he argues that it is useful at this point to accept broad definitions of both control and disease and continue to search for relations between these concepts. Alternatively, I argue that the appropriate strategy at this point is to move toward greater specificity in defining control, in defining disease outcomes, and in explaining how control would influence disease.

The thrust of my argument is that future research in this area should be driven by highly specified models of the relation between control and health that are both biologically and psychologically plausible. Epidemiologic studies are expensive and time consuming and must be designed to be cost effective. Shotgun approaches to this kind of work are neither politically nor scientifically practical. Well-specified models can maximize the economy of such work by providing guidelines for choosing appropriate samples, measures of control, measures of underlying biologic and psychologic mediation, and disease outcomes. Models that provide convincing biologic explanations of why we would expect control to influence a disease process also provide the ammunition necessary to convince the medical community of the importance and the validity of this work.

At minimum, the development of models linking control to disease pathogenesis requires (a) distinctions between various conceptualizations of control, especially in regard to their temporal stability; (b) a strong rationale as to why we think a specific conceptualization of control should influence a disease process; and (c) an understanding of disease processes that allow specific predictions in regard to what diseases (or disease stages) should be influenced by control.

The remainder of this discussion elaborates the minimum requirements for modeling control influences on health maintenance and disease as outlined earlier. I propose a dimension on which to differentiate control and suggest both psychologic and biologic pathways that could link control to various disease processes. My intent is not to provide all distinctions between control concepts or all plausible models linking control to health or disease, but only to exemplify some reasonable approaches to the problem. Hopefully, this discourse will motivate others to develop more sophisticated and detailed models of controls relations to a range of disease processes.

DIFFERENTIATING CONTROL CONCEPTS

There are a number of dimensions on which control concepts could be distinguished (e.g., objective vs. subjective, global vs. specific, and environmental vs. personal). Clarification of the differences between various control concepts on these and other dimensions would be extremely useful in modeling the relation between these concepts and disease. However, for demonstrative purposes, I distinguish control concepts only on the basis of temporal stability. The issue here is whether a measure of control taps an enduring personal or environmental characteristic or whether it taps a short-term state. Examples of concepts that are likely to be very stable over time include locus of control and attributional style. Examples of relatively unstable concepts are self-efficacy and perceived situational control. As discussed in detail later, the plausibility of control-disease models rests to a great extent on the stability issue. In short, we need to know the minimum time that control (or lack of control) must last to influence the disease process under consideration.

WHY WOULD WE EXPECT CONTROL
TO INFLUENCE DISEASE PATHOGENESIS?

This section focuses on the ways in which control may influence health and disease. The models I propose are concerned only with the causal role of control and hence do not address reserve causation (disease causing control) or spuriousness (another factor such as age or social class simultaneously influencing control and disease). The exclusion of these alternative causal pathways is not intended to reflect any hypotheses about their existence.

At the most elementary level, it can be posited that control is linked to physical disease either through its influence on health practices that increase (or decrease) risk for disease or through control triggered biological responses that affect disease onset or progression (e.g., Krantz, Glass, Contrada, & Miller, 1981). Examples of health practices that may be influenced by control and are implicated in various disease processes include smoking, diet, drinking alcohol, exercise, and sleeping. Although a number of biological systems may provide links between control and disease, neuroendocrine pathways provide the most plausible links in this case. The secretion of hormones such as cortisol, norepinephrine, and epinephrine are known to be triggered by psychological states and are suspected of playing a role in both the pathogenesis of immune mediated diseases and of coronary artery disease.

We can also ask why a particular conceptualization of control would influence the behavioral and/or biological pathways to disease. This question has led to the development of two generic models of the influence of control on disease pathogenesis (Cohen & Edwards, 1989). The main-effect model suggests that control has a beneficial influence irrespective of whether persons are under stress. The stress-buffering model proposes that control operates by protecting people from the potentially pathogenic influence of stressful events. Some conceptions of control are likely to operate through main-effect mechanisms, while others operate through stress-buffering mechanisms.

Main-Effect Model

The main-effect model postulates a general beneficial effect of control. The pathways through which such an effect could occur depends to some extent on what is controllable (e.g., information or access to material goods). Some of the mechanisms outlined later assume that control implies the ability to manipulate a specific resource, whereas others address more general psychological consequences of having or not having control over important outcomes. As apparent in the discussion, the applicability of each mechanism depends on the specific conceptualization of control under consideration. An overall summary of possible main effect mechanisms is provided by Fig. 1.

Information-Based Models.   Having control can imply access to good sources of information. Accurate information could influence health-relevant behaviors or help one to avoid stressful or other high-risk situations. Examples of beneficial information include information regarding access to medical services or regarding the benefits of behaviors that positively influence health and well-being. Appropriate information could also aid in avoiding stressful life events, or in avoiding exposure to infectious or carcinogenic agents (Berkman, 1985; Cohen & Syme, 1985).

Tangible Resource-Based Models.   Control can imply access to tangible and economic services that result in better health and better health care; for example, the ability to procure food, clothing, and housing that operate to prevent disease and limit exposure to risk factors or to access health care that prevents minor illness from developing into more serious disease.

Affect and Self-Esteem Models.   Feelings of control may generate generalized positive affect, a sense of predictability and stability in one's life situation, and a recognition of self-worth. These positive psychological states are presumed to be facilitative because they result in increased

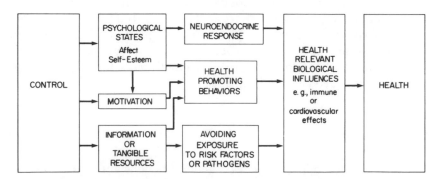

FIG. 1   Main-effect model of the psychological and biological pathways linking control to the onset and progression of disease. All indicated paths move in one causal direction. The exclusion of alternative paths is not intended to reflect any hypotheses about their existence.

motivation to care for oneself (e.g., Cohen & Syme, 1985), or because they suppress neuroendocrine response (Cassel, 1976). On the other hand, it might be argued that relations between control and health are primarily attributable to those suffering from insufficient levels of control. For example, a lack of control may result in less motivation to care for oneself, or in affect mediated elevations in neuroendocrine response (Cohen, Evans, Stokols, & Krantz, 1986; Seligman, 1975).

Stress-Buffering Models

The stress-buffering model posits that control "buffers" (protects) persons from the potentially pathogenic influence of stressful events. The model assumes that stress puts persons under risk for physical disease This risk is presumed to occur either because stress triggers neuroendocrine response, arterial flow disturbances implicated in coronary artery disease (CAD), or because behavioral adaptations to stress often include detrimental health practices (e.g., smoking and poor diet; Cohen, Kaplan, & Manuck, in press). Control operates in these models by decreasing the probability that situations will be appraised as stressful, by directly dampening neuroendocrine responses to stress, by preventing persons from adopting unhealthy behavioral adaptations, or by influencing the ability to control stress elicited emotions. A summary of stress-buffering mechanisms is provided in Fig. 2.

Information-Based Models.   Control can imply having or having access to information about the nature of the potential stressful events or about ways of coping with those events. To the extent that this information (or

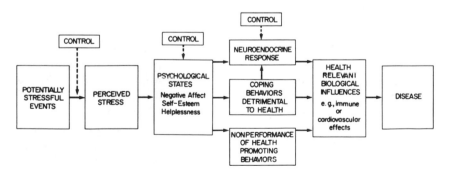

FIG. 2 Stress-buffering model of psychological and biological pathways linking control to health and well-being. All indicated paths move in one causal direction. The exclusion of alternative paths is not intended to reflect any hypotheses about their existence.

access to it) reduces the evaluation of potential threat or harm, the event would be appraised as less threatening and/or harmful and hence the risk of illness decreased. A reduction in stress appraisal would be presumed to reduce negative affect, negative health behaviors, and concomitant physiological reactivity. Information about effective means of coping may also increase appropriate coping efforts.

Affect and Self-Esteem-Based Models. The ability (or perceived ability) to control a stressor often increases feelings of positive affect and self-esteem. As noted earlier, such feelings may influence health through increased motivation to perform health behaviors or through suppression of neuroendocrine responses. Feelings of control that are not specific to coping with the stressor itself may also facilitate coping with the negative affective consequences of stress, or limit generalization of negative affective or cognitive responses to other situations (Abramson, Seligman, & Teasdale, 1978; Cohen, Rothbart, & Phillips, 1976; Seligman, 1975).

Tangible Resource-Based Models. Control can imply the ability to access tangible or economic services. If such resources provide appropriate coping responses to a stressful event, they would reduce the probability of the event being appraised as threatening or harmful and hence reduce the behavioral and affective concomitants of such an appraisal. Again, the mere perception of the availability of resources may operate without actual receipt of help. Tangible resources could also help resolve specific (tangible, related) problems after a stress appraisal is made.

WHAT DISEASE PROCESSES WOULD WE EXPECT TO BE INFLUENCED BY CONTROL?

As discussed earlier, control influences on health and disease are presumably mediated by behavioral and biological factors that have been implicated in a range of disease processes. For example, negative affective responses associated with helplessness could influence cancer and infectious diseases through neuroendocrine-elicited immunosuppression (Seligman, 1975; Sklar & Anisman, 1979; Visintainer, Volpicelli, & Seligman, 1982) and coronary artery disease through neuroendocrine-elicited facilitation of coronary artery occlusion (Glass, 1977). Similarly, cigarette smoking provides a good example of a health practice that has been implicated in multiple diseases including CHD, stroke, lung cancer, and upper respiratory infections (Matarrazzo, 1982). It is clear, however, that generic models that assume psychosocial influences on susceptibility to all or most diseases are gross oversimplifications. Some diseases (and disease stages) seem especially susceptible to behavioral and biological mechanisms linked to psychosocial factors such as control, whereas others are not (Cohen, 1988).

Two questions should be addressed in deciding whether a particular disease is susceptible to control influence. First, is it plausible that behavioral and biological processes presumed to be influenced by control are important precursors of the disease? For example, although modulations of neuroendocrine response and/or changes in health practices are assumed to play a role in the pathogenesis of some diseases (e.g., coronary artery disease), their influence on others (e.g., meningitis or Hodgkin's disease) is less clear. Second, is the conception of control under study temporally stable enough to provide an exposure that is long enough to influence the pathogenesis of the disease under consideration (Cohen et al., in press; Cohen & Matthews, 1987)? The answer to this question depends on the relation between the temporal stability of a particular conception of control and the developmental course of the disease under study. Plausible models assume either that (a) the concept of control under examination is relatively stable over the period of disease development, or (b) a short-term exposure to a particular level of control is sufficient to influence the disease process.

An example of the importance of temporally matching control stability and disease development is provided by the relation between control and the development of atherosclerosis. Locus of control is a temporally stable conceptualization of control, and CAD has a very long and slow course of development (clinical disease generally requiring five decades). Hence, there is a reasonable match here between stability of the control measure and the temporal characteristics of disease pathogenesis. That is, exposure to relatively lower levels of locus of control lasts over the period of disease development. Conceptualizations of control with much shorter temporal stabilities such as self-efficacy or perceived situational control would not be plausible predictors of CAD pathogenesis, although they may be plausible predictors of diseases with very short-term developments like colds and influenza.

It is possible, however, to propose plausible models of slow-developing diseases that focus on control measures with shorter stabilities. For example, we have been discussing control processes that may influence the development of atherosclerosis. As noted earlier, this disease develops over many years. However, for those with clinically significant coronary artery occlusion, a coronary event can occur in relation to a psychosocial factor lasting for a relatively short period. Consider, for example, modeling myocardial infarction (MI) incidence. An MI is a common form of heart attack caused by the death of heart tissue. MIs occur when blood flow through the coronary arteries is interrupted and as a consequence insufficient oxygen reaches the heart muscle. Assume that persons with severe coronary artery occlusion are more likely to manifest this disease in an MI if they experience stress (e.g., Glass, 1977). A severe stressor might trigger the onset of an event, for example, by causing an artery to spasm (Cohen et al., in press). In this case, perceived control over the specific stressor, a control concept with less temporal stability, may be important if it is stable over the course of stressor exposure and operates to buffer persons from stress at the trigger point. In our example, perceived control might ameliorate the experience of stress and thus prevent the stressor from triggering artery spasm. Hence perceived situational control might protect such a person from stress-triggered disease progression.

Finally, there are plausible (but speculative) control-disease models in which short-term exposures to a particular control level triggers the onset of the development of a disease with a long (slow) developmental course. Take for example the possibility that sudden and severe breaches in control such as those often produced by severe and uncontrollable life stressors (e.g., death of a loved one) may be associated with immunologic changes that set a given disease in motion. Hence, a short-term lack of control may hit with sufficient impact to produce a dramatic but short-lived compromise in immune functioning triggering the onset of a disease like cancer that may then be self-perpetuating.

In summary, the question of whether a particular disease is susceptible to control influence depends on (a) whether the conceptualization of control under consideration affects processes that influence disease pathogenesis, (b) on the temporal stability of the control concept, and (c) on the nature and time course of the pathogenesis of the disease.

In short, temporally stable conceptions of control are plausibly related to the onset and progression of diseases with both long- and short-term pathogeneses, and less-stable control conceptions like perceived situational control are plausibly related to both diseases with short-term developments and diseases for whom stressors may act as triggers of progression or onset. Future work on diseases with plausible links to both stable and unstable conceptualizations of control is a high priority at this time. High-prevalence diseases such as infectious diseases (ranging from common upper respiratory infections to AIDS), and cancer provide opportunities in this area that have the potential for both theoretical and practical contributions.

CONCLUSION

How do we proceed from here? We can continue to examine whatever measure of control is easily available, of interest to a study collaborator or consultant, or short enough to include in an epidemiologic questionnaire.

(This comment is unfair to Dr. Syme but is closer to how things are actually done than we would like to believe.) Results from such studies can then be reviewed for consistencies and inconsistencies and a pattern may emerge. Alternatively, future research can be driven by hypothetical propositions based on plausible biologic and psychologic models of the link between control and disease. I have argued that the creation of such models requires a greater specificity in regard to the definition of control and the disease process under study.

Do we need separate models of the relation between control and disease for each individual disease and disease stage? One apparent difference between Dr. Syme's position and my own is his emphasis on general processes applying to all diseases and my emphasis on specifying relevant processes for each disease or disease stage. To some extent our differences on this point are illusory. I agree that common psychologic and biologic pathways can influence multiple disease processes, and hence it is inevitable that certain models will apply across a range of diseases. For example, elevations of secretions of the catecholamines epinephrine and norepinephrine over a prolonged period of time may influence the development of coronary artery occlusion as well as suppress immune function hence possibly increasing susceptibility to infectious and neoplastic diseases. However, not all diseases fit any single pathway model (whether behavioral or biologic). Moreover, the importance of common pathways such as the release of catecholamines varies widely among disease processes. In some cases the common pathways may be an important influence on the etiology and/or progression of a disease, in others the influence is clinically trivial. Finally, as outlined earlier, different disease processes have different temporal courses. Although conceptually mediated by the same processes, they are differentially influenced depending on the temporal stability of the control concept under consideration. In summary, some models may represent processes that influence more than one disease or disease stage, but before assuming such etiologic commonality we need to carefully consider a range of factors influencing the likelihood of a relation between specific definitions of control and specific disease processes.

ACKNOWLEDGMENTS

Preparation of this chapter was supported by a Research Scientist Development Award to the author from the National Institute of Mental Health (K02 MH00721).

REFERENCES

Abramson, L., Seligman, M. E. P., & Teasdale, J. (1978). Learned helplessness in humans: Critique and reformulation. *Journal of Abnormal Psychology, 87,* 49–74.

Berkman, L. F. (1985). The relationship of social networks and social support to morbidity and mortality. In S. Cohen & S. L. Syme (Eds.), *Social support and health* (pp. 241–262). New York: Academic Press.

Cassel, J. (1975). Social science in epidemiology: Psychosocial processes and stress theoretical formulation. In E. L. Struening & M. Guttentag (Eds.), *Handbook of evaluation research* (Vol. 1, pp. 537–549). London: Sage.

Cohen, S. (1988). Psychosocial models of the role of social support in the etiology of physical disease. *Health Psychology, 7,* 269–297.

Cohen, S., & Edwards, J. R. (1989). Personality characteristics as moderators of the relationship between stress and disorder. In R. W. J. Neufeld (Ed.), *Advances in the investigation of psychological stress* (pp. 235–283). New York: Wiley.

Cohen, S., Evans, G. W., Stokols, D., & Krantz, D. S. (1986). *Behavior, health and environmental stress.* New York: Plenum.

Cohen, S., Kaplan, J. R., & Manuck, S. B. (in press). Social support and cardiovascular disease: Underlying psychologic and biologic mechanisms. In S. A. Shumaker & S. M. Czajkowski (Eds.), *Social support and cardiovascular disease.* New York: Plenum.

Cohen, S., & Matthews, K. A. (1987). Social support, Type A behavior and coronary artery disease. *Psychosomatic Medicine, 49,* 325–330.

Cohen, S., Rothbart, M., & Phillips, S. (1976). Locus of control and generality of learned helplessness in humans. *Journal of Personality and Social Psychology, 34,* 1049–1056.

Cohen, S., & Syme, S. L. (1985). Issues in the study and application of social support. In S. Cohen & S. L. Syme (Eds.), *Social support and health* (pp. 3–22). New York: Academic Press.

Glass, D. C. (1977). *Behavior patterns, stress, and coronary disease.* Hillsdale, NJ: Lawrence Erlbaum Associates.

Krantz, D. S., Glass, D. C., Contrada, R., & Miller, N. E. (1981). *Behavior and health* (National Science Foundation's second 5-year outlook on science and technology). Washington, DC: U.S. Government Printing Office.

Matarrazzo, J. D. (1982). Behavioral health's challenge to academic, scientific and professional psychology. *American Psychologist, 37,* 1–14.

Seligman, M. E. P. (1975). *Helplessness: On depression, development, and death.* San Francisco: Freeman.

Sklar, L. S., & Anisman, H. (1979). Stress and coping factors influence tumor growth. *Science, 205,* 513–515.

Visintainer, M. A., Volpicelli, J. R., & Seligman, M. E. P. (1982). Tumor rejection in rats after inescapable shock. *Science, 216,* 437–439.

Personal Control and Health Promotion: A Psychological Perspective

Christopher Peterson
University of Michigan

In his chapter, Syme notes that his studies of the sociology and epidemiology of disease literally drove him to consider control and self-directedness as serious notions. This comment offers a nice counterpoint to my own research career. As a social psychologist interested in personal control, my studies of control literally drove me to consider health and illness. I knew all along that one's physical well-being is important, of course, so what I mean is that I came to regard health and illness as important consequences of personal control.

I address two topics here. Obviously and most importantly, I comment on Professor Syme's chapter, and I do so from the perspective of a psychologist. And then I place the topics of control and health in the context of the life course, mentioning some of the archival work I have done in this area.

COMMENTS ON PROFESSOR SYME'S PAPER

Albert J. Stunkard and I have recently reviewed the theoretical literature on personal control (Peterson & Stunkard, 1989). We identified several dozen similar theories, each with its own focus of convenience to be sure, and we attempted to boil them down to common factors. Professor Syme, in his chapter, agrees with us about several of the common threads running through the psychology of personal control. This convergence is encouraging.

First, Professor Syme speculates that personal control is one of the few social science concepts that can transcend levels of analysis. I certainly agree. Let me give you an example. We can follow the lead of Bandura's (1986) discussion of collective efficacy to label the group or societal manifestation of control something like collective control and expect some interesting giving and taking between personal control and collective control. Perhaps light is thereby shed on opinion leadership, on job burnout, and on alienation. In each case, there is an interplay between an individual's sense of his or her own control over outcomes and beliefs about the control that can be exercised by some larger group of which the individual is a member.

Second, personal control is reality based, as implied by the dramatic socioeconomic status (SES) differences in disease rates—which Professor Syme suggests that control may explain. To argue that control is reality based is not to say that it is perfectly accurate. I sometimes liken the construct more to a promise than to a prediction. Still, personal control cannot be too estranged from the way things really are. Throughout this volume, we have heard several comments concerning "illusory control," and although I wish not to dismiss this phenomenon altogether, I object strongly to the provocative but misleading implication that somehow illusion and mental health are synonymous. Anyone who has worked as a therapist with profoundly disturbed individuals appreciates that psychopathology is characterized by estrangement from reality, not the opposite.

Third, personal control is affected by and in turn affects social relationships. I am frequently asked what can be done to boost someone's sense of control, and I always give two answers: (a) change the world so that it is responsive; and (b) do not forget that the most important aspect of the world is other people. I am not reducing social support to personal control (and certainly not vice versa); I am simply saying that they drag each other along. In a sense, personal control is the Velcro of the social sciences, because it adheres so readily to other social science constructs!

Fourth, personal control is related to the gamut of questions we want to pose about the causes of health and illness. I found Professor Syme's distinctions among the types of causal questions one might ask concerning the onset of illness to be useful. Does control relate the same or differently to the different levels of cause?

Fifth, personal control is a relevant consideration in designing and implementing programs of health promotion. Again, I certainly agree with this conclusion (see Peterson & Stunkard, 1989). I would like to remind you all of a truism within clinical work: One must distinguish the cause of a problem from the solution to that problem. In other words, whether or not personal control is involved in the etiology of some phenomenon has no necessary bearing on whether personal control should be targeted in an intervention. Nor vice versa.

Having made clear these points of agreement, let me move on to disagree with Professor Syme's characterization of personal control as ill-defined. He asks, for instance, whether personal control is a property of the person or the situation. I believe the answer is both, because personal control is almost unique as a truly transactional concept (Peterson, 1988b). It refers to the *relationship* between a person and his or her world, and isn't this sophistication what all theorists eventually call for in the social sciences? Given researchers may focus on one side of this relationship or the other, but the transactional nature of the concept remains.

The concept of personal control helps us resolve the person–situation controversy, and it may similarly shed light on the age-old mind–body problem. If nothing else, the research linking personal control and health forces us to consider these two human spheres at the same time, perhaps in the most productive way since Descartes split them apart. And perhaps we can follow the example of personal control to come up with other transactional notions.

To blunt my disagreement, I think familiarity has something to do with the different reactions by Professor Syme and me to personal control. So, as a psychologist I am puzzled about how to conceive and measure one's physical well-being, a variable that Professor Syme refers to as "hard and quantifiable"! Perhaps here is an obvious place for collaboration, with psychologists measuring personal control and epidemiologists taking care of illness.

Professor Syme warns against prematurely settling on a single definition of personal control, and if he means a single operationalization of the notion, I certainly agree with him. I think it fair to say that the measurement of personal control has lagged behind other aspects of its study, giving us a line of research with poor reliability but spectacular validity. I am reminded of the difficulties some years earlier in deciding how best to measure the related notion of locus of control. Not just more work is needed here, but more careful work.

Regardless, I offer the following truisms about how to proceed in research linking personal control to physical health and illness: (a) employ longitudinal designs; (b) obtain baseline measures of physical well-being; and (c) eliminate common elements from predictors and criteria. I admit this advice is easier to give than to follow.

PERSONAL CONTROL IN THE LIFE COURSE

Perhaps some of you know of the work I have done linking my personal control cognate—explanatory style—to health and illness (e.g., Peterson, 1988a; Peterson & Seligman, 1987; Peterson, Seligman, & Vaillant,

1988). I do not bicker that explanatory style is inherently a better notion than the other two dozen related constructs. But I argue that one of the measures I have developed of explanatory style allows research to be done that is really impossible with other constructs. In particular, research is possible that addresses large questions about the operation of personal control across someone's life.

Let me give you some background. Explanatory style reflects individual differences in how people explain the causes of bad events that befall them (Peterson & Seligman, 1984). These explanations range from optimistic ("It was a fluke") to pessimistic ("I am an inept human being"). Or to use the language of our conference, explanations range from self-directed and efficacious to helpless and hopeless. Causal explanations are ubiquitous in spoken and written material, which means that explanatory style can be assessed through content analysis of documents left behind by subjects quick, dead, belligerent, or ancient (e.g., Zullow, Oettingen, Peterson, & Seligman, 1988). Several studies with archived material show the feasibility of the method and support the hypothesis that lack of control is a risk factor for illness and perhaps early death.

The most extensive of these investigations is one I did in collaboration with Martin E. P. Seligman and George E. Vaillant (Peterson, Seligman, & Vaillant, 1988). From open-ended questionnaires completed in 1946 by participants in the Harvard Study of Adult Development, we extracted causal explanations about bad events and rated them along dimensions reflecting their optimistic versus pessimistic nature. At this point, subjects were about 25 years of age. With respect to their causal explanations, they were consistent within themselves (i.e., an individual tended to offer the same sorts of explanations for different bad events). Further, they differed considerably across themselves (i.e., some were quite optimistic, and others were quite pessimistic).

Available for each research participant at 5-year intervals were global ratings of their health, made by a physician blind to their other characteristics. Pessimistic explanatory style at first showed no particular relationship with health ratings, but by age 35, a significant relationship appeared, peaking at age 45, but continuing to be apparent to age 60. It should be noted that these relationships held even when initial measures of physical and mental well-being were held constant.

This study raises more questions than it answers. First, we have no idea about what mediates the established link between pessimistic explanatory style and poor health. Second, the Harvard Study just described includes only male participants, and so we have no idea about whether our findings generalize from men to women. This is not an idle question, granted the well-documented sex differences in morbidity and mortality (Verbrugge,

1989). Why do women suffer more illnesses than men but nonetheless live longer?

We are currently coding explanatory style of research participants in the Terman Study of Genius. Here we have data from more than 1,500 males and females, followed from the 1920s when they were adolescents until the present. Among the questions we hope to answer in this research are:

- Is explanatory style continuous across the life span?
- What role is played by intervening life events in bolstering or undercutting one's explanatory style?
- More basically, what are the origins of individual differences in explanatory style?
- Are there sex differences in explanatory style, and if so, how do these relate to sex differences in morbidity and mortality?
- Relatedly, are there cohort differences in explanatory style, and if so, do these relate to generational trends in mortality rates (cf. Sagan, 1987)?
- What are the psychosocial mediators of the relationship between pessimistic explanatory style and poor health?

The possible yield of this research is information with which to direct interventions that enhance the quality and quantity of one's life, by targeting for change deficits in personal control. I concur with Professor Syme that research on control is worth our best effort.

REFERENCES

Bandura, A. (1986). *Social foundations of thought and action: A social cognitive theory.* Englewood Cliffs, NJ: Prentice-Hall.

Peterson, C. (1988a). Explanatory style as a risk factor for illness. *Cognitive Therapy and Research, 12,* 117–130.

Peterson, C. (1988b). *Personality.* San Diego: Harcourt Brace Jovanovich.

Peterson, C., & Seligman, M. E. P. (1984). Causal explanations as a risk factor for depression: Theory and evidence. *Psychological Review, 91,* 347–374.

Peterson, C., & Seligman, M. E. P. (1987). Explanatory style and illness. *Journal of Personality, 55,* 237–265.

Peterson, C., & Seligman, M. E. P., & Vaillant, G. E. (1988). Pessimistic explanatory style is a risk factor for physical illness: A thirty-five year longitudinal study. *Journal of Personality and Social Psychology, 55,* 23–27.

Peterson, C., & Stunkard, A. J. (1989). Personal control and health promotion. *Social Science and Medicine, 28,* 819–828.

Sagan, L. A. (1987). *The health of nations: True causes of sickness and well-being.* New York: Basic Books.

Verbrugge, L. M. (1989). Recent, present, and future health of American adults. In L. Breslow, J. E. Fielding, & L. B. Lave (Eds.), *Annual review of public health* (Vol. 10). Palo Alto, CA: Annual Reviews.

Zullow, H., Oettingen, G., Peterson, C., & Seligman, M. E. P. (1988). Explanatory style and pessimism in the historical record: CAVing LBJ, presidential candidates, and East versus West Berlin. *American Psychologist, 43*, 673–682.

Afterword

Carmi Schooler
National Institute of Mental Health

As was the case for its two predecessors in this series sponsored by the Gerontology Center at Pennsylvania State University, this volume examines aspects of the relationship between social-structural and cultural processes, on the one hand, and aging on the other. The first book in the series aimed at breaching the disciplinary walls that limited our ability to explore the causal interconnections between social structures and a variety of psychological aging processes. The second book examined the psychological implications of the different relationships between age and the roles and statuses that have existed in different cultures and in different periods of history. This book has a somewhat narrower focus. Although it has kept a life-course perspective that looks across disciplines and fields, it addresses the causes and effects of two closely related feelings—self-directedness and efficacy.

I hope that readers who have reached this point in the book have not found this narrowing of focus premature. I believe that, taken together, its chapters make a strong case that the study of self-directedness and efficacy provides a key to understanding important aspects of human mental and physical health. Beyond that, the chapters, by ranging in theoretical and empirical level from the sociological to the biological, show how the topics of control and efficacy provide a common ground on which seemingly disparate theoretical and empirical traditions can meet to discover where they reinforce and where they challenge each other.

A large part of this bringing together of diverse perspectives is foreshadowed in Rodin's introductory chapter. In this chapter, she reviews the research literature on control and delineates the various definitions of control and their implications for how control has its effects on people's mental and physical health. Among the definitions she examines are desire for control perceived self-efficacy, potential controllability, and perceived control. She shows that, although these different perspectives are not necessarily incompatible, they may lead to quite different generalizations about the causes and effects of control throughout the life span.

Wishing her chapter to reflect the general state of the field, Rodin intentionally takes an ahistorical and acultural viewpoint. My chapter takes quite a different approach—adapting an historical and cross-cultural perspective. Doing so readily reveals that being a self-directed and efficacious individual is far from a universal human goal. Focusing on the concept of individualism, I examine how historically determined cultural and socioeconomic factors affect people's desires for self-directedness and efficacy. Exploring a range of historical and socioeconomic circumstances where such desires were or are particularly strong (certain hunting–gathering societies, England from the 14th century on, 17th-century Japan, and the modern industrialized West), I try to come to grips with the question of the nature and direction of the causal connections between individualism and the socioeconomic conditions in which it is found. One clear conclusion is that differences among people and societies in individualism and the value placed on self-directedness and efficacy must be taken into account before any generalizations about the effects of feelings of self-direction and efficacy on people's physical and psychological functioning can be reached.

In his elegant critique of my chapter Meyer, a sociologist, departs even further than I do from the ahistorical, nonsociologically influenced approach that is generally taken by psychologists studying self-directedness and efficacy. He legitimately chides me for underestimating the importance of cultural and social institutions in developing and supporting individualistic ideologies. Meyer sees my historical and comparative evidence as showing how important it is for individualism to be culturally institutionalized if it is to have any profound effects. He concludes that "self-direction and efficacy may be more significant as cultural elements than as experiential realities, both in predicting our individual orientations and in accounting for social change."

Heise, in his chapter, takes a somewhat different sociological approach. His fundamental theme is that a sense of efficacy has sociocultural determinants, some of which derive from the structure of career patterns. Borrowing taxonomic methods from anthropologists and biologists, he develops a taxonomic approach to careers. Using this approach on several sets of empirical data, he concludes that careers are cultural structures that unfold in accordance with institutional rule systems and that career roles differ in the esteem with which they are held and in the power they are seen to have and hence on their sense of self-efficacy.

Heise sees individuals as accumulating more roles as they move from youth to middle age. He views those who have a larger set of roles, such as adults in their mid-years, as being more self-directed and efficacious by virtue of their being able to match the roles they choose to play to their personal needs. Heise notes, however, that, although younger people may not have as much control as may older ones, they may feel more potentially efficacious because various attractive role possibilities that may already be foreclosed to older people are still open to them.

In her comments on Heise's chapter, Foner takes a much less sanguine view of the potential effects of multiple roles and career lines. Taking the perspective of sociological role theory and using examples such as that of the working mother, she sees the holding of multiple roles as limiting people's ability to chart their own courses as they please. She also shows how peoples' career paths are affected by the career paths of others in their own social networks. Foner, however, does not one-sidedly emphasize the constraining influences of social structure. Drawing on examples from the studies of industrial workers and her own research on societies that use age as a major element in their social organization, she provides evidence that the self-directed actions of individuals can impact not only their own lives, but also the social institutions of which they are a part.

In his comments on Heise's chapter Abeles shifts to a somewhat more psychological perspective. He focuses on the question of the psychological mechanisms through which culturally provided schemas of the type that Heise describes, might affect a person's sense of control. Synthesizing major strains in the current psychological literature, Abeles presents a schematic diagram that conceptualizes control in terms of subjective experiences. The model is characterized by a feedback loop so that accumulating experiences result in both short term changes in sense of control and longer term changes that occur with aging.

Weisz shifts to a more clinical perspective in his chapter. He examines the development of control-related beliefs, goals, and styles and links various aspects of this development to psychological adjustment in childhood and adolescence. He defines *control* as the causing of an intended event and sees such control as a function of contingency (i.e., the extent to which human behavior can influence an event) and competence (i.e., the degree to which an individual can manifest the relevant behavior). He shows how as children grow, their ability to make and integrate appropriate judgments about contingency and competence increases. Weisz also distinguishes between primary and secondary control. The former involves attempting to change objective conditions so that they match one's desires; the latter involves altering one's desires to effect a satisfying fit to objective reality. Weisz' evidence indicates that secondary control occurs developmentally later than primary control.

Although Weisz' major interest is in the psychological functioning of the individual, he is clearly open to the possibility that such functioning can be affected by cultural factors. His distinction between primary and secondary control developed out of his cross-cultural comparisons of Japanese and American ways of coping. In his chapter, he examines two forms of control styles, overcontrol and undercontrol, and tries to link them to the reports of the behavior of Thai and American children. Although as suggested by their pattern of socialization, Thai children tend to be more overcontrolled than their American counterparts, the expected greater level of undercontrol of American children did not occur consistently. As Weisz notes, his apparent disconfirmation of what had seemed an obvious hypothesis clearly calls for more research. Nevertheless, Weisz' work presents an exemplary example of how an awareness of psychological, cultural, and developmental phenomena can lead to an insightful, yet methodologically sophisticated research program on control in normal and psychologically disturbed children and adolescents.

Rosenberg's comments on Weisz' chapter focus on two points. The first is Rosenberg's suggestion that people attempt to control their emotional experiences not by acting on their emotions, but by acting on the causes of their emotions. This occurs, he maintains, because people can exercise more control over the thoughts that they believe arouse them than they can over their emotions or over the objective circumstances that may lead to unpleasant feelings. Rosenberg supports this view by describing some of the forms that such cognitive self-regulation may take.

Although he is a sociologist, Rosenberg's second general point—an alternative explanation of why secondary control tends to develop later in children than primary control—is in part based on Piagetian psychological theory. Rosenberg views this delay as occurring because "as Piaget expresses it . . . 'the child is not conscious of his own thought' " so that younger children are unlikely to direct their attention to the internal world of experience. Only when children become attentive to their own inner states can they come to recognize that they can deal with their problems by regulating their own thoughts.

In her chapter, Berg deals with one of the oldest and still central issues in field of psychology—the nature and determinants of intellectual efficacy. She is particularly concerned about how the nature of such efficacy may shift during the life course. She argues for the advantages of a contextual theoretical perspective based on an examination of adults' conceptions of what defines intellectual efficacy. Using such a perspective, she presents the beginnings of a conceptualization of what constitutes intellectual efficacy across the life span that uses, together with standard measures of intelligence, people's own beliefs as revealed by both closed and open-ended questionnaires. She concludes that perceived and measured ability to solve novel problems decline much earlier and more markedly than other abilities. At the same time, such ability is seen as becoming a less important component of competence in meeting everyday problems as one ages.

In their comments on Berg's chapter, Evans and Lewis express skepticism on relying on people's beliefs and self-reports for gaining a contextual perspective. They maintain that more thinking is needed about how to measure problem solving as it unfolds naturalistically or in response to experimental situations. They also offer a general caveat about what they see as the underlying premise of the whole volume—that greater self-efficacy is a good thing. Having expressed these concerns they then describe some of the coping processes that accompany aging. In doing so, they speculate on the nature of the intellectual skills necessary to adapt competently. The types of abilities they discuss as intellectual skills include such diverse ones as the abilities to meet new people and make friends, to cognitively map new locations, and to regulate one's sources of stimulation.

Herrmann's chapter deals with the effects of self-perceptions of efficacy on a particular aspect on intellectual efficacy—memory performance. Reviewing the literature, he finds that although self-perception of memory performance is a reliably stable characteristic of individuals, it is not a particularly valid estimate of such performance. He provides evidence about how inaccurate self-perceptions about memory ability can affect performance by influencing what tasks people try, how much effort they expend, and their use of both external memory aids, such as notepads, and internal ones, such as rehearsal strategies. Herrmann describes studies in which memory self-perceptions were altered by providing relevant experience or feedback. Citing evidence that memory perceptions can be influenced by stereotypical prejudices, he calls for more attention to be paid to social level phenomena, frequently overlooked by memory researchers. He also shows how memory self-perception, and to some extent memory performance, can be improved by instructions designed to rectify self-perceptions arising from false stereotypes about such groups as the aged.

Syme's chapter completes the volume's general progression from concern over how self-directedness is related to cultural and social-structural level phenomena, through its examination of relationships between self-directedness and various aspects of psychological functioning to the examination of the relationship between control and the biological determinants of physical health. He notes that he came to the study of concepts such as control and self-directedness, not because he was interested in them per se, but because he was reluctantly driven by the data to the belief that the idea of control is necessary to explain disease patterns that are otherwise inexplicable. Having controlled the effects of a whole series of factors, such as inadequate medical care or poor nutrition, he still could not account for the gradient of disease rate by socioeconomic status that has been observed for many body systems and a very wide range of diseases. Especially difficult to account for are differences between those at the top of the hierarchy and those just one or two steps down. The hypothesis that Syme feels most easily fits the facts is the control hypothesis. This hypothesis states that the negative relationships between various illnesses and position in the socioeconomic status hierarchy come about because the lower one is in that hierarchy, the less control one has over the factors that affect the conditions of one's life.

Syme is well aware that the mechanisms through which lack of control increases the incidence of various illnesses are still far from known. He sees the concept of control as being at this point primarily integrative and sketches two general models that may account for how the absence of control may be related to such a wide range of diseases and conditions. One is that the concept of control includes a diversity of elements each of which separately influences the likelihood of different diseases and conditions. The second model is that stressors associated with breakdown of control depress the body's defense systems so that those affected are made vulnerable to a wide range of disease agents.

Cohen, in his comments on Syme's chapter, argues strongly that research in the area of control and illness should be driven by highly specified models. Such models should include the careful differentiation of alternate concepts of control, as well as the specification of the causal pathways through which a particular type of control may have its affect on a particular disease process. Cohen goes beyond making a general call for specificity. He lays out a variety of models through which control may have its effects (e.g., tangible resource models, psychological state models) and diagrams the various paths (e.g., neuroendocrine response, health-promoting behavior) through which these effects may occur for different types of disease.

Peterson finds himself in agreement with Syme on most points. In fact, he begins his discussion by strongly supporting Syme's contention that a wide range of data and theories converge in their agreement about the nature and importance of personal control. Nevertheless, as a psychologist, he is amused that he views as problematic the measurement of physical well-being, a variable that Syme sees as much more readily quantifiable than is sense of control. Peterson also responds to Syme's concern over whether personal control is a property of the person or the situation by arguing that personal control is almost unique in being a truly transactional concept in that it refers to the *relationship* between a person and his or her world. Summarizing his own research indicating that an optimistic, personally efficacious way of explaining events predicts good health decades later, Peterson also provides further evidence of the relationship between a sense of personal control and health.

It seems appropriately fitting to the task of concluding what should be gleaned from this volume that Peterson, the last discussant of Syme's chapter, the last chapter in this book, begins his comments by strongly approving of Syme's conclusion that personal control is one of the few social science concepts that transcends levels of analysis. I believe, that this is, in fact, a central conclusion of the book as a whole. Two points about the path that Syme took in reaching his conclusions about the importance of personal control support me in this belief. The first is that he is a practicing epidemiologist primarily interested in the study of disease, who was "driven" to the study of psychosocial concepts such as control and self-directedness, not because he was interested in them per se, but because he found them necessary to explain disease patterns that seemed to him otherwise inexplicable. The second point is that, as Syme ironically noted in his chapter, he started out as a sociologist. Clearly, the keeping in mind of levels from the sociological to the biological is so difficult that even someone trained as a sociologist may forget the possible relevance of the one level to the other. Equally clearly, as Syme himself has shown us, it is necessary to bear all these levels in mind if we are to fully understand many important biological, psychological, and sociological phenomena and how these phenomena interact to affect the individual's well-being.

Hopefully, the chapters and discussions in this book have shown that maintaining such a wide perspective is neither a hopeless nor a thankless chore. Looking back on the volume as a whole, it is my belief that its component chapters and discussions have not only dealt with self-directedness and efficacy and their causes and effects throughout the life course from a variety of perspectives, but have done so in ways that are not mutually contradictory or basically incompatible. I say this although the authors may disagree about whether control is internal or external, is perceived, actual, or potential or whether what does the controlling or is controlled is physiological, psychological, or social in nature. Nevertheless, although all of the definitions presented or approaches suggested are not necessarily in agreement, their differences are generally those of disciplinary perspective or of narrowness of focus. Thus, I am reasonably optimistic, that at least in this area, theories and research programs that stretch their perspectives will not run into untoward or irreconcilable difficulties.

The contributors to this volume have, I think, made a strong case that their various findings and approaches must be taken into account if we are to have a basic understanding, not only of self-directedness and efficacy, but of what happens to people psychologically and physically as they develop and age. Besides its own inherent interest, such a basic understanding is necessary if people are going to be successfully helped with the difficulties they encounter as they grow older. As always seems to be the case, further research is needed. Hopefully, the perspectives of those readers of this book who may do such research will have been jiggled a bit wider.

Author Index

Subject Index